The Fallacies of Racism

For all the Adjuncts

The Fallacies of Racism

Understanding How Common Perceptions Uphold White Supremacy

Jennifer Patrice Sims

polity

First published in 2024 by Polity Press

Polity Press
65 Bridge Street
Cambridge CB2 1UR, UK

Polity Press
111 River Street
Hoboken, NJ 07030, USA

ISBN-13: 978-1-5095-5347-1
ISBN-13: 978-1-5095-5348-8(pb)

A catalogue record for this book is available from the British Library.

Library of Congress Control Number: 2023919912

Typeset in 10.5 on 13pt Swift
by Cheshire Typesetting Ltd, Cuddington, Cheshire
Printed and bound in Great Britain by TJ Books Ltd, Padstow, Cornwall

The publisher has used its best endeavours to ensure that the URLs for external websites referred to in this book are correct and active at the time of going to press. However, the publisher has no responsibility for the websites and can make no guarantee that a site will remain live or that the content is or will remain appropriate.

Every effort has been made to trace all copyright holders, but if any have been overlooked the publisher will be pleased to include any necessary credits in any subsequent reprint or edition.

For further information on Polity, visit our website:
politybooks.com

Contents

Acknowledgments

This book is rooted in my experiences teaching. So my first thanks are to all of my students! I taught my first courses as Instructor of Record in spring 2007 as a part-time Adjunct at Nashville State Technical Community College and Volunteer State Community College. Since then, I have taught as a Graduate Lecturer at the University of Wisconsin–Madison (UW–Madison), as a full-time Adjunct at the University of Wisconsin–River Falls (UW–River Falls), and as an Assistant and now Associate Professor at The University of Alabama in Huntsville. All that to say: thank you to the thousands of students across three states who passed through my classrooms. Your questions and comments not only helped make me a better instructor but they gave me the glimpses into how people perceive racism that led to this book. I'd like to give a special shout out to Maci Panariello and the other members of my fall 2021 Honors Introduction to Sociology class for the media references that y'all identified as connecting to class material and by extension this book.

Next, thank you to my editor Jonathan Skerrett. I greatly appreciate your close read of my proposal, support of this book project, your amazing feedback on chapter drafts, and so much more. To the rest of the team at Polity, y'all were amazing from start to finish. Thank you so much to: Karina Jákupsdóttir, Jason Anscomb, Ian Tuttle, Neil de Cort, and Polity's indexer.

Thanks, too, to the following family, friends, colleagues, and one outstanding undergraduate student for reading draft materials and/or providing invaluable comments and constructive criticism: Stephanie Anderson, Alondra Delgado, Nick Jones, Candice Lanius, Whitney Laster Pirtle, Anne Marie McCabe, Chinelo L. Njaka, Jillian Paragg, Zawadi Rucks-Ahidiana, Brittany Sims Nwankwoala, Pamela

Sims, and Oliver Sims. For her patience and understanding during many long nights at my office: Thank you to my amazing daughter Roxie.

Finally, I would like to take a moment to certify that no artificial intelligence (AI) was used for any part of this book. All materials reviewed, analysis conducted, themes identified, and writing performed for this book were done manually by me.

Introduction

In September of 2012, I stood behind a podium in an auditorium-style classroom, shaking as students filed in and took their seats. I was a graduate student at the University of Wisconsin–Madison, and while the course was not my first as the instructor of record, it was the first time I would be teaching 200, mostly White, students specifically about race and racism in the United States. "What have I gotten myself into?" I texted my mother. The start of a new way to teach about race and racism as it would turn out.

The semester passed in a whirlwind of typical new-class stressors: overpreparing for lectures, learning how to manage a class of 200, supervising two teaching assistants who were otherwise my peers, realizing I had brought too few scantrons to the exam. As a young Black woman teaching at a primarily White institution (PWI), I also faced being challenged and insulted by White students when they preferred their own racist stereotypes to the data and data-informed explanations presented in my class.

Since that first class over ten years ago, I have come to recognize this as a situation of many students coming to my classroom with ideas about race and racism that are, put most kindly, problematic. Inaccurate ideas like "Immigrants don't pay taxes," when sales *taxes* are a thing in most states, are frustrating; but racist/sexist ideas like "Black women should stop having children," especially when stated matter-of-factly to my face in the middle of class, represent one of the hardest parts of teaching.[1]

Recognizing that students more than likely entered my classroom ignorant of academic conceptualizations of racism and/or believing misinformation from their prior schooling and the media, when I first began teaching Race/Ethnicity I was extremely focused on presenting academic definitions, showing lots of empirically accurate information, and debunking stereotypes. I used a textbook that defined racism as social domination that arranges life "in such a way that its ordinary, everyday workings serve to benefit certain racial groups (predominantly Whites) at the expense of others (predominantly non-Whites)."[2] My lecture slides showed the latest data and numbers on racial trends and disparities from reputable organizations like the US Census, Bureau of Labor Statistics, and Federal Bureau of Investigation. To my mind, these statistics provided facts and disproved stereotypes. I emphasized the normality and logic of an evidence-based approach with a statement in my syllabus that "In no field do professors purposefully teach *inaccurate information* about their topics."

When my first student evaluations arrived, they were split. Some students said I was teaching my "opinion" and that I marked off when students did not share my "opinion." Others accused me of being biased against White men. At the same time, I received comments like, "I loved this class. It was very interesting and eye opening." In addition, I received official recognition from three students via their campus organizations' "Honored Instructor" or "Influential Instructor" award program.

Due to some students "getting it" from my data-driven approach, I stayed the course. I thought that if I showed and explained the numbers clearly enough, that more students would come away with an empirically accurate picture of race and racism in the US. For example, in covering race and the economy, I showed data demonstrating that the numeric majority of US Americans on "welfare" are White, not (Black) "welfare queens" or (Latina) "illegals." I believed that if I closely stuck to the numbers that students would be unable to dismiss information, even information that contradicted common but racist stereotypes, as merely my "opinion" or "bias."

Then, one comment shattered this delusion. A student wrote: "I will never believe a word she says no matter how many statistics she shoves down my throat." While of course no instructor can expect that every student in their class will learn, appreciate, or even believe the topics they teach, seeing that even cold hard numbers – in a science class no less! – could be rejected in favor of racist beliefs was humbling. The comment was an example of the "militant" and "aggressive" commitment that many US Americans have to remain ignorant of the empirical reality of racism.[3]

Fortunately, the comment also shone a light on a pedagogical way forward, for it made me realize that before I could hope to get some students to even consider a data-informed perspective on race and racism, I had to first actually address the entrenched "culture-serving distortions" with which they entered my classroom.

In his now infamous book *Lies My Teacher Told Me* (2018 [1995]), sociologist James Loewen argues that adults have problematic ideas about race and racism in large part because middle- and high-school history/social studies classes teach "culture-serving distortions." That is, for their first education people are taught lies, such as the myth that Reconstruction failed because Black people mismanaged it as they "weren't ready" for full citizenship, which supports a "white supremacist ideology and material social structure."[4] Though he originally wrote the words while I was in junior high school, by graduate school I had joined the population of "[s]ociology professors [who] are amazed and depressed at the level of thinking about society displayed each fall, especially by white upper-middle-class students in their first-year classes."[5]

Psychologists have found that "[i]f prior knowledge is inaccurate and consists of misconceptions, new learning can be particularly difficult and 'resistant to correction.'"[6] I realized that it was not enough to present students with data and expect that they would, upon comparison of it with their first education, be able to recognize that social science offers a more rational and systemic view of society than high-school history books, click-bate media, or their cousin's boyfriend's hot takes on social media. So I decided to teach my students to think critically about the common yet distorted ideas about race and racism that so many of them brought to the classroom. In this pursuit, I dedicated first a half, and then eventually a whole, lesson to what racism is *not*.

Exploring a topic by focusing on what it is not has been found to be a useful way to gain key insights into the properties of a phenomenon.[7] The first chapter of the race textbook I use lists "Five Fallacies about Racism," and the authors, sociologists Matthew Desmond and Mustafa Emirbayer, explain that:

> There are many misconceptions about the character of racism. Americans are deeply divided over its legacies and inner workings,

and much of this division is a result of the fact that many Americans understand racism in limited or misguided ways.[8]

The authors go on to define fallacies as "logical mistakes, factual or logical errors in reasoning" that they say "are recurrent in many public debates about racism."[9] Likewise, early in sociologist Crystal Fleming's *How to Be Less Stupid About Race* (2018), she details six "fallacious ideas about white supremacy that I'd like to address up front," half of which overlap with those described by Desmond and Emirbayer.[10] In both of their books, the concept of fallacies helpfully functions to debunk common but problematic perspectives on racism before readers dive into the deeper content. Desmond and Emirbayer say it plainly, writing: "Before we articulate what we believe race to be, however, perhaps the best way to start off is by offering some suggestions on how *not* to think about race."[11]

Situated within sociological theories of racial epistemology, *The Fallacies of Racism* focuses deeply and wholly – not just passingly for a few introductory pages – on ignorance of racism, that is, what it is not. I build on the concept of fallacies of racism by analyzing a dozen common perceptions that, upon closer examination, are revealed to be rooted in an "epistemology of ignorance" that functions to uphold White supremacy. Some of the fallacies that will be discussed are expansions of those that Desmond, Emirbayer, and Fleming briefly mentioned, but the majority are culture-serving perceptions that I have identified from my teaching and research. Below, I summarize the theoretical framework within which fallacies are conceptualized, briefly layout the twelve fallacies that will be discussed in the coming chapters, and offer my own introductory ("getting on the same page") caveats.

An Epistemology of Ignorance

Many social theorists have discussed how dominant patterns of thinking in society exist to maintain the legitimacy of society. Karl Marx, for example, famously said that the ruling ideas are the ideas of the ruling class. Antonio Gramsci coined the concept of *hegemony* to describe ideas that are dominant, dominating, and culture-serving yet unnamed. Pierre Bourdieu wrote of the *illusio* in society, that is the ideas that justify the current terms of capital transfer that must be "bought into" in order for social exchanges to proceed in any given field.

With respect to dominant patterns of thinking about race and racism specifically, there is an emergent body of scholarship in sociology that focuses on theorizing the role of ignorance in justifying and (re)producing inequality.[12] Charles Wade Mills' theory of the Racial Contract, in particular his concept of there being an epistemological aspect to it, offered one of the first powerful explanations of how patterns of thinking function to support White supremacy. In brief, the "Racial Contract" is the term Mills gives to the typically unacknowledged yet guiding agreement among White people to support the White supremacist status quo. Mills further suggests that "we can think of [the epistemological aspect of the Racial Contract] as an idealized consensus about cognitive norms and . . . an understanding about what counts as a correct, objective interpretation of the world."[13] When it comes to race and racism, the "cognitive norms" and "what counts as a correct, objective interpretation of the world" are actually "to *mis*interpret the world. One has to learn to see the world wrongly, but with the assurance that this set of mistaken perceptions will be validated by white epistemic authority."[14] This is a racism-specific application of the more general philosophical understanding that "the powerful have no interest in achieving a proper interpretation [of society] . . . They have a positive interest in sustaining the extant misinterpretation" since that is what favors those in power.[15]

Mills calls societal-level patterns of thinking that utilize misinterpretation to maintain inequality an "epistemology of ignorance." He asserts that "misunderstanding, misrepresentation, evasion, and [Whites'] self-deception on matters related to race" are "in no way *accidental*, but *prescribed*" and are "among the most pervasive mental phenomena of the past few hundred years."[16] Historically, these inverted patterns of thinking regarding race and racism were "required for conquest, colonization, and enslavement" to reconcile calculated economic exploitation with, first, Christian religious doctrines like "Love Thy Neighbor" and, later, secular ones like "All Men Are Created Equal."[17] However, an epistemology of ignorance was not just necessary in the *past* during eras of infamous, overt, and large-scale racist projects; it continues to function in the *present* by undergirding perceptions of contemporary racism. As in the past, thinking about race and racism today, "requires a certain schedule of structured blindness and opacities in order to establish and maintain the white polity."[18] As such, both historic and contemporary "pattern[s] of localized and globalized cognitive dysfunctions" are "psychologically and socially functional" in that they not only justify but (re)produce White supremacist material structures.[19]

Building on Mills and other Critical Race Theory scholars such as Joe Feagin, Eduardo Bonilla-Silva, and Moon-Kie Jung, sociologist Jennifer Mueller's Theory of Racial Ignorance (TRI) "conceptualizes ignorance as a cognitive accomplishment grounded in explicit and tacit practices of knowing and non-knowing."[20] Mills' Epistemology of Ignorance is the first tenet of TRI. The second tenet of TRI, that ignorance is an "Ends-Based Technology," describes how its function is to provide specific outcomes that members of society, especially members of the dominant group, are "motivated to pursue."[21] These include not only the material spoils of White domination, such as greater opportunity to obtain quality goods like housing[22] and services like health care,[23] but also psychic outcomes such as being able to feel one legitimately "earned everything."[24]

Mueller's third tenet, "Corporate White Agency," describes how, in addition to individuals' ignorance, "structural and institutional mechanisms facilitates white ignorance."[25] The US state of Florida offers a clear example: In 2023, the governor signed a bill that banned teaching about systemic racism in public schools. Regardless of whether this ban stands or ultimately crumbles under the weight of legal challenges, organized efforts like it to regulate what information schools can teach on racism demonstrates how institutions can contribute to maintaining widespread ignorance of racism.

A focus on the "Centrality of Praxis," TRI's fourth tenet, draws attention to the "specific social processes and many practical ways ignorance manifests and can be observed in social life."[26] This includes "what people *do* (i.e., practice) as a reflection of racial logic" and also "what people *write* and *say*" because of it.[27] Understanding actions and thinking means that TRI is able to identify how "a wide variety of white racial projects, including the most well-meaning and progressive," actually stem from the culture-serving commitment to ignorance.[28]

Theorizing how all of the foregoing phenomena evolve and change is the final tenet of "Interest Convergence." Mueller explains that because "white ignorance advances white people's material and psychic interests, large segments of society have little incentive to alter or eradicate it."[29]

In sum, Mills' Epistemology of Ignorance, Mueller's Theory of Racial Ignorance, and the many scholars who lay the foundation for a general sociology of ignorance have established that "ignorance is a bona fide if often vexing social fact."[30] Considering "the dangers of scientific illiteracy and 'post-factual' societies," Mueller asserts that examining the place of ignorance within systems of racism is timely and necessary for anti-racist progress. It undoubtedly has great potential to illuminate how common thinking about racism is marred in a White supremacist logic of distortion that there are material and mental benefits to protecting. However, it would be impractical and ineffective in most undergraduate classrooms, not to mention in casual conversations, to take a deep dive into the scholarship of epistemology. Using a condensed, portable synthesis such as fallacies, though, can help bring this understanding from behind pay walls and erudite language and into everyday usage.

The Fallacies of Racism

From historic Indigenous resistance to the nation's first racist project of European colonization to the contemporary rejection of White beauty standards that is Black women wearing our natural hair, the idea that White domination is natural and just, versus human-imposed and immoral, has been constantly challenged since its inception. To reassert a Bourdieusian *illusio* in such a clearly unjust system, though, takes "specific *cognitive tactics*" born of "white agency motive, and creativity."[31] The coming chapters describe examples of "practical ways racial ignorance manifests and is observable in social life."[32] I call these fallacies of racism. As will be shown, fallacies are perceptions, but they are not simply thoughts. As patterns of thinking, they are *tools* that are used in writing and conversations to (knowingly or unknowingly) maintain White domination by obscuring the operation of it and/or (attempting to) neutralize challenges to its legitimacy. Within Mueller's TRI framework, the fallacies of racism are a part of her tenets of praxis and ends-based technologies.

After this Introduction, the book presents a dozen common perceptions about racism. Some of these fallacies are expanded treatments of those that Desmond, Emirbayer, and Fleming briefly mentioned; but the majority are additional perceptions that I have identified from my teaching and research. Throughout these chapters, I not only describe common patterns of thinking regarding racism but also demonstrate how they are ends-based. In other words, the chapters will demonstrate how perceptions function to maintain White supremacist logics and, by extension, material practices of oppression, even in the absence of active or conscious White supremacist beliefs.

The first section of the book presents the first three fallacies of racism. The Individualistic Fallacy (chapter 1) is the notion that racism only exists at the individual level; in other words, it is the view that there is nothing systemic nor structural about racism. The Token Fallacy (chapter 2) is the idea that racism only exists if all power and resources are held by Whites; and conversely, it is the idea that if so much as one member of another race has any power or resources, then racism against that group does not exist. The Familiarity Fallacy (chapter 3) is the belief that a person cannot possibly be or act racist against a given group if that person has a relationship with a member of that group. Because these fallacies share the common feature of being individual-focused, taken together they are called the Micro-Level Fallacies.

The five fallacies that are the focus of Section II are called the Meso-Level Fallacies. Meso, i.e., middle or "in-between," level analysis within sociology studies localized norms and processes within groups, organizations, and social institutions. Privileging what a person says over what they do is the Simon Says Fallacy (chapter 4). Named for the childhood game, it is the perception that if Simon says "jump" then the group jumps, and if Simon says "I'm not racist" then the group believes that he is not racist. The Mens Rea Fallacy (chapter 5) is the perspective that pre-meditated, malicious intent is a pre-requisite for racism to exist or have occurred. The Innuendo Fallacy (chapter 6) is the view that coded language and behavior do not exist with respect to racism. In other words, it is the perception that only explicitly hateful speech and actions are racist and that it is invalid to claim that euphemisms or codes can be racist too. The perception that pointing out instances of racism is problematic, or even constitutes an act of racism itself, is the

Recognition Fallacy (chapter 7); and the perspective that collective action to defend or protect minorities against racist oppression is just as harmful as oppression itself, and thus is "wrong," is the Self-Defense Fallacy (chapter 8).

Section III examines four Macro-Level Fallacies, that is, perceptions that are socio-historically focused, structural, and systemic. The Legalistic Fallacy (chapter 9) is the perspective that having a law against racism means racism no longer exists. The Fixed Fallacy (chapter 10) is the perspective that racism does not modernize over time and thus only specific types of historical actions are racist, not anything in the present. The perspective that those past actions did not create, and in fact have nothing to do with, the state of current conditions is the Ahistorical Fallacy (chapter 11). Lastly, the Silence Fallacy (chapter 12) is the assumption that talking about race at all is harmful and that silence is the best way to solve racism.

The Conclusion contains a summary of my overarching argument about fallacies of racism. Far from being specific ideas that people actively subscribe to in order to create racist disparities, fallacies are instead unexamined general patterns of thinking that are rooted in an epistemology of ignorance. As such, if they are not interrogated, they will function to justify and (re)produce White domination, both ideologically and materially. The Conclusion of the book also acknowledges that many, if not all, of the fallacies can apply to gender inequality, sexual orientation inequality, and other systems of oppression as well. While it is outside the scope of one book to cover all manifestations of fallacy-based perceptions about inequality, the Conclusion highlights the possibilities. The final section of the Conclusion and book contains suggestions for incorporating the lessons in *The Fallacies of Racism* into our thinking and action in multiple areas of everyday life.

Caveats

There are a couple of important caveats to address before diving into *The Fallacies of Racism*. First, this book covers twelve fallacies; however, that is not to say that these are the *only* fallacies in the past, present, or future. Psychologists use Systems Justification Theory to explain the phenomenon of people using "ideas about groups and individuals to justify the way things are, so that existing social arrangements are perceived as legitimate, desirable, and fair."[33] As existing social arrangements shift, so too must patterns of thinking about them, though always in service to maintaining their legitimacy. Thus, specific fallacies of racism will wax and wane; but the existence of White supremacist system-justifying patterns of thinking persists.

A ready example of this is my non-inclusion of a chapter on the Biological Essentialism Fallacy. When Western elites' religious (Christian) understanding of society gave way to scientific "reason," the pattern of thinking about the origins of groups likewise changed. Dominant Western understanding of human difference shifted from religious frameworks like Africans carried the curse of Noah's son Ham to "scientific" ones like Native Americans and Africans are subhuman. Notice, though, that within both frameworks, the perception of White superiority vis-à-vis non-White inferiority is maintained. Having now mapped the entire human genome, science is clear that members of all races are equally human and that there are not even sub-species divisions like there are breeds of dogs or types of flowers.

Even before the twenty-first century offered the technology to peer into humans' genetic makeup, though, it took commitment to an epistemology of ignorance to maintain the perception of race as biological. During the seventeenth through nineteenth centuries, for example, the fact that the widespread sexual assault of enslaved Black women by White men led to mixed-race children who were themselves fertile, *unlike* the mule from which the word "mulatto" was derived, was proof that members of different races were equally human from a biological perceptive. However, in order to justify enslavement, walking, talking, and procreating proof of Black and White biological equality was ignored in favor of the culture-serving Biological Essentialism Fallacy that assigned non-Whites subhuman status.

Racial groups are "socially constructed," meaning they have been created by context-specific social events (colonization, war, enslavement, classification laws, etc.) that used arbitrarily selected characteristics – some biological, some not – to classify people into groups and then use that classification as justification to (mis)treat them accordingly.[34] Presently in the twenty-first century, the *dominant pattern of thinking* about racial groups is no longer that Western minorities are biologically *subhuman*. Likewise, while there are certainly those who believe that members of different races have different biological predispositions in some specific areas, for example there are perceptions that Whites and Asians are innately intelligent while Blacks are innately athletic, biology is no longer the *dominant* explanation for group difference. Research on White US Americans' analysis of the origins of racial disparities in housing and wealth, for example, does not find any assertions of biological difference.[35] Because social conditions have changed from the seventeenth century to now, new – albeit equally distorted – dominant patterns of thinking have arisen.

The coming chapters focus on these contemporary fallacies; but, as will be made clear, regardless of *which* fallacies of racism exist at a particular point in time, they are all ends-based epistemological technologies that function to justify and (re)produce White domination. The point, then, as discussed in the Conclusion, is not to view the fallacies as a taxonomy to be memorized. The goal is to analyze current fallacies in order to learn how to identify how patterns of thinking can function to maintain inequality.

Second, this book is written to make dense theoretical concepts regarding racism and cognitive science accessible and memorable. However, unlike other books on the topic of racism and cognition, *The Fallacies of Racism* is *not* "mainly writing to a white audience."[36] To be sure, numerous scholars have given ink to the observation that it is most frequently White people who, when confronted with empirically accurate information about racism, respond with emotional "fragility" and the cognitive gymnastics that characterizes an epistemology of ignorance.[37] However, as Black thinkers from Frantz Fanon to Malcolm X to Kehinde Andrews have explained, "the effects of colonialism were not just physical" but also "profoundly cultural and psychological," with the result that many minorities have been conditioned "to believe in White supremacy."[38]

Thus, this book is written with the understanding that some members of oppressed racial groups also think in ways that align with fallacies of racism. Whether due to having been miseducated,[39] conventionally socialized within the dominant Western culture[40] or under colonialism,[41] or due to the influence of experiences based on their gender, sexuality, or non-race social statuses,[42] non-White people are not a monolith who are immune to society's common patterns of thinking about racism. To quote Andrews: "the delusions of Whiteness disturb all of our thinking."[43] In sum, as Mueller explains, analysis of racial ignorance "recognizes that all groups can engage in practices of racialized ignorance and not-knowing," although it is clear on the fact that White people have been and continue to be the group who are most "committed to 'thinking badly' on such matters."[44] Learning to think critically is a skill that is important for all members of society; thus, as a book about identifying the inequality-sustaining function of normative thinking, *The Fallacies of Racism* is written for a diverse audience.

Third, while each fallacy is discussed singularly within its own chapter, like the colorblind racist phrases that Bonilla-Silva analyzed in his book *Racism Without Racists: Color-Blind Racism and the Persistence of Racial Inequality in America* (2018 [2003]), the patterns of thinking that I am labeling fallacies also "bundle with each other." This means that two or more fallacies can co-occur in an individual's thinking, in social discourse, and as the basis for institutionalized policies. In other words, though highlighted in discrete chapters, these common patterns of thinking work together to maintain the status quo.

Finally, two meta-notes on the text. Regarding terminology, I use the terms White supremacy and White settler colonialism interchangeably to refer to the overall hierarchical (Whites on top, all others stratified below) social arrangements in the United States and other "Western" countries like the United Kingdom, Canada, and Australia that were created from Europeans dispossessing Indigenous peoples of their land. I refer to the action of creating and maintaining the unequal ideological and material aspects of these societies with words like White domination or simply racism; and I refer to specific outcomes of those processes as racial/racist disparities or inequality. Lastly, for ease of reading, most citations are included as endnotes. Additional discussion related to the content is also included in endnotes.

Section I

Micro-Level Fallacies

With regard to sociological analysis, focusing on small-scale manifestations of social phenomena, such as individuals' actions and face-to-face interactions, is taking a micro-level approach.[1] The micro level is "the most intimate way of thinking about social life" and "typically focuses on interaction, communication, and relationships."[2] Micro-level sociological analysis highlights individual, psychological, and cognitive processes, though it differs from the discipline of psychology in that it centers the role of social experiences and context for those processes. This is in contrast to meso- and macro-level analysis, which focus on groups and structures, respectively.[3]

Within the study of race and racism, micro-level analysis focuses on individual racism, which sociologist Tanya Maria Golash-Boza defines as "individual acts of racial discrimination or bigotry."[4] The concepts of prejudice, i.e., an individual's holding of pre-conceived, often negative and stereotypical, ideas about different groups and of microaggressions, that is the "daily commonplace insults and racial slights that cumulatively affect the psychological well-being of people of color" are both micro-level analytical concepts.[5] They both describe racial phenomena that occur either with respect to a given individual or during a small-scale (one-on-one) interaction.

The three chapters in this section describe fallacies that are all individual or one-on-one relationship focused; thus, they are called the Micro-Level Fallacies. Chapter 1 addresses the perception that individual prejudice and individually committed bigoted actions are the only type of racism that exists. Chapter 2 analyzes the perception that (strategically selected) individuals who are different than the majority of their race negate the reality of the majority. Chapter 3 uses the intimate, one-on-one interaction focus of micro-level analysis to debunk the perception that people having cross-racial relationships is incompatible with racism.

Social scientific research shows that most people have difficulty understanding racism beyond the micro level.[6] As common patterns of thinking that reproduce the view that racism is strictly an individual issue, the Micro-Level Fallacies function to maintain racial inequality. As will be seen in the chapters that follow, these culture-serving micro-level perceptions contribute to maintaining White supremacy beyond individual thinking and one-on-one interactions.

1

The Individualistic Fallacy

Research shows that the majority of people, especially but not exclusively White people, think about racism "as personal prejudice rather than as systematic or institutional."[1] Prejudice, an individual form of racism, is defined by sociologists as the holding of preconceived ideas about groups' innate hierarchal differences that are resistant to change even in the face of empirical evidence to the contrary.[2] Institutional racism, on the other hand, is defined as "policies, laws, and institutions that reproduce racial inequalities."[3] Sociologist James Loewen blames high school history textbooks for the fact that so many people in the US have "no understanding of the ways that opportunity is not equal in America and no notion that social structure pushes people around, influencing the ideas they hold and the lives they fashion."[4]

Explaining that racism exists *not only* as personal prejudice *but also* as institutional discrimination is a key goal in college-level Race/Ethnicity books and courses.[5] For example, throughout her book *Getting Smart About Race* (2020), sociologist Margaret Anderson stresses to readers that structural-level racism exists.[6] Other sociologists name the perception that racism is strictly individual as a "fallacy" about racism and debunk it at the beginning of their book. Sociologists Matthew Desmond and Mustafa Emirbayer call the perception the Individualistic Fallacy. In their textbook, *Race in America* (2020 [2010]), they state that "racism is assumed to belong to the realm of ideas and attitudes."[7] It is seen as "only the collection of nasty thoughts a 'racist individual' has about another group," and is only "a matter of personal 'prejudices' . . . and of 'stereotypes.'"[8]

Sociologist Crystal Fleming's KKK Fallacy, the first to be debunked in her book *How To Be Less Stupid About Race* (2018), is the common perception that racism is an isolated "cancerous tumor you can remove" from otherwise healthy systems.[9] From this view point, racism only manifests as specific "extremists such as the Ku Klux Klan or the Nazi regime."[10] Fleming also discusses the perceptions that only people of a certain class or political party are racist, calling these her Class Fallacy and Political Fallacy, respectively. I see these two perspectives as part of an expanded Individualistic Fallacy, though, because at their root is the idea that racism is not systemic but isolatable to individuals, be that individual people or one specific group.

To be clear, naming the Individualistic Fallacy is *not* to suggest that individual-level racism (prejudice) *doesn't exist*. The fallacy is the perception that it is the *only* type of racism. I have seen people fall into this fallacy in three main ways. First, I have seen them have a difficult time understanding the concept of there being an unequal social structure. Second, more abstractly, I have seen them struggle to accept the existence of phenomena that they have not personally witnessed or experienced. These patterns of thinking mean that when tasked with problem assessment and problem solving, the Individualistic Fallacy, third, manifests as individual-focused proposed solutions to social inequality. As such, this fallacy is revealed to be not "illogical thinking" or "a mistake" but a common-sense ends-based perspective that functions to support White supremacy by limiting development of effective interventions.

Personal Troubles vs Social Issues: Racism Edition

Psychologist Cyndi Kernahan explains that the idea that racism is structural (that is, patterned in the society) and systemic (that is, existing in multiple ways and parts of a society) is rejected because these ideas are "deeply threatening to the idea of meritocracy, that one's own effort and hard work are the main reasons for one's success."[11] I would add, too, that in the United States specifically, a culture of rugged individualism bordering on arrogance makes people remiss to admit that any part of one's fate is impacted by something other than their own actions. For people of color, the

realization that racism is not just individuals or just a few extremists is resisted because it is "angering and disempowering, making
it difficult to feel in control of one's own future."[12] In my experience, I have seen middle- to upper-income second-generation Asian
Americans whose immigrant parents worked hard and "made it"
have a difficult time recognizing that there are structural con-
straints that prevent immigrants from different backgrounds from
following that straight line assimilation pathway. For White people,
Kernahan says that "the understanding that racism creates a kind
of privilege that benefits them every day in ways seen and unseen
comes into conflict with the belief that they are good people. Not
racist people."[13] The Individualistic Fallacy is a perception that
allows people to maintain their view of their nation as meritocratic
and themselves as agentic.

The Individualistic Fallacy can be seen in the difficulty of apply-
ing the sociological imagination to problems of race. Like many
sociology instructors, one of the very first lessons in my classes
is C. Wright Mills' (1959) concept of the Sociological Imagination,
which is the ability to recognize, understand, and articulate structural social phenomena and their mutually determining relationship with individual and group aspects of society. Mills' classic
example is the case of unemployment: if there is one unemployed
man [sic] out of 50,000 that is that individual's "personal trouble,"
while if half of a city's men are unemployed that is a "social issue."
Mills explained that solving a personal trouble is accomplished
via one's own actions. That one hypothetical unemployed person
could get better transportation to get to work, go back to school to
get more education, or simply "stop being lazy."

The resolution of social issues, by contrast, is *not* within the
singular power of any one unemployed person. Recent events
such as the Great Recession, Trump Administration, and Covid-19
pandemic offer quick examples of how economic circumstances
like outsourcing of jobs, an economic downturn, discrimination
against a whole class of people, or mass illness are all potential
causes of unemployment. These examples illustrate how sometimes no one person alone can solve the problem of their unemployment. Instead, collective efforts like unionizing or structural
changes like introducing small business loans are the needed solutions. Historically, government programs like the New Deal's Work
Progress Administration did in fact create jobs for out of work US

Americans during the Great Depression of the 1930s. On their first exam, the majority of my students correctly explain the difference in wrecking one's car because of a personal trouble versus wrecking it because of a social issue. Popular answers include texting while driving for the former and poor traffic signage for the latter.

Yet too often when this perspective is applied to the study of race and racism, the dominant epistemology of ignorance triumphs over the sociological imagination. For example, research on racial disparities in heterosexual marriage rates show that economic factors (e.g., income inequality) and social factors (e.g., mass incarceration, sexual racism) explain why Black US American women have lower rates of marriage than other demographic groups. Once, after I presented this information in class, a White man raised his hand and asked if the "real reason" for marriage rate differences was not simply "because Black women are less attractive than other women."

I have written elsewhere about the impact that this public racist insult had on me and the Black woman who sat in the front row;[14] so for the purposes here, I want to focus on the speaker. The epistemology of ignorance, here manifesting as clinging to the Individualistic Fallacy, compelled him to reject the data-supported idea that the economy and society have an influence on marriage rates. His thinking, here rooted first in sexism and second in racism, is that attractive women get married, ergo if fewer Black women are married than others it is because they are not as attractive as others. Whiteness Studies scholar Tim Wise has commented on this pattern of thinking saying that, "It becomes very logical. Albeit flawed. I mean it's wrong. But it's very logical to come to that conclusion."[15] Thus, one's ability to understand the difference in personal troubles and social issues when it comes to some types of problems but then resist perceiving social factors as creating racist disparities makes plain that the latter pattern of thinking is an attempt to maintain the legitimacy of the status quo by refusing to acknowledge its unequal design.

From just one "Bad Apple" to "I Don't See Any Bad Apples": Contradictory Manifestations of Racism Denial

The Individualistic Fallacy manifests outside of university classrooms, too. In the media, for instance, there is often more outcry over an individual's racist behavior than over their or their nation's structural and systemic racism. Race scholar Alana Lentin has analyzed media firestorms in the US and Australia demonstrating how the Individualistic Fallacy serves the function of deflecting, distancing, and denial, which she coins "the three Ds of post-racial racism management."[16] In the US, she analyzes the public reaction to tapes being made public that reveal that Donald Sterling, the then-owner of the US basketball team the Los Angeles (LA) Clippers, made anti-Black comments like "don't bring Black people [to my games]."[17] Citing news reports, Lentin explains that Sterling was "already well known" as a "verbally abusive bigot" and she reveals that the US Department of Justice had brought a lawsuit against him for racial discrimination in housing rentals.[18] "[S]o it is not the words themselves nor Sterling's known racist practice, but rather his being caught that appears to have been the problem," Lentin concludes.[19]

The perception that racism is only one Bad Apple's personal beliefs, words, or inter-personal interactions, i.e., the Individualistic Fallacy, ensures that hot-mic situations like Sterling's are recognizable as "racist." But the myopic focus on personal prejudice means that structural forms of racism can be overlooked. As Sterling's housing discrimination has a much larger and more wide-reaching negative impact on others than who his friends bring to a basketball game, the Individualistic Fallacy is revealed to function to protect macro-level forms of inequality from identification and challenge.

Regarding Australia, Lentin analyzes the case of a Chinese immigrant coffee shop owner who refused to hire a Black barista simply because of the latter's race. During the media coverage of the story, the owner told journalists that, "'There are a lot of white customers at the café and I think the clients here want local people, not African [sic] people' and 'We need to offer good service at this café and I think the coffee culture is more about white people.'"[20] Australia's own systemic anti-Blackness was sidelined, however, as "[c]ommentators used the experience to perform a denial of Australian racism, underline the exceptionalism of the event, and applaud the public's reaction, casting it in terms of the national character [of being committed to racial equality]."[21] In this case, not only was individual anti-Blackness highlighted to the exclusion of structural manifestations of it in the nation, but also, since the offender was an immigrant, the Individualistic Fallacy allowed his prejudice to be framed as a foreign import rather than a local practice.

While not at play in the Australian coffee shop case since the owner admitted to engaging in hiring discrimination, in other cases when someone is accused of racism others express surprise or disbelief because they have never seen such behavior from the accused person. Crystal Fleming names denying that racism exists "simply because they haven't experienced it – or because they don't want to believe those who have been targeted" as her Gaslighting Fallacy.[22] Rather than having the humility to accept that there are things that they cannot or simply have yet to perceive, they instead think that if they don't see someone behaving like a Bad Apple then the alleged racism couldn't possibly be real. Philosophers use the term "epistemic arrogance" to describe this pattern of thinking, which by default assumes one's own knowledge is complete.[23] Resistance to new information, especially information that would challenge one's assumptions or positions, is called "epistemic laziness" and "epistemic closed-mindedness."[24]

Another theoretical term that captures this phenomenon is "internalism." Internalism is "the perspective that unless a thinker can determine whether something is true from their own internal sensory experience, they cannot conclude that something is true."[25] Theoretical physicist Chanda Prescod-Weinstein asserts that this perspective is an issue because we live in "a world where sensory experiences are necessarily diverse and where the distribution of these experiences tends to correlate heavily with ascribed identities such as one's race, gender identity, sex identity, and gender expression."[26] The "I don't see any Bad Apples" manifestation of the Individualistic Fallacy is the mental gymnastics to negate this observation; that is, it functions to deny that there are many diverse experiences in the social world, that perhaps, due to one's position in society, there are some things one will not have personal access to witness or experience.

Sociologist Erving Goffman would say that people actually know this because in their daily lives their presentation of self involves acts of audience segregation, that is showing different sides of oneself to some people versus others. For example, most people can accept, albeit with exaggerated faux-retching, that their parents engage(d) in sexual activity. Indirect evidence, such as one's own existence, is sufficient to accept that their parents act differently

with each other than how they act with their children. With regard
to racism, though, the Individualistic Fallacy means that not seeing
someone, or a group, act in a discriminatory manner can be the
basis for not "believing" that they do. My students often cite seeing
the video of police officers murdering George Floyd as what made
them "believe" in racist police brutality. Many students admit to
having heard of it before; but unlike their parents' sex lives, indirect evidence was insufficient regarding racism. It was seeing it for
themselves that made them "believe."

The need for first-hand experience or witness to accept the
existence of racist behavior, when that standard is not required to
accept the existence of other types of social behavior, has conveniently developed during the present era when there is less direct
racism in public for people to witness.[27] The young people of today
were not taken as children to lynchings like the White children of
the Silent Generation were. Unlike the explicitly racist comments
made in the media consumed by Baby Boomers in their youth, the
news today presents a color-blind façade by mentioning any and
everything other than race as reasons for any observable racial differences.[28] It is no wonder, then, that so many people today say
they haven't seen racism or White privilege. What they have been
told racism is (mid-twentieth-century Klan values and actions, see
chapter 10), is not on display in most people's daily lives; and so the
Individualistic Fallacy misleads them to believe that if they individually don't see it, then it does not exist.

Donate to End Racism

Viewing racism as only individual thoughts and behaviors does not
only limit what is perceived as racism but it also limits the solutions
proposed to address it. Kernahan explains how the Individualistic
Fallacy is an ends-based tool that functions to maintain White
domination: "[i]f it is just about one person, then our society will
not have to contend with the larger currents of racism and White
supremacy that underlie such incidents. We will not have to consider solutions beyond just getting rid of those few 'bad apples.'"[29]

The offering of solutions to address individual Bad Apples is
another way I have observed the Individualistic Fallacy manifest.
When I first began teaching, I concluded inequality lessons with

brief references to hopeful future developments and I concluded the semester with lessons on social movements and change for equality. One student commented on this practice in their evaluation, saying, "The instructor was very good at balancing the difficult topics and making sure we didn't want to go hang ourselves after lecture by ending on a good note." Nevertheless, other students wrote that they were left "feeling helpless" after learning about racism in the US. In order to help students discover their own agency, versus just hearing me point out examples of agency in general, I changed the conclusion section of the paper assignments on inequality to task students with brainstorming their own structural solutions to racism. The social structure is the durable patterns of social life within the various institutions of a society, and structural racism is the "interinstitutional interactions across time and space that reproduce racial inequality."[30]

Developing structural solutions to racial inequality requires thinking outside of the Individualistic Fallacy; and this is difficult for the majority of people. For example, analyzing her own students' racial wealth gap research assignments, sociologist Jennifer Mueller found that even when "racist asset-policies were a primary focus of students' research and policy remediation was covered in course lectures and readings, only two students [of 105] invoked related public interventions."[31] A common suggestion that my students make – despite my specification that proposed solutions be structural – is to call for an increase in individual philanthropic efforts. In other words, like Ebenezer Scrooge at the end of Charles Dickens' *A Christmas Carol*, well-off members of society should "donate more" to the less fortunate. Other common non-structural solutions include being "nice" to everyone, "educating yourself," and simply "stop discriminating."

While individual efforts are wonderful, they are nonetheless not structural solutions. Mueller found in her analysis that her students resisted learning about racism in their own families' history via not following the directions to research it.[32] In this way, feelings like guilt or culpability (which students who did the assignment correctly admitted to experiencing upon discovery of their family's financial benefit from historical racist policies) can be kept at bay by literally refusing to face the information. Likewise, my students who write individual solutions to racism when I specifically asked them to brainstorm structural ones may be engaged in a similar tactic. If one is unaware of structural solutions, then one can remain innocent and non-culpable (that is "not racist") when one does things like vote for candidates who vow to roll back programs that represented attempts at structural solutions to racism. One can, when one is graduated and employed, be innocent of perpetuating institutional racism when one abides by versus challenges biased workplace policies.

Beyond donating, another common way the Individual Fallacy manifests regarding solutions to racism is via appropriation of concerns for mental health, which are perceived as more empathetic solutions than "political" solutions. For example, the day after the July 4, 2022 mass shooting by an outspoken White supremacist, the US's *Fox News* reported that one witness was already "putting politics aside" and instead "demands answers on alleged shooter's mental health."[33] The interviewed man is quoted as saying that when his children "had many questions after the shooting," he responded:

> By explaining the individual needed more mental health support and his mind was not "correct". . . . I explain to my kids that his mind wasn't correct. He didn't know or maybe didn't know, but he wasn't sure what was the correct way of expressing his anger and his frustration.[34]

He further revealed that his family is "rooted in empathy" as they suffer from mental health issues and therefore "understand some of the social judgments and the frustrations" the shooter was feeling.[35] Regarding solutions, he explained:

> We don't care about politics. We don't have concern about the gun debate. We want to know why someone with a neurological [sic] who wasn't right, who lived in our community, didn't get the support and resources that my children are getting right now, so they can be as best as possible.[36]

To be clear, at that point – the day after the shooting – there was *no* basis for any of this man's assumptions nor for his implicitly proposed solution of expanding whatever "support and resources" his children were getting to others. For one, the police had not released any information whatsoever about the shooter's health status, mental or otherwise, beyond saying he was taken in alive. In other words, there was no reason to think the shooter had mental health issues. What is more, even if the shooter *did* have mental health issues, as no information on that had been released there was no basis for this witness, who is assumedly unacquainted with the shooter, to make assertions regarding what support and resources he did or did not get. Second, on July 5, the public had not yet been told the shooter's motive. Thus, there was no reason to assume he felt any anger and frustration, let alone the same anger and frustration the witness admits his family has felt.

The only information that *was* known at the time of this interview was the shooter's politics. Before his social media profiles were deleted, internet users saved pictures he had posted of himself that revealed him to be an avid Trump Republican. Photos circulated online of him draped in a Trump flag and there were others showing him attending Trump rallies dressed as the literary character Where's Waldo. The interviewed witness, *Fox News*, and millions of others were compelled by the Individualistic Fallacy to fervently desire to "put aside" concrete sociopolitical information – i.e., group-level information – in favor of assumptions and conjecture about an individual's mental health.

Research analyzing shootings in the US has shown that sociological explanations are superior to psychological ones. By the end of the twentieth century, the lower income, "inner city," and "gang" violence associated with racial minorities in the 1970s and 1980s had given way to middle-class White boys in Republican-controlled states being the majority of random, mass shooters. Concurrently, the explanatory narratives and proposed solutions that flowed from them changed as well. Gone were the group-level explanations like the Culture of Poverty thesis and government reports on the pathology of shooters' family structure. Sociologists explain that:

> As the shooters have become White and suburban middle-class boys, the public has shifted the blame away from group characteristics to individual psychological problems, assuming that these boys were deviants who broke away from an otherwise genteel suburban culture – that their aberrant behavior was explainable by some psychopathological factor.[37]

It is the Individualistic Fallacy that pivots thinking away from group-based explanations when a White person's violence is under consideration. This attempt to set the national thinking about a White supremacist terrorizing the public as about an individual's mental health versus the pathology of a group is so ubiquitous that it has been memed. In one version of the meme, Peter Griffin, the White man lead on the animated television show *Family Guy*, is sitting in his car with his window rolled down as a chart is held up to his face. The chart has three light skin color shades, marked with individual labels like "lone wolf" and "mentally ill" and three darker shades with group labels like "thug" and "terrorist." In short, the epistemology of ignorance not only favors individual explanations for racism but also individual solutions because it means "our society will not have to contend with the larger currents of racism and White supremacy that underlie such incidents."[38]

So great is the focus on individual psychology that a common structural solution is directed at it: to make laws requiring sensitivity, cultural competence, and/or anti-racism trainings. In her book *Flatlining: Race, Work, and Health Care in the New Economy* (2019), sociologist Adia Harvey Wingfield explains that these trainings address the cultural competency of individual workers, not the structural inequality of the workplace as an organization or social context. Moreover, while training efforts may lead to improved patient outcomes, they do not address the racism faced by marginalized workers nor its impact.[39] In short, such trainings, which many organizations have actually required, at best do nothing for employment discrimination and at worst have been shown to make White men even more hostile to anti-racist efforts.[40]

Social scientists contend that these trainings become little more than a "shield against lawsuits" and a "box to check."[41] "Diversity" statements and initiatives at the hiring stage are also "limited to face-saving statements that are not supported by actions."[42] One example Wingfield recalls from her research came from a Black doctor whose White partners in the practice agreed to diversify the practice but then made excuses when faced with minority applicants. In one instance, the White partners expressed concern over a Latina applicant's bilingualism, perceiving it as a weakness rather than as a potential asset to the practice, in order to remove her application from further consideration.[43] Sociologist Eduardo Bonilla-Silva calls this the Abstract Liberalism frame of Colorblind Racism for it exemplifies the post-Civil Rights era phenomenon of positioning oneself as in favor of racial equality in theory while taking action, always justified via non-racial factors, to block attempts to make greater equality an actuality. Bonilla-Silva's data shows that 96 percent of White interviewees and 35 percent of Black interviewees used an Abstract Liberalism in their responses to interview questions about racism.[44]

While increasing diversity, equity, and inclusion is on a lot of companies' minds, the Individualistic Fallacy is impacting these efforts. Take beer, for example. In their analysis of the homogeneous Whiteness of the craft beer industry, sociologists Nathanael Chapman and David Brunsma discuss the Brewers Association's (BA) "three key ways in which craft brewers can advance their diversity."[45] The first and third, "identify and address unconscious bias" and "make sure everyone feels invited and welcome at your brewery," respectively, focus on changes in thinking and behavior to be made by *individual* owners/employees.[46] In their interviews, Chapman and Brunsma found that "*none* of our white male respondents" saw the Whiteness of craft beer as being due to "barriers and lack of resources," and only half of their non-White interviewees mentioned it.[47]

The Individualistic Fallacy thus facilitates the continued functioning of White domination in the craft beer and other industries by thwarting understandings of the structural origins of racial disparities within them. Racism will not be solved primarily by encouraging individual actions. Four centuries of structures of exclusion do not disappear just because a few individuals decide to donate some of their clothes, take online training, or invite people of color to an event.

The second suggestion from the BA is double-barreled (pun intended): "hiring a diverse set of staff and attracting a diverse set of customers."[48] These two reveal the White centeredness in the industry, as "diversity" is seen as getting more dark bodies into White spaces (and having minorities feel "invited and welcome" there). Nonetheless, the first part of the suggestion regarding hiring a "diverse set of staff" does at least hint at changing the structure of one aspect of craft beer as an *industry*.[49] Unlike other suggestions, a focus on hiring is a noticeable departure from the more frequent focus on changing hearts to the exclusion of improving material conditions. Chapman and Brunsma comment that the Brewers Association's steps "are in the right direction; however, more needs to be done."[50]

Conclusion

The view that racism only exists within individuals is common. However, social scientists have produced millions of pages both theorizing and empirically demonstrating that "[r]ebel flag waving white supremacists are not the only ones invested in preserving white spaces in the interests of prosperity, privilege, and comfortableness."[51] Although social structure plays the largest role in (re)constructing inequality, the Individualistic Fallacy places both causes of and responsibility to correct racism on the shoulders of individuals not the society. The moral panic over teaching that the structure is the issue has led to "critical race theory" bans in red states in the US; and these would be humorous in their ridiculousness if not for the fact that if enforced they would do real harm to what little sociohistorical education is currently offered.

And that, of course, is the goal. The Individualistic Fallacy that the West does not have structural racism is a perfect example of the epistemology of ignorance. The mental gymnastics allows people, Whites in particular but not exclusively, to explain the empirical data on disparities while fulfilling the Racial Contract to always view Whiteness as innocent. In so doing, it thwarts attention to potential structural solutions and thereby, and by design, also thwarts development and implementation of substantive changes that would begin to dismantle White supremacy.

2

The Token Fallacy

Although the Individualistic Fallacy is one of the hardest perceptions to relinquish, it can be done. However, just because someone is able to perceive how a system *can be* constructed unequally, does not mean that they will see that society *is* constructed unequally with respect to race. Like the mythical Hydra, White supremacy has many heads; as such, if the logic of one fallacy of racism is fallen in any given situation, then others will spring forth to take its place.

The Token Fallacy is one that easily follows a forced acknowledgment that social structures do exist. Sociologists Matthew Desmond and Mustafa Emirbayer, who called it the Tokenistic Fallacy, defined this line of thinking as one that "assumes that the presence of people of color in influential positions is evidence of the complete eradication of racial obstacles."[1] In other words, high-achieving minorities (tokens) are perceived as proof that, though a current structure exists, it is equally accessible to all. Sociologist Crystal Fleming mentioned this pattern of thinking, too. She defines her Whites-Only White Supremacy Fallacy as "a simple-minded view of racism [that] holds that white supremacy only exists if and when all resources and all power are held by 'whites only.'"[2] She considers it a "foolish idea that proof of white supremacy requires every single person of color to be deprived of all rights and resources."[3] Given that nothing in life is always and completely 100 percent homogeneous, setting that as the bar to establish that racism exists means that "[i]f any person of color holds a position of authority or experiences any degree of success, their mere existence is taken to be evidence that systematic racism and white privilege do not exist."[4]

In other words, the Token Fallacy functions to deny the existence of structural racism while simultaneously justifying it. Its logic is that within a just system those who fail do so on account of their own actions/inactions or lack of merit. Apropos to the Individualistic Fallacy of the previous chapter, unequally structured opportunities and life chances are ignored. In a nut shell, then, the Token Fallacy legitimizes the White supremacist-serving perception that observable racial disparities are because most racial minorities are not as smart or hardworking as White people. This perspective not only justifies the status quo but helps reproduce it given that a system that is considered fair is not one in need of fixing.

Building on and expanding upon Desmond, Emirbayer, and Fleming, I see the Token Fallacy as manifesting in three ways: first, by perceiving statistically outlying non-White "success" as if a few people beating a rigged system is evidence the system is not, in fact, unequally structured; second, by perceiving cherry-picked White "failure" as proof that White privilege does not exist, as if poor performance after a head start means you didn't actually have a head start; and third, by the differential majority response to non-Whites who align with White domination compared to White people who challenge it. The third point here especially gets at how the root of the Token Fallacy is not about actual numbers or the sincere perspective that 100 percent consensus is necessary for a phenomenon to exist; it is about using that perception *when it is convenient* to protect the perception that racism is not what is responsible for racial disparities.

Who Can Go into Space: Outliers, Averages, and Racism

The Token Fallacy can be seen in action in racism-denying bleats like, "But the US had a Black president!" and, "But Rishi Sunak is prime minister of the UK!" However, a person from a racial minority group achieving an impressive thing does not mean that everyone in society, regardless of group membership, has the same opportunity to do so. One person also does not mean that the structure that causes different opportunities is not there.

Since I live in Huntsville, Alabama, and the National Aeronautics and Space Administration (NASA) is literally down the street, let's back up and take the example of human space travel. The way life currently is structured on earth, not all people have an equal opportunity to go into space. The way the social structure is right now, occupational groups like astronauts and scientists (and bored trillionaires and their guests) are the ones who have the opportunity to go into space. The ability of those few token humans to go to space, though, does not change the fact that the rest of humanity is earth-bound.

The culture-serving perspective that the existence of outliers negates the data points that are clustered around the mean is common when discussing racism. Speaking of the barriers for women and racial minorities to careers in science, theoretical physicist Chanda Prescod-Weinstein estimates that every Black woman physics PhD she has talked to has been told, "Your success is proof that the system isn't rigged."[5] She rejects the Token Fallacy plainly: "Of course one token, or even a few, getting their foot through the door doesn't signal that the playing field is level."[6] Likewise, Prescod-Weinstein reminds her readers that the "personal success" of one able-bodied, light-skinned, middle-class person like herself "will not end the structural racism that keeps so many Black people and refugees, especially single mothers, their children, and trans folks, in poverty."[7] Holding on to the Token Fallacy is part of the White supremacist-serving epistemology of ignorance as it functions to protect the status quo, in Physics and beyond, from being recognized in its true – unequal – form.

In her book *Teaching About Race and Racism in the College Classroom* (2019), psychologist Cyndi Kernahan reveals that she has many times experienced students making comments in her class that align with the Token Fallacy. In one example she offers, a White student responds to her presenting data on racial wealth disparities by "bringing up the fact that there are many relatively wealthy and prosperous Black Americans (e.g., LeBron James, Ben Carson)."[8] Kernahan recommends "modeling the use of scholarly evidence to try to answer" such comments by staying focused on the evidence, which is that "there are certainly people who are above or below the average [for their race] when it comes to wealth . . . but that does not change the overall pattern of greater wealth for Whites."[9] Notice, though, that cited alongside billionaire athlete LeBron James was Ben Carson, who despite being a millionaire is nonetheless better known for his politics – he is a Black conservative and Republican – than his wealth. In other words, in using the Token Fallacy to deny racist wealth disparities, not only are wealthy minorities cited, but minorities who voice support for White supremacist views and policies are cited too.

Another example of this is US Supreme Court Justice Clarence Thomas. Thomas infamously characterized his professional success as "pulling myself up by my bootstraps," a White supremacist-serving perspective that aligns with the Individualistic Fallacy in that it ignores both the existence of structural racism and the structural solutions that made it possible for a Black man to succeed despite them. As an individual, Thomas could not have pulled himself to law school, pulled himself to a judgeship, or pulled himself to the altar to marry a White woman were it not for generations of civil rights activists giving their literal blood, sweat, tears, and lives to topple the structural barriers that previously prevented Black people from doing all of those things. Thus, Thomas's claim of self-made status is rooted in the White supremacy-serving epistemology of ignorance and it has a status quo legitimating and tokenistic air of "If-I-can-do-it-then-there-is-nothing-stopping-other-Black-people." Moreover, a look at his voting record reveals a White supremacy-aligned consistent distain for policies like affirmative action and voting rights protections, i.e., policies that acknowledge the continued operation of White domination in thwarting many US racial minorities' efforts to "pull up." For their support of White supremacy, minorities like Thomas and Ben Carson are pointed to, alongside wealthy minorities like James, as supposed evidence that racism does not exist.

Minorities who show strong support for White domination are statistical outliers on opinion polls; and although progress has been made, there are still racial disparities in average income and wealth. But the Token Fallacy ignores the math of outliers and averages to zero in on these tokens because "the sight of relatively successful racialized minorities feeds into the delusion that we have moved into a post-racial society."[10] Here "successful" means achievement of wealth and acceptance of the epistemology of ignorance. In his book *The Psychosis of Whiteness* (2023), Black Studies professor Kehinde Andrews explains that "the notion that Black people breaking through glass ceilings into the halls of presumed power represents progress is a key delusion of the psychosis of Whiteness."[11] In a chapter titled "Black skin, white psychosis," Andrews offers examples of people of color who he characterizes as "sucking and jiving to the tune of White supremacy to pocket some pieces of silver."[12] Among those he discusses are South Asian British politician Priti Patel, the former UK Home Secretary who "hated" Black Lives Matter demonstrations "so much that she put forward a bill that might make those kinds of protests almost impossible" and whose administration conducted "mass deportations which took place late at night."[13] He also discusses Suella Braverman, the second South Asian woman to be UK Home Secretary, whose "distain for asylum seekers was such that she ignored legal advice" and allowed migrants to be placed in an overcrowded detention center that led to "dangerous conditions" which drew criticism even from her predecessor Patel.[14] Andrews reminds his readers that people like Thomas, Carson, Patel, and Braverman are not new. He writes: "The current crop of Black and Brown people promoting White supremacy are just following in the footsteps of the chiefs, administrators and soldiers who took a salary in the service of Western imperialism" and of the plantation "House Negros" who were content to "live near the master, to accept the scraps from the table and defend the racist system that keeps all Black people down."[15]

The historical fact that some members of oppressed groups have always materially supported White supremacy reveals the illogic of perceiving modern tokens as evidence that racism does not exist. Andrews' chapter "The post-racial princess" exposes a second illogic of the Token Fallacy: The fact that, unlike politicians, other high-profile tokens who supposedly are proof of equality actually have no power. Discussing Meghan Markle, the Black/White mixed-race woman who married Prince Harry, as a symbolic token, he states: "Celebrating a Black princess may make us feel better, but it does not change any of the realities of the structural racism" because Meghan "did not even have [the Queen's] ceremonial power, let alone access to any of the levers of power necessary to make substantive change."[16]

According to Andrews, the public's hasty perception of Meghan's marriage into the Royal Family as sign of racial progress was due to an "intersectional failure." While statistically the Token Fallacy ignores the mathematics of outliers and averages, theoretically it ignores intersectionality. Coined by legal scholar Kimberlé Crenshaw in the 1980s, intersectionality is the critical, social justice-oriented theoretical perspective that acknowledges that

experiences of racial oppression differ based on other social strati-
fications such as gender, class, and sexual orientation.[17] An intersectional failure is "an inability to analyze through a lens that includes
both race and gender."[18] Such a failure meant that the public did not
perceive how being not only mixed-race (race) but also a woman
(gender) would influence the social impact of Meghan's addition
to the "deeply patriarchal institution" of the Royal Family.[19] Given
the conservative, gendered expectations of royal wives, an intersectional perspective would have quickly dashed any dreams that
Meghan could affect any change. Andrews points to her husband's
mother, Princess Diana, and the fate she suffered from the Royal
Family and British press, as evidence of what awaits a woman who
departs from royal tradition.

Intersectional failures also prevent dominant thinking from
taking into account the fact that within any given racial group,
certain experiences will not afflict, or even be visible, to all group
members because of other non-race group memberships. The
reason that minorities like Thomas, Carson, Patel, and Braverman
view society differently from the majority of their races is not
because they are "right" that society is not racist but is because
gender, class, and more mean that people of the same race nonetheless have different social experiences. In other words, they share
a race but other statuses mean they inhabit different places within
what Black Feminist Theorist Patricia Hill Collins calls the "Matrix
of Domination."[20]

The Token Fallacy is a perception that fails to acknowledge this.
The different treatment of Asian men versus women on dating apps
offers a ready example of its folly. In the US, sexual racism negatively stereotypes Asian men as less masculine and thus undesirable, while conversely, Asian women are exotified as highly feminine
and desirable. Research on online dating shows that Asian men
receive lower interest from other app users while Asian women,
especially White/Asian mixed-race women, are one of the demographic groups who receive the most interest on apps.[21] It would
be committing an intersectional failure, therefore, to assume that
there is not systemic anti-Asian racism on dating apps simply
because some types of Asian users are highly successful on the
apps. Pointing to a hypothetical Asian woman who sees no racism
on the apps would be an example of the Token Fallacy since gender
(as well as age, phenotype, and sexual orientation) influences one's

experiences of racism. Purporting that token minorities who have different experiences than the majority of their race are proof of the illegitimacy of the majority's perspective or experiences is thus a tool to ignore the fact that sexism, classism, homophobia, and more influence how racism manifests in society.

The Other Response to Minority Tokens: Know Your Place Aggression

The dominant thinking that happily points to successful minorities to negate claims of racism can quickly be revealed to be a smoke-screen when one considers another frequent response to minority tokens. As dramatized in the movie X about the life of Civil Rights Activist Malcolm X, when faced with a highly successful racial minority, another common response is, "That's too much power for one man to have." The powerful mental framework of the perceived hierarchical positioning of the races is at play here. White settler colonial societies were originally built on the myth of natural White superiority vis-à-vis natural Black and Indigenous inferiority. High-achieving and powerful racial minorities, therefore, represent a threat because their existence is proof that the White superiority/minority inferiority assumption on which those societies are based is a lie. Thus, in addition to embracing some minority tokens who succeed within the system as proof that the system is fair, the legal and extra-legal enforcers of White supremacy *also* attack and attempt to push them back. Sociologist James Loewen explains that "Particularly in the [US] South, whites attacked the richest and most successful African Americans, just as they had the most acculturated Native Americans . . . [for example] Black jockeys and mail carriers were shut out, not because they were inadequate, but because they succeeded."[22]

Theoretically, the dueling desires to celebrate and destroy minority tokens can be explained via sociologist Herbert Blumer's theory of racism as group position. In 1958, Blumer broke with the then dominant (White) academic thinking that racism was rooted in individual prejudiced sentiments and instead offered that racism was more about a concern with the position of racial groups than about individuals' feelings towards other individuals. He explained:

[T]he positional relation of the two racial groups is crucial in race prejudice. The dominant group is not concerned with the subordinate group as such but it is deeply concerned with its position vis-à-vis the subordinate group. This is epitomized in the key and universal expression that a given race is all right in "its place." The sense of group position is the very heart of the relation of the dominant to the subordinate group. It supplies the dominant group with its framework of perception, its standard of judgment, its patterns of sensitivity, and its emotional proclivities.[23]

In a society that professes to value meritocracy, high-achieving members of "the subordinate group" represent a threat to the sense of superior position of "the dominant group." In post-colonial scholar Edward Said's terminology, the orientalist ideology of the West (White, Euro-American) always imagines itself positioned above "the rest." This "framework of perception" applies even when all empirical evidence points to the contrary, that is, when it is clearly evident that a non-White person is more successful, qualified, etc., than a White person by currently accepted assessment criteria. Like Jesse Owens' track and field wins during the 1936 Olympic Games in Nazi Germany, achievements by "the rest" demonstrates that innate White superiority is a social fiction. Therefore, in order to bring the world back in to making sense, that which contradicts the dominant ideology must be neutralized.

When Western minorities, especially Black people, excel, the response from a large number of White people is "know-your-place aggression." Literary historian Koritha Mitchell defines this as "the flexible, dynamic array of forces that answer the achievements of marginalized groups such that their success brings aggression as often as praise."[24] Know your place aggression often takes the form of physical violence. A classic example occurred in June 1921. When legalized segregation and anti-Black discrimination structurally barred them from homes, jobs, business, banks, etc., in the early twentieth century, a Black community in Oklahoma built their own. The Greenwood District of the city of Tulsa was called "Black Wall Street" as it was a successful and thriving Black community. Instead of being highlighted to claim that Jim Crow racism was not actually what was keeping the majority of US Black Americans in poverty at that time, the now infamous Tulsa Massacre was the White response. According to the Tulsa Historical Society and

Museum, the violence lasted 24 hours after which "35 city blocks lay in charred ruins, more than 800 people were treated for injuries and contemporary reports of deaths began at 36. Historians now believe as many as 300 people may have died."[25]

Those who uncritically use the Token Fallacy conveniently ignore the bloody history of White supremacist attacks on "successful" minorities – unless of course that acknowledgment can be used to further White domination. Clarence Thomas did this when he asserted that backlash to his assent to the US Supreme Court was "a high-tech lynching." His invocation of lynching specifically to characterize backlash against him reveals that he is aware that White people attack minorities for "getting above their station." Pointing to the success stories while ignoring *both* the larger majority who were impeded from success *and* the successes who were bombed, burned, fired, or otherwise beaten back (figuratively and literally) for making a fool of the innate White superiority assumption lays bare the logic of the Token Fallacy. It is a perception that is rooted in the epistemology of ignorance and that functions to maintain White supremacy.

"Is that something Mom can pick up at Walmart?" Selective White Tokens

Following her citing of a few high-profile Black men as tokens that supposedly prove structural racism does not exist, Kernahan's student quoted above "goes on to say that her own White family is not wealthy and then compares herself to a wealthier Black person she knew in high school."[26] The "It's not race it's class" claim mars dominant thinking about race. Educator Robin DiAngelo, author of *White Fragility: Why It Is So Hard for White People to Talk About Racism* (2018), lists it as one of the go-tos that White people use when responding to the unease they feel (White fragility) upon being exposed to information on racism.

The White man cousin of a White woman Facebook friend of mine once shared a meme that exemplifies this version of the Token Fallacy's use in public discourse. My Facebook friend had shared a post about White privilege and her cousin responded with a gray-toned meme of a poor White family captioned with "White Privilege: Is that something Mom can pick up at Walmart?" Since

I had time that day, I replied that yes, actually, it is! I explained that when a poor White mom goes to a store like Walmart to buy shampoo, she's getting Pantene Pro-V Classic. Actually, even if she can't afford to buy name brand shampoo, she can look at it on the shelf and see that "regular" and "classic" and "normal" versus racially specified personal care products are for White people like her. Shampoo and other personal care products, whether she can afford them or not, are not in a small (or locked!) "ethnic" section of the store. That is a psychological privilege, part of the "wages of whiteness" in DuBoisian terms, that non-White people don't get to enjoy, no matter how famous, successful, or rich.

This meme girl's mom can go to Walmart and, even if she is too poor to afford it, can see foods that are common to her race in the masses of regular aisles. She does not have to find the one designated "ethnic" aisles nor does she have to drive to a special area of town to buy food from specialty grocery stores. Any Walmart, Target, Publix, or Wawa carries food that is typical to the average White US American. Also, if someone donates shampoo, food, or toys like a doll from a store like Walmart to this poor family, the chances are very good that they will all be in alignment with their race.

The meme that my friend's cousin shared specifically mentioned "Mom," but Dads go shopping too. So if the dad from this hypothetical poor White family decided to pick up a toy gun, even if he cannot afford to buy it, he will have the privilege of not being shot dead by police, unlike John Crawford III, because the stereotype of his race/gender is not that he's a dangerous thug. And if the meme dad was able to afford to buy a toy gun, their son could sit holding it on a playground and not be shot dead within seconds of police laying eyes on him, unlike Tamir Rice. In fact, if the White mom or dad were to purchase a real gun for their son, he could travel across state lines, kill peaceful protestors, receive an outpouring of support and money from White people around the country, and then be acquitted of any wrongdoing, just like Kyle Rittenhouse in 2020 in Kenosha, Wisconsin.

In sum, while in no way dismissing the *economic* hardships of White people who live in poverty, invocation of the class oppression of a small portion of White people to deny the existence of *racial* privilege in general is plainly committing the Token Fallacy. Like those who name a few wealthy minorities to reject the idea that racism hampers minorities' life chances, noting the existence of White statistical outliers to deny Whites' statistical average stems from a pattern of thinking that seeks to dispel challenges to the dominant ideology of a meritocratic status quo.

Moreover, invocation of White "failures" like poverty as evidence that structural and systemic White privilege does not exist ignores the fact that current racist structures oppress some White people for the utilitarian reason of ability to claim that the structures are not actually biased by race. Internationally, in 2017 we saw this when then US President Donald Trump imposed a travel ban on seven Muslim-majority countries in Africa and the Middle East. Breaking the norm of what we will see in chapter 7 is called the Recognition Fallacy, people called out the policy as racist. The Trump Administration "scrambled to say it was not a ban on Muslims," but the legislation was blocked by courts.[27] A subsequent travel ban list included one majority non-Muslim (Catholic) country along with the Muslim-majority countries; and this tokenism was enough for lawmakers to accept that the legislation was not discriminatory and pass it.[28] Years later, Trump would admit that the bans were in fact targeted. Since his successor Joe Biden had repealed the ban, one of Trump's 2024 campaign promises was: "I will restore my travel ban to keep radical Islamic terrorists out of our country."[29]

On the US home front, the contemporary criminal justice system uses the same tokenizing strategy by oppressing some Whites along with the main targets of minorities to maintain the myth that racism isn't at play. In her book *The New Jim Crow: Mass Incarceration in the Age of Colorblindness* (2012 [2010]), legal scholar Michelle Alexander explains that one difference between the criminal justice system of the past (e.g., during the anti-bellum and Jim Crow eras) and the present is that the former overtly targeted non-Whites while the latter uses color-evasive policies. Discussing the reason for the late twentieth-century US prison boom, the "War on Drugs," Alexander explains how racism harms some Whites, literally treating them as the "collateral damage" in its modern assault on minorities:

> If 100 percent of the people arrested and convicted for drug offenses were African American, the situation would provoke outrage among the majority of Americans who consider them-

selves nonracist and who know very well that Latinos, Asian Americans, and whites also commit drug crimes. We, as a nation, seem comfortable with 90 percent of the people arrested and convicted of drug offenses in some states being African American, but if the figure were 100 percent, the veil of colorblindness would be lost. We could no longer tell ourselves stories about why 90 percent might be a reasonable figure; nor could we continue to assume that good reasons exist for extreme racial disparities in the drug war, even if we are unable to think of such reasons ourselves. In short, the inclusion of some whites in the system of control is essential to preserving the image of a colorblind criminal justice system and maintaining our self-image as fair and unbiased people.[30]

Given that the vast majority of White people who are incarcerated for drug and other crimes are not members of the wealthy class, we once again see perception that ignores intersectionality. In this way, poor White tokens are again used to obscure the existence and operation of structural racism.

The Non-Token Status of Race Traitors

The White supremacist-serving basis of the Token Fallacy is revealed even more plainly by looking at the examples of when White outliers (tokens) are *not* brought up. Sociologists have pointed out that "the US has always loved the rare story – that which masks the more general reality for the vast majority."[31] Tokens are not invoked when their existence or actions cannot be used to support the status quo, though. When it comes to racism, the rare story needs to legitimize White supremacy. History shows us that White tokens who *un*mask White domination, by contrast, are not at all loved.

The story of civil rights activist Viola Liuzzo illustrates this point. Viola was a White woman from the northern US who worked registering Black voters in Mississippi in the 1960s. She demonstrates what Mills distinguished as "whiteness as phenotype/genealogy and Whiteness as a political commitment to white supremacy."[32] The decoupling of commitment to White supremacy from White racial status makes conceptual room for people who are White to reject White supremacy. Sociologist Jessie Daniels notes, though, that "There weren't thousands, hundreds, or even scores of White women risking their lives for the [Black civil rights] movement."[33] Nevertheless, the existence and efforts of even just a "handful" of White anti-racists is a threat to the myth of legitimate White domination because it reveals that the commitment to White supremacy of the majority of White people is a voluntary choice, not an intrinsic part of being White.

Throughout history there have been White people who were "anticolonialists, abolitionists, opponents of imperialism, civil rights activists, resisters of apartheid" who "have recognized the existence and immorality of Whiteness as a political system, challenged its legitimacy, and insofar as possible, refused the [Racial] Contract."[34] Examples in US history go back as far as the nation: Second President John Adams opposed slavery in the 1700s. Supreme Court Justice John Marshall led the Court in ruling in the 1830s that Cherokee land should not be seized by southern states. Abolitionist John Brown led the Harpers Ferry Raid trying to start a movement to end slavery in the 1850s. Representative Charles Sumner spoke out against the evils of slavery in the 1850s. And every day White people like Viola Liuzzo joined racial minorities throughout the twentieth century to struggle against White supremacy.

For breaking solidarity with White oppression, these tokens were not lauded. Unlike non-Whites who align themselves with White power, White anti-racists are not considered evidence that the majority perspective of their race is wrongheaded. Instead, they are disparaged as "White reengages," "race traitors," various types of "RacistSlur-Lovers," and even plain "crazy." In addition to stigmatizing labels, the White tokens mentioned above were, in order: ignored, defied, hung, publicly beaten almost to death (on the floor of the Senate no less), and murdered by the Ku Klux Klan. The reaction continues in the twenty-first century, with White protestors like Heather Heyer in Charlottesville, Virginia, and Joseph Rosenbaum and Anthony Huber in Kenosha, Wisconsin, being murdered by White supremacists just like Viola Liuzzo.

What these historical and contemporary examples have in common is White supremacists' violent contempt for token White people who do not share their commitment to White domination. James Fields, the man who killed Heyer, called her mother a "communist" and "anti-white supremacist," and when he was told that

Heyer had died, he remarked that it "doesn't matter" and called her mother "the enemy."[35] Thus, rather than being trotted out like poor Whites are during discussions of racism, anti-racist Whites – despite being just as much of a statistical outlier as poor Whites – are at best ignored and at worst murdered. This is because, first, they cannot be used to reject epistemological challenges to White supremacist views and, second, because "the mere fact of their existence shows what is possible, throwing into contrast and rendering open for moral judgement the behavior of their fellow whites, who chose to accept Whiteness instead."[36]

The violent response to White tokens when they cannot be used to justify the status quo also occurs even for just one single outlying action. For example, when James Meredith integrated the University of Mississippi in 1962, White students who showed him even a moment of collegiality were attacked by fellow White students. For the crime of sitting with Meredith at lunch, two White students' rooms were "wrecked" and "nigger lover" was painted on their walls; and another was surrounded and screamed at. For sitting next to him in class, a White woman received such "vicious" harassment that she left Ole Miss and her family in fact left the state.[37]

More recently in 2021, Mike Pence, at the time the US Vice President, found himself targeted by White supremacists. Pence rejected the lie that the 2020 election was stolen from his party and did his constitutional duty as Vice President of the United States to certify the election results. Though it was unused, the symbolism of the noose that was allegedly hung for him during the January 6 riot could not be clearer: White people who, for even a moment, do not show commitment to White supremacy are not considered trend-debunking tokens to be highlighted or memed. They are traitors to be eliminated.

Conclusion

Looking at the ignored cases of White tokens and comparing them to typical trotted-out cases of White and non-White tokenism shows how the Token Fallacy is a perception that is White supremacist and culture-serving in nature. Rooted in the epistemology of ignorance, as in literally ignoring mathematical concepts of outliers and averages, theoretical concepts like intersectionality, and utilitarian practices, it pretends that certain tokens prove that an unequal system does not exist while ignoring other tokens that contradict that perspective.

Using the Token Fallacy when faced with the reality of racial disparities is disingenuous. The claim has never been "that *all* whites are better off than *all* nonwhites, but that, as a statistical generalization, the objective life chances of whites are significantly better."[38] The willful disregard for the fourth-grade-level concept of an arithmetic mean coupled with the cherry-picking of which outliers to marshal for rhetorical utility shows how the Token Fallacy is rooted in the epistemology of ignorance that upholds White supremacy. Regardless of how a token is used, and especially when the token is *not* used, then, the point is to maintain the White supremacist perception that social structures do not unequally influence people's life chances by race. For if anyone can succeed within the system, then the races being situated as they are – with Whites in more favorable positions on average – can be perceived as legitimate.

3

The Familiarity Fallacy

In a highly anticipated tell-all interview with Oprah in 2021, Meghan Markel and Prince Harry cited racism as one of the reasons for their departure from the UK and their life as working royals. Together they gave concrete examples of anti-Black comments from Royal Family members, discussed how the four-quarters White great grandchildren not in direct line to the throne were nonetheless granted titles (and protection therewith) while the great gran who is three-quarters White was not, and shared the devastating mental health impact on them of media coverage that, as Malcolm X observed of the media 70 years before, could make readers/viewers "hate the people being oppressed."

Soon after the interview, *The Telegraph* ran a story in which Seyi Obakin OBE, a Black (Nigerian) British accountant, charity executive, and UK Social Security Advisory Committee (SSAC) member asserted that his friend Prince William was not racist. The two met in 2009 when William joined him sleeping under a cardboard box on the street for one night. It was a part of the annual "sleep out" event hosted by the charity for homeless youth that Obakin leads. Based on this night and Williams' official patronage of the charity, which he took over from his mother Princess Diana, he and Obakin are characterized as having an "enduring friendship." Obakin told *The Telegraph*, "I have never seen a hint of racism. Never. I have worked with him in close proximity for years. He has met my family. He's never treated us with anything other than decency, dignity and respect."[1]

Even a committed Royalist would be forgiven for being confused about this enduring friendship. Obakin was not in attendance at

William's wedding, it seems, despite UK and other cultures affording "friends" invites. A 2023 Google search for Obakin returned his UK.Gov page, LinkedIn page, and several pages pertaining to his charity work; and the latter showed that, well prior to 2021, Obakin and William had a working relationship. In a 2020 piece in *The Mirror*, Obakin spoke at length about William's work on behalf of homeless youth in general and with Centrepoint, Obakin's charity, in particular.[2] In short, the British media's response to the Royal Family being accused of racism against a mixed-race American woman and her unborn child was to re-interview a Nigerian British man who William occasionally works with. An apparent periodic business associate was morphed into an endearing friend.

The appeal to the existence of one non-White person that someone accused of racism knows, as if that is proof that the accused is neither racist nor engages in racist actions against anyone else, is common. I call this thinking the Familiarity Fallacy. Regardless of two people's actual level of friendship, familiarity with someone of a different race than yourself is not a "Get Out of Racism Free" card. Yet that is exactly how many people think. I have observed the invocation of familiarity to both individual minorities and to a minority group as a whole. What is more, the familiarity often claimed is specifically with Blackness, even in cases concerning other races or cases that don't primarily concern race at all. In sum, the Familiarity Fallacy is not about real friendship; it is a perception that seeks to use a claim of friendship as a tool to neutralize accusations of racism.

"I Have Black Friends"

In his book *Racism Without Racists* (2018 [2003]), sociologist Eduardo Bonilla-Silva describes claims like, "Some of my best friends are ..." as "standard fare of post-civil rights racial discourse."[3] In his research, one in five interviewees in his student sample and one in six in his community sample used this version of the Familiarity Fallacy while answering questions about race and racism in the US.[4] Bonilla-Silva conceptualizes the phrases as "rhetorical shields to save face" given that the so-called "'best friend' is never identified by name."[5]

Black family members are also used in service to attempting to prove that a nice White person cannot possibly be racist.[6] For example, in the wake of the US Supreme Court overturning *Roe v. Wade*, Illinois Representative Mary Miller spoke at a rally thanking former US President Donald Trump for the "victory for white life."[7] Miller's campaign representatives explained that she stumbled over her written notes, which they say said "right to life";[8] but her Freudian slip is not the point here. The Familiarity Fallacy is what took center stage when her campaign's explanation not only stated what she supposedly misread but also "that she is the grandmother of several nonwhite grandchildren, including one with Down syndrome."[9]

Unless they are in attendance or mentioned in the speech, a politician's grandchildren are not mentioned in standard news coverage of their political events. Even more rare is a campaign doing PR damage control by telling folks unrelated information about the grandchildren. However, in this case, Miller's statement was considered racist. Thus, the idea to include the fact that some of her grandchildren are non-White was related because it stems from the thinking that familiarity with minorities has a bearing on the racism of her statement.

There is a longstanding fantasy that the mere existence of non-White children makes racism a non-issue for White family members. The nineteenth-century French scholar Alexis de Tocqueville even theorized this at the national level. In his 1835 book *An American Dilemma* based on his travels around the US earlier that decade, he assessed the US as seemingly hopelessly unequal but predicted that perhaps a member of the mulatto class (what we now called Black/White mixed-race people) would unite the two races.[10]

My own and other research with mixed-race people reveals that to be a delusion.[11] My first interviewee, Dave (UK, Black/White, 30 in 2011), told me that he was named for his White father's father, his paternal grandfather, but that he had never met him:

> Dave: I'm named after his dad who was the much more conservative guy who opposed his relationship to my mother. Him naming me after his father I think was, again, an expression of his naivety and idealism in that, you know, I'd be this kind of racial bridge builder and would be able to, you know, by taking on my grandfather's name, would be able to somehow bring him around as it were.

Jenn: Did it work?
Dave: Not at all no [laughs].
Jenn: Oh!
Dave: So I'm just named after this guy who doesn't think I should exist really.

In the US, Bo (US, Black/White, 36 in 2012) was born to a White mother and Black father. When I asked about his family, he only mentioned his Black family. Of his mother's family, he said:

Bo: I've never seen none of them.
Jenn: Oh, never?
Bo: Yeah. They totally disowned my mother. Because she had a child by a Black man.

Mixed-race people who do have a relationship with their White grandparents also report that this relationship did not mean the absence of prejudice. Former US President Barack Obama, for instance, has spoken publicly about how his White grandmother who raised him nonetheless was still afraid of other Black men. Regarding women, in my research Black/White mixed-race women recalled how their White mothers' anti-Blackness was expressed via disparaging and devaluing their hair. Sarah (UK, Black/White, 38 in 2011) recalls how as a child she had "never been able to have long hair" because her White mother "used to freak out and she used to say to me 'You look like a witch doctor.' So and then she'd cut my hair." Sarah entered into the foster care system by the time she was a teenager, and her White foster mum forced her to have her hair "thinned out" because of the sexually racist notion that thin hair looks more "lady-like" than thick hair. Aaliyah (US, Black/White, 25 in 2012) remembers that as a child her hair was either "a frizzy mess" or in braids that occasionally became so matted they had to be cut because her White mom "did not know what to do with my hair." Aaliyah says that when she looks at old pictures of herself "I feel bad for myself. It was so bad."

This theme of White mothers' neglect of their daughters' mixed-race hair is found in other qualitative interview studies as well.[12] In their book *Raising Biracial Children* (2005), sociologist Kerry Ann Rockquemore and family therapist Tracey Laszloffy remind parent readers that hair care is not trivial. They explain that "how parents respond to a child's physical characteristics sends the child direct and indirect messages about race . . . and what is considered valuable."[13] White mothers' racist insults ("witch doctor," not "lady-like") and their refusal to learn to care for their children's body (hair) stems from an anti-Black beauty standard that was not disrupted simply by having non-White children.

The familial experiences of mixed-race as well as interracially adopted Asians also lays bare the fallacy of thinking that having family or friends of a given race has bearing on that person's ability to be racist or not. Janette (US, Asian/White, 24 in 2018) shared that her ex-partner's family had "derogatory ways of thinking about Asian language" and mockingly used fake "Chinglish." As will be discussed in chapter 8, the family attempted to convince Janette that this behavior was not racist. In her book *The Racism of People Who Love You* (2023), mixed-race White/South Asian scholar and essayist Samira K. Mehta writes of similar types of microaggressions and gaslighting that she has faced from mainly White family and friends.[14] She tells readers, "When I experience racism from the people whom I love most and, perhaps more importantly, from people who love me, I am always surprised, taken aback, and disappointed."[15] Given both general cultural scripts (especially for women) to be "nice"[16] to others even when they act in hurtful ways and the desire to maintain good relationships with loved ones, Mehta explains that "It is hard to know what to do when the racism is present in your private space, your home, your family."[17] In fact, she says that it is often hard to even name the behavior of her relatives as racism to herself "because they are not often deliberate and because sometimes they looks simply like interpersonal conflict."[18] Because she often feels that she cannot name her relatives' racist comments and behaviors as racism, she says that "the racism of people who love me, the racism that I don't know how to see, or talk about or name" is "the racism that hurts me the most" and that "ends up making me feel crazy."[19]

Non-mixed-race people can suffer in White families as well. In her book *Nice White Ladies: The Truth About White Supremacy, Our Role in It, and How We Can Help Dismantle It* (2021), sociologist Jessie Daniels devotes one chapter to analyzing how "the white nuclear family is one of the most powerful forces for reproducing white supremacy."[20] Regarding non-White children adopted into White families, Daniels' analysis of multiple headline-grabbing cases reveals a disturbing pattern of adopted Black children being abused and killed by their White adoptive parents.[21] Daniels also covers the case of a White couple who adopted then "re-homed" a toddler from China. Research on parents' decisions to adopt internationally has shown that if the child is from a country/culture that bourgeois White people exoticize and value, then nurturing an adopted child's racial identity via involvement in the child's birth culture can "add to a parent's status as well-educated travelers participating in high-end globalization."[22] In the case analyzed by Daniels, though, it tran-spired that the child had special needs. Thus, since easy Instagram worthy globe-trotting was out as it was a "struggle . . . to be a parent to a special-needs child . . . back he went, like a defective appli-ance."[23] In the wake of the rise of anti-Asian prejudice and violence that followed the global Covid-19 pandemic, Asian adoptees who were not "re-homed" by their White adoptive parents nonetheless penned essays, op-eds, and Twitter threads like those in Mehta's book about the racism of the people who love them.

Research on heterosexual interracial coupling also finds that having a partner of a different race than oneself does not make one free of prejudice against that or any other race.[24] The higher rates of interracial coupling among queer couples does not make lesbian, gay, bisexual, transgender, queer/questioning, intersex, or asexual (LGBTQIA) couples immune to sexual racism, either.[25] Finding a partner who is not racist was mentioned by several of my queer interviewees as a goal. Sociologist Katie Acosta's research with queer step-families reminds us that the extended families of partners also matter. She described how one of her queer women interviewees reported that her partner's brother "'makes really racist comments, especially when he's drinking. The first time I met him, he said something about Mexicans being lazy."[26]

To be clear, social scientists do *not* point to White friends', parents', and families' racism to suggest that White people are the *only* ones who are harmful to members of their family. People of all races abuse and even kill their friends/children/partners/relatives. What highlighting cases of White abuse against non-White family members (and against White family members who marry across the color line) does is show the illogic of thinking that non-White familiarity is evidence of lack of racism. No one else can speak to the quality of relationship between Representative Miller and her grandkids; but we can all look at academic research, published memoirs, and clickbait news to see enough examples to know that mere cross-racial relationships are no guarantee of lack of racism. Thinking that racism is not something that people in racially diverse families do, though, is rooted in an epistemology of ignorance that supports White domination by resisting knowledge that contradicts it.

"There is a Slave Cemetery down the Road"

The thinking that underlays the "I have a minority friend" or "They adopted Black children" retorts is also responsible for thinking that invoking a minority as a group likewise can be used as a rhetorical shield. In his classic book *Lies My Teacher Told Me*, sociologist James Loewen recounts the story of a sixth-grade class in Illinois who were "outraged" when their teacher passingly mentioned that "most presidents before Lincoln were slave owners."[27] After the teacher encouraged the students to each select an early president and look up his biography, the students discovered that the teacher was correct. Now outraged at their whitewashed history textbook, the students wrote a letter to the author and publisher. The response they received told them to look later in the textbook where there is "substantial treatment of the Civil Rights Movement."[28]

In similar fashion, in 2019 my daughter's first-grade class visited a children's museum that has an outside area containing a recreation of colonial era blacksmith and carpenter work spaces. At the end of the tour, the guide told the crowd that additional recreations would be available for touring later in the year to celebrate the state's bicentennial. Before leaving, I asked the guide if there would be any recreations of Black or Native American life from 1819, given that both groups lived differently than Whites at the time. She responded that there was a slave cemetery down the road.

In both of these cases, it is clear that the person to whom the query was addressed sidestepped providing a relevant answer. As cases in which the queries called attention to a company's erasure of US minorities from the thing in question, they were both likely received as subtle accusations of racism. Facing that, neither the textbook publisher nor the museum guide acknowledged nor explained the oversight. Instead, they both pointed to other things that were associated with Black people, that is, to other parts of the textbook and city respectively, as if showing familiarity with something Black over there was enough to neutralize the original criticism of omission of it over here.

In short, they both relied on a group-based version of the Familiarity Fallacy by citing not an individual but something about Black people in general. As with those who invoke the familiarity of a non-White friend or family member, claiming that one has indeed engaged with minorities, even though not in the manner asked about, is a rhetorical strategy. Asserted familiarity functions to absolve the person of the racial shortcoming that was exposed. This reveals invocation of familiarity to be perceived as a way to dismiss challenges to White domination thereby leaving it intact.

"... If We're Willing to Work With them"

While the students in Loewen's story specifically asked about enslaved Black people, notice that my question, by contrast, inquired about *two* racial minorities: Black Americans *and* Native Americans. Yet the response to me contained *only* mention of something Black. If the Familiarity Fallacy was simply pointing out anything related to a minority group in response to a suggestion of your omission of them in some way, then we would expect the museum employee to have mentioned the slave cemetery *and* something regarding Native Americans, such as Trail of Tears historical markers that are all around downtown Huntsville, Alabama.[29] Her only mentioning something Black, though, is illuminating.

In the US, "Black people" (understood as US-born, US slave descent Black people) occupy the most socially abject position in the collective conscience.[30] Even though data show that reservation-bound Native Americans and some Latino and Asian ethnic groups actually have lower education or lower income averages than Blacks in general, "Black" is thought of as the lowest of the low. In *Colormute: Race Talk Dilemmas in an American School* (2004), education scholar Mica Pollock explains the power of even just the word black. She says to "Imagine that every word is a stone. While some words drop into an existing pool of talk with no more consequence than a pebble, dropping certain heavy words creates noticeable social waves."[31] Black, she says, is a heavily weighted word, as evidenced by the fact that White people "stuttered, mumbled, and paused measurably even in private" when saying it while they did not speak like this when using any other racial label.[32]

To be clear, the heaviness and stigmatization of Blackness does not only exist among White people. My grandmother used to say that the worst thing someone could call you when she was growing up in the 1930s was "Black." Anti-Blackness is pervasive in other racial communities besides White and Black as well, manifesting as colorism as well as the color black's association with and use to indicate badness and evil.

Thus, one pattern of thinking that arises when one is feeling accused of racism appears to be to specifically invoke familiarity with Blackness. The originator of the term "White privilege," Women's Studies scholar Peggy McIntosh, described the apparent thinking behind this version of the Familiarity Fallacy. She recalls that when she and other White women were accused of being "oppressive to work with" by Black feminist academics in 1980, her initial thoughts were "I don't see how they can say that about us. I think we're nice" and the self-described "outright racist" follow-up thought of "I especially think we're nice if we work with *them*."[33] In other words, since Blackness is so utterly devalued, any association with Black people, including just admitting knowledge of anything about or related to Black people – is evidence that the person in question is not racist. How can they be racist if they are willing to associate with *them*?

Within this mindset, it makes sense to point to a later chapter that mentions Black people and to mention a Black cemetery down the street as responses to being asked about minorities' omission in an earlier chapter and at the current location. As such, the Familiarity Fallacy allows one to sidestep and never address the questions at hand: Why don't early history textbook chapters mention that most first presidents were enslavers? and Was the museum going to include Black and Native Americans in the bicentennial recreations? Those questions can remain unanswered and, more importantly, the Eurocentrism they betray can remain unchanged.

Bonilla-Silva explains that claims drawing on the Familiarity Fallacy "act as discursive buffers before or after someone states something that is or could be interpreted as racist."[34] However, when specifically drawing on the abject position of Blackness, citing familiarity can even be used when an accusation was of a completely *non-racial* type of social bias. A story from my home state of Tennessee offers an illustration. During the 2019 US presidential primaries, Sevier County Commissioner Warren Hurst alluded to Democratic hopeful Pete Buttigieg, who is gay, saying that "a queer running for president" was "about as ugly as you can get."[35] He also said that there are "better people" in the local jail than the Democratic candidates.[36] Unlike private conversations caught on "hot mics" or via secret recording, Hurst made these comments in public, in the middle of a County Commission meeting.

As an open and public meeting, several news stations were present and recording. The off-topic comments were apparently several minutes long and also included the "I'm not prejudiced, but ..." rhetorical move Bonilla-Silva has discussed, classically positioned, as Bonilla-Silva's research shows it always is, before his objectively inaccurate assertion that "by golly, a white male in this country has few rights and they're getting took [sic] more every day."[37] Other claims included that liberals "don't want you to protect yourself and your home" and "they'll kill babies just as fast as they can get them." In apparent reference to Republican conspiracy theories that former US President Barack Obama is not a lawful US citizen, Hurst said that the US was "being run by these thugs from other countries."

News station WFTV9 reported that in response to Hurst's comments, "Some of the 25 county commissioners, who are all white and, all but one, male, could be seen laughing openly. Many audience members clapped and cheered, and there were a few shouts of 'Amen.'"[38] One woman in the audience, though, got up and walked out. According to WVLT Knoxville, she said, "Excuse me. This is not professional. This is [explicative]."[39] In an interview with WVLT the next day, the woman, Sara Thompson, who was chair of the Sevier County Democrats, elaborated explaining that: "I was actually incensed. I think that was a very demeaning and nasty thing to even talk about."[40] Thompson was not the only one to think Hurst's comments (at least made publicly as he did) were inappropriate. The City of Sevierville, Dollywood, and individuals such as the Mayor all condemned the comments via official statements and on social media as the video of the rant went viral.

WVLT Knoxville reported that Hurst spoke with them via telephone and defended himself saying "that some of his best friends were African American, but he stands by his comments because he's entitled to his opinions."[41] The fact that he thought to include a claim to have best friends who are Black in defending himself against accusations of not just racism but more prominently homophobia reveals a number of things. First, as will be discussed in the Conclusion of this book, Hurst's comments and his statement to the news show how race and other forms of inequality such as homophobia are interrelated. Fallacies are thus patterns of thinking that can be and are used to attempt to position bigoted views of all stripes as unproblematic. This reveals fallacies to be patterns of thinking that function to maintain not only racial inequality but other forms of inequality as well.

Second, this case shows how familiarity with the abject category of Blackness is literally thought to be so magnanimous that it proves a person is beyond touch of any manner of criticism. As such, it is a powerful rhetorical tool, and people wield it not only when they do actually have Black friends/family but also even when there is little evidence of any such real relationships. We can notice that, unlike Prince William, no Black friend came forward willing to declare how decently Hurst had treated their family for the last decade. Also, like the people interviewed by Bonilla-Silva, Hurst's supposed Black friends have no names. Lastly, the Black population of Sevier County, where Hurst had been for over 30 years, is less than 1 percent; that is, there are fewer than 800 Black people total in the whole 600 square mile county.[42] Based on this, we can make a wise bet that a homophobic birther who thinks liberals kill babies and that White men's rights are being eroded does not actually have Black *best friends*. The statement, then, as Bonilla-Silva originally wrote 16 years before this incident, was not representative of real friendship but was simply a hallow "semantic move" used to "talk nasty about minorities without sounding racist."[43]

"I Myself Am a Minority, Therefore I Don't Have any Advantage"

The Familiarity Fallacy can also manifest as an example of what educator Robin DiAngelo calls "credentialing." In her book *Nice Racism: How Progressive White People Perpetuate Racial Harm* (2021), she defines credentialing as "the ways in which white progressives attempt to prove that they are not racist."[44] Assertions, made to minorities as well as to other White people, include, but are not limited to, "My best friend or partner is Black," "I was on a mission in Africa," and "I adopted children of color."[45] She says these come up "whenever race enters the conversation and white people feel the need to establish their goodness. It functions as a kind of certificate of completion that preempts any further discussion."[46]

In addition to references to racial minorities, the Familiarity Fallacy can also manifest as a person citing a marginalized aspect of themselves. DiAngelo includes the claim "I am a minority myself" as a White progressive attempt at credentialing, but I have also seen it marshaled as supposed proof that a type of marginalization the person does not experience does not, therefore, actually exist. For example, a middle-class White man was once struggling to write his paper analyzing a system of inequality in which one's own group occupies the position of privilege. This student's family were immigrants and so had had the difficult experience of navigating a confusing US immigration system. Since their immigration, he had become very aware of the subtle ways that nativism privileges those born in the US. Rather than apply his first-hand understanding of structural inequality by nationality to understand structural inequality by race, class, or gender, though, his first line of thinking led him to tell me that as an immigrant he had no White, middle-class, or male privilege.

Psychologist Cyndi Kernahan explains the psychology she sees underlying this thought pattern: "One escape hatch that can provide relief [to the discomfort learning about racism] is claiming hardships of one's own."[47] While it is about the self not another, the logic is the same as the other manifestations of the Familiarity Fallacy. In all cases, the logic is that because of one's association with a devalued thing, one cannot be implicated in prejudice or racism of any kind.

DiAngelo, too, hones in on this dynamic as an attempt at self-soothing:

> White progressives are more likely to acknowledge shared dynamics such as white advantage but may still want to be granted exceptions and be seen as unique. Our own minority status is especially useful to this end, e.g., *I myself am a minority, therefore I don't have any advantage; why aren't we talking about xyz oppression (the one I suffer from)?*[48]

DiAngelo writes that discourse that seeks to center one's own group's trauma "can function as a kind of protective wall, warding off outsiders. This exempts us from accountability and responsibility."[49] Thus, as with claiming familiarity to a minoritized person or an oppressed group, citing familiarity with minoritization stems from an attempt to avoid thinking about racism.

Conclusion

Speaking specifically of White women married to Black men, though the process is the same regardless of gender or race, DiAngelo reminds us that being in a relationship with someone of a different race "potentially offers deep insights into cross-racial dynamics."[50] This is psychologist Gordon Allport's classic "contact hypothesis," that is, that personal prejudice can be reduced by intergroup contact and friendship.[51] Combined with the fact that all people are multi-situated, DiAngelo reminds us of the potential to "use our own experiences with oppression and the experiences of our loved ones as a way in to understanding racism."[52]

Unfortunately, she continues, cross-racial familiarity is all too often simply "announced to establish a complete lack of racism."[53] Regarding a person's own minority status within other systems of oppression, she says that too often people "use the forms of oppression we experience as a way out" and are "defensive and resistant when challenged on racism."[54] I call this pattern of thinking the Familiarity Fallacy. As we have seen, the Familiarity Fallacy classically takes the form of evoking the specter of a non-White friend or family member, typically a Black one, to absolve oneself or another of accusations of racism. This pattern of thinking also manifests as attempting to provide a "Get Out of Racism Free" card to anyone who can so much as name one thing about people of color, even if that thing has nothing to do with the topic at hand.

Like the Token Fallacy of the previous chapter, the Familiarity Fallacy upholds White supremacy by setting the mathematically impossible standard of complete homogeneity for racism to be acknowledged. If anyone with a non-White friend or family member, anyone who knows of the existence of information about non-White people, and anyone who has familiarity with oppression themselves cannot think or act in a racist manner, then literally no one meets the criteria. But as my interviewee Sarah stated of her White mother "Just 'cause you go out with someone different doesn't mean to say you're not racist at the end of the day."

Section II
Meso-Level Fallacies

Meso-level analysis within sociology studies localized norms and processes within groups, organizations, and social institutions. These phenomena are seen functioning to "link individuals to the larger society."[1] In other words, they represent the mechanism by which micro-level interactions and macro-level structures are linked.[2]

Regarding race and racism in particular, meso-level analyses look at institutional racism, which sociologists define as the "policies, laws, and [social] institutions that reproduce racial inequalities."[3] In his book *The Racialized Social System* (2022), sociologist Ali Meghji explains that meso-level analysis is important because "it allows us to avoid falling into a structuralist 'grand theory' approach and helps us avoid a micro-oriented myopia that turns a blind eye to social structure."[4] Sociologist Adia Harvey Wingfield's concept of racial outsourcing emerged from meso-level analysis of Black health care workers' experiences within the medical field. Focusing on processes within health care organizations as the connecting link between individual medical providers and the White supremacist social structure, she reveals that "organizations fail to do the work of transforming their culture, norms, and workforces to reach communities of color and instead rely on Black professions for this labor."[5] In other words, as sociologist Victor Ray's theory of racialized organizations explains, "race is constitutive of organizational foundations, hierarchies, and processes" and "both state policy and individual attitudes are filtered through – and changed by – organizations."[6] The fact that the additional unpaid labor that Black health care workers do is an unwritten organizational norm, not a society-wide official mandate, reminds us of the importance of the "in-between" social spaces for understanding the workings of inequality.

The five chapters in the Meso-Level Fallacies section all describe fallacies that are rooted in institutional, organizational, or group-based logics and norms. Chapters 4 and 5 both address inequality in common patterns of thinking regarding various types of institutional racism. Chapter 6 analyzes the perception of language, i.e., the system of symbols that a group uses to communicate meaning to each other and others,[7] and then chapter 7 analyzes the perception of using language to call attention to the harmful actions of members of dominant groups. Both of these are considered meso-level insofar as language, in particular linguistic exchanges, represent a middle ground between the individuals who use it and the social structure that stratifies it with respect to power and legitimacy.[8] Chapter 8 closes the section by interrogating the perception that attempting to defend or protect minority groups from institutional racism is "just as bad as" or worse than racism itself.

As common patterns of thinking about the processes that occur within institutions, organizations, and groups, the Meso-Level Fallacies reveal how logics of White domination are institutionalized. In addition, to again cite Ray, they also reveal how meso-level social phenomena are "central to contestation over racial meaning, the social construction of race, and stability and change in the racial order."[9]

4

The Simon Says Fallacy

While Meghan Markle and Prince Harry characterized the British press and the Royal Family as racist in their 2021 interview with Oprah, internet users had been saying that for years. Regarding the British press, articles with images juxtaposing headlines about Prince William's wife Kate Middleton and Meghan frequently circulated online. One showed that *The Sun* had characterized Kate as glowing as she touched her stomach during pregnancy; but then it wrote that Meghan touching her stomach was "contrived," "just for a photo op," and that she "should take her 'Baby Bump Barbie' act down a notch."[1] *The Mail Online* also covered their pregnancies differently. Their headline about Kate was that she "tenderly cradles her baby bump;" but of Meghan their headline rhetorically asked if "pride, vanity, or acting" was the reason she couldn't "keep her hands off her bump."[2] Another UK paper, *Express*, wrote of how William "gifted" Kate avocados wrapped in a bow when she had morning sickness; and then it headlined avocados' link to "human rights abuse and drought, millennial shame" when reporting that a pregnant Meghan "is wolfing down a fruit linked to water shortages, illegal deforestation and all round general environmental devastation."[3] Regarding the Royal Family, many had already noticed that they did not defend Meghan against the media's villainous portrayal of her, even after she revealed the toll it was taking on her mental health. To the contrary, in their interview Meghan and Harry detailed how she was literally confined to the home, not even being allowed to go out to lunch with friends.

In her textbook *Race and Racisms* (2018 [2015]), sociologist Tanya Maria Golash-Boza defines institutional racism as "the policies, laws, and institutions that reproduce racial inequalities."[4] The glaringly unequal treatment that Meghan received from two of the UK's most powerful institutions is an example. After the Oprah interview, race scholars were zoomed into news studios around the world to discuss institutional racism. In my comments on BBC World News regarding why the interview resonated with US women, I explained that the specific type of institutional racism Meghan faced, workplace discrimination, is experienced by many women across nationalities. When Meghan mentioned going to Human Resources and reaching out for institutional support in the face of distorted media stories and the negative impact that was having on her mental health,[5] that resonated with many women who have gone to their boss or HR department noting concerns about sexism or racism, too. Like Meghan, women of color in particular are often seen as complaining and are brushed aside.

I don't flatter myself that Prince William saw my BBC interview, or any scholars' interviews perhaps. If he saw any of his brother's Oprah interview, though, the concept of institutional racism went right over his head. For in addition to trotting out a "Black Best Friend" as discussed in the previous chapter, William's first public comment on the matter was to say, with conviction, authority, and finality, "No, we're not a racist family."

Elected politicians offer us numerous examples of this type of attempt to make one's word count for more than empirical evidence of one's actions. During the UK's Covid lockdown, Prime Minister Boris Johnson claimed he attended a "work event" (allowed under certain circumstances) even as pictures from it very clearly showed it to be a social gathering (not allowed). In the US, former President Bill Clinton famously stated, "I did not have sexual relations with that woman" even though he definitely received blow jobs from his intern. Before him, Nixon famously said, "I am not a crook" even though he attempted to cover up the illegal actions of his administration. In short, whether sticky fingered toddlers or national leaders, when asked, "Did you do it?" the desire to avoid the consequences of one's actions prompts many a person to unreflexively yelp, "Not me, not me!"

Within a society in which the dominant thinking patterns are predisposed to accept the word of a person of high status over others, though, a childish bleat of "Not me" and "See, not him" in response to accusations of racism takes on a more nefarious character, one that raises it to the level of fallacy. I call this the Simon Says Fallacy. I named this after the children's game in which a caller orders a crowd of kids to do silly things like jump up and down by saying, "Simon says jump up and down." According to rules, players are not supposed to perform actions unless they have been prefaced with "Simons says." With regard to thinking about racism, philosopher Nicholas Jones explains that we can analogize Simon's commands to an accused person's testimony regarding their behavior and we can analogize players' action to people accepting that testimony.[6] The rule in both the game and life is that Simon is the authority to be followed. Thus, Jones continues, if "Simon says 'jump'" it is correct to jump, and if "Simon says 'What I did was not racist'" it is correct to accept that what he did was not racist. In this way, the Simon Says Fallacy elevates how the accused *speaks* about their actions as more credible than their actual *observable behavior*.

To be clear: any given individual believing another when the latter says, "I am not racist" is *not* the Simon Says Fallacy. The fallacy refers not to believing/disbelieving a specific individual but to a *habituated cultural pattern of thinking*, what philosophers call a "social imaginary," which reflects the social inequalities of the society.[7] There is a maxim that "Actions speak louder than words." The Simon Says Fallacy is the invisible ink addendum of "except when powerful people are accused of racism."

It is also important to be clear that the question of William's, or anyone's, sincerity in their testimony is being bracketed for the moment. Scholars from numerous academic disciplines have explained that people of high status often do not see how objectively harmful actions toward those of lower status are problematic; and regarding race in particular, social analysts have long observed that many White people do not see mistreatment up to and including violence against people of color as "racist."[8] The opening of Prince Harry's memoir SPARE (2023), for example, reveals that his brother and father did not understand why Harry left the UK. "You left, Harold," William told him; "Yeah – and you know why," Harry replied. To this, Harry writes that William said, "I don't . . . I honestly don't." Then Harry says he "turned to Pa. He was gazing at me with an expression that said: Neither do I. Wow, I thought. Maybe they really don't. Staggering. But maybe it was true."[9] Like many people, Harry's relatives did not see the disparate and negative treatment of a racial minority, Meghan, as disparate, negative, problematic, and certainly not as "racist" enough to warrant a Prince leaving his homeland.

The burning questions regarding the sincerity, motive, and culpability of those individuals and institutions accused of racism will be addressed in later chapters. The focus of this chapter is not on the accused, but on others' tendency to defer to what they *say* despite evidence of what they *do*. In other words, this chapter is on the cognitive predisposition to accept testimony that denies that a given behavior is racist. Philosophers remind us that "the powerful have an unfair advantage in structuring collective social understandings," and that with regard to testimony and counter-testimony in society ("he said, she said"), unequal social power relations result in the collective cognitive habit of uncritically classifying someone's statement as valid or not based on their status, versus on the quality of empirical support or logic for their assertion.[10]

Feminist philosopher Miranda Fricker characterizes this as "a distinctively epistemic kind of injustice."[11] She defines "epistemic injustice" as "a wrong done to someone specifically in their capacity as a knower."[12] With regard to members of society giving testimony as to this or that, she explains that "Testimonial injustice occurs when prejudice causes a hearer to give a deflated level of credibility to a speaker's word."[13] Fricker labels "receiving less credibility than she otherwise would have – *a credibility deficit*," and she labels "receiving more credibility than she otherwise would have – *a credibility excess*."[14] Fricker takes credibility deficits, which she theorizes as stemming from negative identity prejudice, as her focus since her "aim is to highlight the injustice that is occurring."[15]

However, philosophers of race have demonstrated that undue credibility excess from positive identity prejudice can be considered a form of inequality, too.[16] The Simon Says Fallacy is thus a pattern of thinking that privileges denials of racism, even in the face of contradictory evidence, due to the epistemic excess granted to the accused. I have observed this manifest in two ways: First, as people saying, and others accepting, that they are not racist despite clear evidence of racism. The second manifestation is people saying/accepting that a person or organization values diversity, equity, and inclusion (DEI) or anti-racism despite their actions demonstrating the literal opposite. In both cases, epistemic excess works to maintain not only epistemological but also material racial inequality.

"He Did Not Mention Race"

In matters of accusation of racism, a credibility excess is given to accused (typically White) people such that their simply testifying that race/racism was not a factor in their actions is sufficient for many to cast doubt on the accuracy of the accuser, if not to exonerate the accused completely. For instance, in 2021 a 21-year-old White man killed eight people at Asian-owned spas in Atlanta, Georgia. The fact that the spas were all Asian-owned and that six of the victims were Asian women immediately led to public outcry to classify this particular mass shooting as a racist terrorist attack or at least a hate crime. However, in his police interview, the shooter told authorities that his motivation was not racism but sex addiction; and he said he targeted the spas because they were "a temptation for him that he wanted to eliminate."[17] His word was enough for many US Americans, including the Director of the Federal Bureau of Investigation (FBI), to accept that the shooting was not racially motivated.[18] The city Police Chief also believed the shooter. He came under fire for sympathetically describing the massacre as the result of a man who "was pretty much fed up and kind of at the end of his rope" and committed the murders because he was having "a really bad day."[19]

Experts such as sociologist and Media Studies scholar Nancy Yuen publicly explained that when the women targeted by sexism are one particular *race* that the violence is both sexism *and* racism. They then received emails from strangers saying that their expert analysis was wrong because "[t]he perpetrator admitted the reason for the attack was sexism. He did not mention race." Sharing a screenshot of that particular emailer's letter on social media, Yuen quipped: "Because racism doesn't exist unless racists admit that they're racist."[20] This is one version of the Simon Says Fallacy in a nutshell.

The emailer Yuen quoted also cited the two White people killed as support for their rejection of the idea that the attack was racist. In this, we see an example of both the Token Fallacy (chapter 2) and the Simon Says Fallacy "bundling together" as this emailer engages in mental gymnastics to deny that a White man killing mostly Asian women at an Asian business is not attributable to racism.

Dominant patterns of thinking set as normal the exonerations of people involved in objectively racially disparate acts just so long as they *do not say* they are acting in a racially discriminatory manner. This directly supports White domination. While the Atlanta shooter was ultimately prosecuted for his crime, though it was not framed as a racist hate crime, in other instances when one "did not mention race," that absence was enough for complete exoneration.

An example of this occurred in 2006 in the US state of Louisiana. A night club named Club Retro that was minority-owned and -serving was "targeted for a preplanned, violent SWAT team raid" while a similar but White-owned and -serving club just a half mile away had "never been raided in a manner similar."[21] The owners of Club Retro filed a civil rights action against the police for "unlawful search and seizure, false arrest, and equal protections violations" among other charges.[22] In line with what we will discuss as the Mens Rea Fallacy in the next chapter, the court focused on the individual officers' supposed intentions. The Club Retro owners were able to show that "[Club Retro] patrons were insulted [by officers] with 'profanities and racial slurs'" as well as show that the nearby White club had never been targeted by law enforcement.[23] Use of racial slurs and disparate treatment of similarly situated White versus non-White venues should be clear evidence of racist animus; however, these were ruled "immaterial to the question of discriminatory intent" because the officers had not made *explicit statements* that "Club Retro was specifically targeted because it was 'minority-owned and attracted a mixed-race and mixed-ethnicity crowd.'"[24]

The fact that there was evidence of disparate racial abuse in both the Georgia salons and Louisiana night club, and yet some people just uncritically accepted the White men perpetrators' classification of their behaviors as not racist, places the Simon Says Fallacy in logicians' category of "suppressed evidence fallacies." Philosophers Douglas Walton and Thomas Gordon explain that in cases such as these, what is occurring is not an *inferential* error but a *procedural* one.[25] In other words, these are not cases of people erroneously "drawing the wrong conclusion from a set of premises" but cases in which cognitive habits of epistemic excess work to prevent people from being able to give credibility to evidence that is at odds with the testimony.[26]

Here we see the maintenance of White supremacy at work in the moving of the goal post, that is the constantly shifting standard, which is done within a White supremacist society to avoid holding racists accountable for their actions. Officers' use of racial slurs as well as their difference in behavior towards a White vs non-White club are both clear evidence that racism played a role in the raid. However, in the face of this evidence, the court simply moved the goal post and pivoted to using the Simon Says Fallacy to avoid holding racists accountable by saying that since the officers did not *state* they raided because of race, no racist discrimination had occurred. As will be discussed in chapter 6, explicit statements of discriminatory intentions have been largely abandoned in favor of proxies, codes, and innuendos that communicate the same sentiments in plausibly deniable ways. Thus, a perspective that demands that Simon Says "I did it because of racism," especially within a society where saying that is no longer the dominant linguistic norm, is nothing more than a blatant attempt to shield discriminatory actors from consequences.

Regarding impact, testimonial injustice does not only shield discriminatory actors from consequences. Fricker explains how it harms those who are not believed due to social prejudices in ways that go beyond any one instance of contested speech. The primary harm is that one is "wronged in their capacity as a knower," which is a "capacity essential to human value ... [meaning that] one suffers an intrinsic injustice."[27] From a philosophical point of view, Fricker states that "in contexts of oppression the powerful will be sure to undermine the powerless in just that capacity, for it provides a direct route to undermining them in their very humanity."[28] In other words, "When someone suffers a testimonial injustice, they are degraded *qua* knower, and they are symbolically degraded *qua* human."[29]

"Committed to Providing a Diverse and Inclusive Learning Environment"

A second way that I have seen the Simon Says Fallacy manifest is when individuals or organizations assert their commitment to DEI and/or anti-racism, while behaving in ways that are counter to those aims. Sociologist Eduardo Bonilla-Silva characterizes this behavior as Abstract Liberalism, that is, supporting racial equality in principle while opposing concrete actions that attempt to make it a reality.[30] In the two large-scale interview projects that provided the data for his groundbreaking book *Racism Without Racists* (now on its sixth edition), he and his team found that one-third of Black interviewees and almost all White interviewees discussed racism within an Abstract Liberalism framework. A prominent example is the many interviewees who expressed support for racial equality but who then equivocated or were downright opposed to any suggested measure, such as affirmative action, that is an attempt to take a step closer to equality as a reality.

Institutions of higher education are notorious for playing Abstract Liberal Simon Says. Despite recent political attacks on DEI efforts, many US universities nonetheless have statements asserting, at the minimum, that they do not discriminate on the basis of race, color, or creed in accordance with federal laws. Some universities go beyond just stating that they follow the law by asserting that they actively value having a diverse student body, faculty, and staff workforce. And yet, in 2023, a survey found that "Nearly three-quarters of the colleges responded that their mission statement 'explicitly supports diversity, equity, and/or inclusion.' But only a fifth of respondents said their colleges were making expected progress toward meeting their DEI goals."[31]

An example of a university saying they support DEI while their actions suggest otherwise was observed in December 2022 at Purdue University Northwest's (PNW) commencement ceremony. According to video that circulated online, after the keynote speaker concluded his speech with a reference to his having made up his own fake language, the university Chancellor "uttered a gibberish aside" and then "said 'That's sort of my Asian version of his, uh . . .' before trailing off and moving on to the next matter of business."[32] The Chancellor's gibberish was meant as a joke, which is in line with social science research that shows that the White majority consider comments that ridicule racial minorities to be "harmless," "honest," and "legitimate" forms of humor.[33] In his apology a few days later, the Chancellor wrote that "my comments do not reflect my personal or our institutional values."[34]

While I cannot speak to the Chancellor's personal values, publicly available data allow us to take a cursory look at the institution to ascertain their valuation or lack thereof with respect to Asian people. Beginning with their curriculum, of the 74 undergraduate majors offered at the time, none were related to Asian or Asian American Studies, Ethnic Studies, or Diversity Studies. There was a Diversity Studies minor; however, according to the 2022–2023

Academic Catalogue, none of the required or elective courses focused on Asians or Asian Americans even though there are specific courses on African Americans and Hispanic Americans. The curriculum of their Global Studies minor likewise omitted Asia/Asians. For example, a note on the bottom of the curriculum page online listed Global Studies Area Studies courses as "(e.g., Latin America, Africa, Middle East, Europe)." Using the website's catalogue search feature returned exactly two courses at the whole university with the word "Asia" in their titles.

Regarding people, 3 percent of the student body was Asian that academic year according to the US National Center for Education Statistics. This is about half of the national percentage, though it is on par with the state percentage. There were larger numbers of students from other US racial minority groups, and this was highlighted a month before the Chancellor's "joke" in an article asserting that "PNW is committed to providing a diverse and inclusive learning environment for its campus community that values students and employees from multiple backgrounds who contribute to a vibrant metropolitan university."[35] That article also mentioned the university's many Hispanic Heritage Month events, Juneteenth event, and its clubs and organizations for Hispanic and Black students. It did not mention anything at all regarding Asian students beyond their 3 percent presence.

In sum, an outsider looking on cannot be faulted from concluding that in December 2022 PNW was not actually behaving in a manner that suggests they value Asians as equal to other racial minority or majority groups. The Chancellor's claims that his mocking gibberish does not represent the values of the institution, therefore, look suspiciously like the Abstract Liberalism version of the Simon Says Fallacy. He and PNW said they value students from multiple backgrounds, but both of their actions – his interpersonal racism of mocking and the university's institutional racism of curricular erasure – prevented equal valuation from being a concrete reality.

The Chancellor of a university making a gaff at commencement is a high-profile phenomenon; however, quotidian examples of academia's Simon Says Fallacy thinking with respect to Abstract Liberalism abound as well. An experience I had on an email thread offers a ready exemplar of average professors saying they value diversity and equality while engaging in actions that run counter to that assertion.

In early fall 2020, following a summer of "racial reckoning," I received an email from a senior colleague that they said was sent to those who had "expressed interest in being part of an effort to think about the sorts of curricular reforms we might undertake to promote equity and fight injustice."[36] The email was intended to kick off a conversation on what that might look like. Short-term options that had been seen elsewhere included efforts such as writing a document for faculty that offered "practical recommendations directed toward making some progress, however minimal, toward a curriculum that promotes equity, inclusion, and justice."[37] Longer term options included changes such as implementing a university-wide ethnic studies or justice studies course requirement. I chimed in to say I would be happy to contribute if the goal would be policy changes, but not if it was raising awareness or making recommendations.

I offered the example of my alma mater UW–Madison because the Wisconsin System has an ethnic studies requirement. All UW System students must take at least one class that does not center straight White men and their ideas. Just one. While not a golden bullet to end racism, the requirement nonetheless is a structural policy solution that has greater impact on diversifying the curriculum than an awareness-raising email that many faculty will not even read. Having taught courses that satisfy the ethnic studies requirement for five years, both my official evaluations and unsolicited emails from former students confirm the positive impact on critical thinking and racial (racism) awareness of requiring just one class.

Since going from zero to university system-wide curriculum change is unfeasible, in my email I offered the hypothetical example of a new policy that the reading lists for all classes could be required to contain at least one reading by a gender minority and one by a racial minority. I elaborated upon this hypothetical policy by offering ideas for sanctions for repeated failure to comply, and then I ended my email quipping that there would be wailing, gnashing of teeth, and excuses when inevitably a surprising number of our colleagues resisted a teeny tiny challenge to their academic freedom to perpetuate White male curricular authority.

The predicted excuses came in the very next reply to the thread. Another senior colleague wrote that they were on board with providing suggestions and education materials to faculty but not with forcibly mandating course content since they saw that as violating academic freedom. To be clear: recognizing that White men are not the only ones to have contributed knowledge and requiring that university-level courses acknowledge that fact *once during a 15-week semester*, is *far* from "forcibly mandating" what faculty teach.[38] However, Bonilla-Silva's research found that the view that "nothing should be forced upon people" is "used in the modern era to justify keeping racial affairs the way they are."[39]

And to be clear: I did not say that my hypothetical policy was the only way forward or even the best way forward. I offered it as an *example* of *creating structural change* versus *suggesting individual actions*. People like my colleague and Bonilla-Silva's interviewees, though, uncritically accept the perception that addressing racism should only be done through "educating" and "encouraging."[40] This is culture-serving thinking because Western history tells us that structural racism has never been solved from just suggestions, recommendation, guidance, or education.

This is not to say that suggestions and education are worthless. Literature and social scientific research that raises awareness and educates have always played a role in anti-racist efforts. Harriet Beecher Stowe's 1852 novel, *Uncle Tom's Cabin*, exposed more US Northerners to the horrors of slavery and helped increase support for abolition. In the 1940s, the doll experiments of psychologists Kenneth and Mamie Clark demonstrated that children had internalized anti-Black messages by their repeated preference for White dolls over Black dolls. Their work was cited in the *Brown v. Board of Education* US Supreme Court case as evidence of the detrimental impact of separate but unequal schooling.

But there comes a point when continued suggestions, recommendation, guidance, and education becomes little more than lip service that allows inequality to thrive. Notice that while Stowe's and the Clarks' awareness-raising and education *helped*, it was the subsequent institutionalized actions – war, a Constitutional amendment, and a lawsuit that went all the way to the nation's Supreme Court – that were ultimately what *brought about* change. To be fair, within a political context in which some governments are dismantling DEI offices and restricting the teaching of history and sociology in schools, it can feel refreshing to hear verbal commitments to anti-racism. Nevertheless, if those verbal commitments are not followed by *actions* to make them a concrete *reality*, they should ring hollow. The Simon Says Fallacy and continued racial inequality occur when they don't.

Conclusion

Speaking as a Black man in the 1960s, James Baldwin observed that "One is in the impossible position of being unable to believe a word one's countrymen say. 'I can't believe what you say,' the song goes, 'because I see what you do.'"[41] The Simon Says Fallacy is the culture-serving pattern of thinking that resists acknowledging that "actions speak louder than words" applies to racism. Too often the words "I'm not racist" trump even the most violent actions against racial minorities. Likewise, simply *saying* that one does value ideals of justice, diversity, equity, inclusion, or anti-racism is too often considered all that is necessary for it to be true.

Philosophers explain this as testimonial injustice. Given the social inequality in society by race, gender, class, sexual orientation, and more, it follows that one way such inequality manifests is as higher status group members' statements (e.g., "I'm not racist") carrying more weight than others' statements or even their own actions. The differential believability afforded to people based on racial status occurs in all areas of life, from formal courtroom testimony to casual family conversations; thus, we see that "testimonial injustice is a normal feature of our testimonial practices."[42]

This is *not* to say that all charges of racism are accurate or that anyone who believes someone who claims not to be racist is wrong for believing them. But the *ease* with which statements asserting racism are rejected while disavowals of racism are accepted, even in the face of contradictory evidence, reveal both epistemic inequality and Abstract Liberalism within society's collective cognitive habitus.

Moreover, the PNW Asian language "joke" case reminds us that the Simon Says Fallacy can be a part of an otherwise admirable thought process. The Chancellor issued an apology and said the university would be taking steps to address its treatment of Asians.[43] This case reminds us that culture-serving thinking is not the same as being "racist," and it is not a mode of thinking that is restricted to committed White supremacists. Like all of the fallacies in this book, the Simon Says Fallacy – whether manifesting as

"I'm not racist" or as "We value diversity" vis-à-vis clearly contradictory actions – is a habituated perception within society at large.
While not consciously "racist," if not recognized and interrogated,
this cognitive predisposition can perpetuate epistemic excess and
deficit and thereby contribute to the reproduction of racial inequality. As all systems of material stratification are legitimized via
epistemologies, inequality in the latter by definition supports inequality in the former.

5

The Mens Rea Fallacy

Since different individuals perceive situations differently, the question of which to accept is an ancient one. As explained in the previous chapter regarding the Simon Says Fallacy, epistemic injustice occurs when social status, not logic or empirical support, determines the validity of what one says. When what a person says is believed simply by virtue of their being a member of a higher status social group it is called credibility excess; and when a person's statements are discounted simply due to membership in a lower status group, it is called credibility deficit.[1]

Epistemic injustice helps explain the frequency with which aggressors' perception is centered rather than their victims' perception, a thinking pattern that can be seen as societal attempts to maintain legitimized domination as the status quo. There have been legal cases, for example, in which a White aggressor's interpretations of their actions were what the court considered the legal "benchmark" against which to consider if the civil rights of the victims had been violated.[2] This perception that the aggressor's view of the situation is what matters leads to a focus on their perspective, in particular their motives, which sidelines the matter of the *harm experienced* by those subjected to their actions.

Though not named or fleshed out as its own fallacy, Desmond and Emirbayer mention the irrelevance of perpetrators' intentionality when they write "intentionality is in no way a prerequisite for racism."[3] Sociologists' focus on social structures allows us to identify and understand that, once in place, systems of oppression "will continue to work largely independently of the ill will/goodwill, racist/antiracist feelings of particular individuals."[4]

Being a *Legally Blonde* fan, I labeled the perception that racism requires conscious malicious intent the Mens Rea Fallacy. At the climax of the 2001 movie, Harvard Law student Elle Woods is defending her sorority sister Brooke Taylor-Windham against murder charges. Elle opens her remarks to the court by reminding them that in a murder trial no crime (first degree murder) can exist without mens rea, that is malicious intent. After being mocked by judge, jury, and audience for the unnecessary "vocabulary lesson," Elle attempts to show that her client, the deceased Mr. Windham's much younger second wife, had no motive to kill her husband. She ends up catching the victim's daughter, Chutney, in a lie about her alibi, though. Chutney dramatically confesses to shooting her father by accident. It was her same-age stepmother, she yells, that she was trying to shoot. Thus, Elle ends up proving Brooke's innocence not via establishing her lack of mens rea but because the real killer confessed on the witness stand.

Though the movie's coverage of the trial ends here, viewers can surmise that Chutney was charged with something like involuntary manslaughter or wrongful death for accidently shooting and killing her father. She was likely also charged with attempted first-degree murder of Brooke. This is because, in both movies and real life, the US legal system recognizes that some killings are accidental while others are attempted/committed on purpose. The former, though, are still considered *crimes*. Mr. Windham is still dead and Brooke is still a grieving widow even though Chutney killed the former without mens rea. As a society, we do not typically punish accidental and purposeful crime the same way; but we do acknowledge that *both* cause *harm* and that for that perpetrators should be held *responsible*.

The Mens Rea Fallacy manifests as denials that unintentional racism is racism. It stems from the cognitive compulsion to root the ontological status of racism in the intent or lack thereof of the White majority. Whether it manifests as the comments of individuals or as the collective actions of groups, when racist behavior is not acknowledged as racism due to perpetrators' lack of mens rea, it not only re-centers dominant groups but also allows the unequal status quo to continue unobstructed and legitimated. After all, that which doesn't exist doesn't need fixing.

Motives in the Classroom: Teachers, Students, and the Mens Rea Fallacy

Given that *Legally Blonde* is approaching its Silver Anniversary, when I discuss the Mens Rea Fallacy in class, I use the example of a car crash. With a cartoon picture of a rear-end collision displayed on the board, I ask if students would still have whiplash if the driver of the car that slammed into them did so on accident. Everyone agrees that they would still be hurt. I then ask what the driver's revelation to them that "I didn't mean to hit you" would mean for their injuries or the damage to their car. Though they say it would be nice to know no one was trying to hurt them, they all agree that they would still need medical attention, their car would still need to be repaired, and that the perpetrator's insurance should take care of both.

As with Chutney in *Legally Blonde*, it is easy to understand the irrelevance of a driver's mens rea regarding the injuries to their victims and regarding their responsibility for remediation. Yet too often when it comes to racism, this understanding breaks down. Rather than focus on addressing victims' injuries, a common contemporary pattern of thinking is to look for the perpetrators' mens rea and assert "no harm, no foul, no racism," if conscious racist intent cannot be firmly established. In this way, the Mens Rea Fallacy manifests as denials that "implicit bias" or "tacit racism" exists.

Psychologists' concept of "implicit bias," that is subconscious and habituated biases, has become a "master narrative of American race relations."[5] With regard to implicit racial biases specifically, sociologists use the concept of "tacit racism." Sociologists Anne Warfield Rawls and Waverly Duck define tacit racism as the "vast amounts of hidden unconscious" racial bias that structures social expectations and interactions.[6] An example they offer in their book *Tacit Racism* (2020) is when minorities are told that we are not like others of our race simply because we do not fit the speaker's unexamined racist stereotypes. For instance, when she wrote my letter of recommendation for college, my high school Algebra teacher said of me that "Jenn is a minority, but she doesn't act like one."[7] When I took the letter back to her to ask what that meant, she turned red, said to white out that line, and practically ran away from me.

A few days later, she held me back after class and apologized for the comment and her brush off. She had realized that she was comparing me to negative stereotypes about Black people's supposed laziness and poor work ethic. She said she didn't even realize that was what she was doing and she looked so genuinely sorry. She seemed sorry not just because I had to send in a letter of recommendation that had a line whited out, but also I feel like she was sorry upon having realized that unconscious anti-Black bias had guided her actions. Rawls and Duck offer many such examples in their book, thereby demonstrating how tacit racism is a part of the fabric of society.

With regard to the Mens Rea Fallacy, my Algebra teacher could have said that she "didn't mean anything negative" by the minority comment about me; but instead, she owned up to her tacit racism, apologized, and revised the letter of recommendation for my next round of applications. That is rare. A more typical response can be seen in the energetic appeals to the Mens Real Fallacy that used to come during the section of my White privilege lecture on Band-Aids.[8] In the lecture, I recount my excitement as a child at seeing flesh-colored Band-Aids and my beeline to my parents to ask them to buy them for me. My father, a tall dark brown-skinned man, replied by simply asking me, "Whose flesh?" After pausing as he did for me, to let the silent answer of "White/light-skinned people" sink in, I used to explain that products like Band-Aids, Ace bandages, crayons, panty hose, etc., that were (back then) made only for White/light-skinned people but were labeled neutrally as "flesh" or "skin" colored were an example of the White privilege side of racial inequality.

When I first began teaching in the mid-2000s, i.e., before companies like Band-Aid began making products in multiple skin tone shades, students were very resistant to the idea that lack of dark brown skin tone products was racist. A common first rebuttal was that companies are focusing on economics, so they logically make products that match the largest consumer group's skin color; but this was easily debunked. For one, globally, the majority of humans are brown skinned, not the shade of light beige so often labeled "flesh." But also, even if we only look at the US context where I was teaching and where White/light-skinned people are the majority, that still does not explain away why the products were labeled "skin" or "flesh." Color labels like "beige" would have functioned just as well.

Still resisting admitting that it was racist of companies to only make beige-colored products and then to label them skin/flesh, the next rebuttal was the Mens Rea Fallacy. Inevitably, someone in class reminded us all that the companies did not "do it on purpose to be discriminatory." The focus on White actors' good, or at least non-malicious, motivations makes the Mens Rea Fallacy a pattern of thinking that represents what sociologist Jennifer Mueller called a "tautological ignorance" maneuver.[9]

From analysis of university students' papers about racism and White privilege, Mueller found that about a third of the White students' papers "embed morally laden assumptions of White's sincere, passive ignorance" of the racism they perpetuated/benefited from.[10] In other words, they didn't know they perpetuated or benefited from racism. They had no mens rea. Mueller characterized this retreat to White innocence as tautological. A statement or argument is tautological when it repeats or circles back upon itself. Mueller's students' papers showed that when they recognized the existence of racism they would then circle back to ignoring it via "the soothing, parallel logic of sincere, white ignorance" that the behavior in question is racist.[11] Likewise, my students in the mid-2000s could only recognize that beige "flesh"-colored Band-Aids were racially discriminatory (i.e., racist) by focusing on the fact that the company did not create and name it thusly intentionally to discriminate, which circles it back to the view that the products were not actually racist per the Mens Rea Fallacy.

Sociology classes are not the only ones in which the Mens Rea Fallacy surfaces when racism is brought up. Literary historian Koritha Mitchell has observed this compulsion in her literature classroom when she teaches *Incidents in the Life of a Slave Girl*, the 1861 novelized autobiography of Harriet Jacobs. Within the book, the narrator, Linda, details the harassment she, an enslaved Black woman, faced for most of her life from a powerful White man, Dr. Flint. Dr. Flint began attempting to force Linda to have sex with him when she was just a teenager. She chooses to become the mistress of another White man, thinking that that would make Dr. Flint cease his pursuit of her; but it did not. Eventually Linda and her children make their way to freedom in New York, only for Dr. Flint to continually hunt them; so they move multiple times. Even after Dr. Flint dies, Linda is not free of him. His daughter continued her father's attempts to take possession of Linda, seeing her as a part of her rightful inheritance. It is only when Linda's Northern employer pays Dr. Flint's heirs after his death that her freedom is secured and the decades-long harassment ends.

Mitchell notes that her students often ask "why Dr. Flint is obsessed with Linda." They want to know his perspective. In response, Mitchell says that she explains: "Jacobs wants you to see that his reasons matter less than the structures & people empowering him to torment her – because not noticing those is the problem."[12] Flint was able to hunt Linda in the north because of the Fugitive Slave Laws. His daughter was able to continue his pursuit because inheritances included slaves. How these and other institutionally racist structures ordered the lives of enslaved US Americans in the nineteenth century is the point of the book. But the epistemology of ignorance, here manifesting as the Mens Rea Fallacy, attempts to re-obscure the reality of structural and systemic racism by focusing on one man's reasons for his actions.

To be clear, Mitchell does not say the author wants readers to consider her tormentor's reasons *irrelevant*. The issue at hand with some manifestations of the Mens Rea Fallacy pattern of thinking is not a compulsion to establish a presence or absence of motive in the perpetrator (as Elle Woods was attempting to do in *Legally Blonde*) but to simply focus on his motive more than his behavior, as if his motive is what matters most. When faced with practically indisputable evidence of White people's racism against minorities, one common thinking pattern is to be *more* or *firstly* interested in the experience of those who perpetrate harm. In this way, the Mens Rea Fallacy subordinates curiosity about the negative impact of racism on marginalized people to curiosity about those who caused that negative impact.

Readers of fiction also often look for mens rea with respect to accusations of racism. After revealing that Lord Voldemort's pet snake, Nagini, was previously a human Asian woman, *Harry Potter* author J. K. Rowling faced backlash for anti-Asian racism. Unlike my Algebra teacher who had the humility to consider then accept that the ambient racist stereotypes in Western society had influenced her writing, J. K. Rowling and her supporters would not even consider the possibility that her making an Asian women a White man's pet was racist. For her part, Rowling responded by inaccurately explaining the origin of the mythical Naga.[13] Her supporters, for their part, reached for the Mens Rea Fallacy and claimed Rowling had "good intentions."[14]

Regardless of Rowling's intentions, however, perpetuating Orientalist stereotypes has negative consequences for real minority women.[15] Dismissing that fact in a rush to claim that no racism occurred because a White woman had good intentions is what makes the Mens Rea Fallacy an ends-based pattern of thinking. Normalizing the centering of dominant group member's motive and then rushing to assert that no harm occurred simply because no mens rea is present functions to keep objectively observable racial disparities from being legitimately recognized as racist. As with all fallacies, this reveals how the epistemology of ignorance works to try to maintain the current racial hierarchy, in movies and in real life, as legitimate.

Primary and secondary grade classrooms also do not need teachers to have malicious intention for disparate outcomes and/or racist harm to occur. Research shows that the majority of teachers in the US, even in schools that serve predominantly racial minority populations, are White and that they harbor the same racist stereotypes of people of color as others in society.[16] One way this manifests is via the assumptions about and expectations for students that teachers hold and the behaviors toward students that stem from them. For instance, in his ethnographic study of digital technology at White, Asian, and Latino schools, sociologist Matthew Rafalow found that teachers viewed wealthy White students as "future Bill Gates," Asian students as model minorities or future hackers, and Latino students as hardworking immigrants or future gang members.[17] Accordingly, despite the fact that across all three races students were equally adept at using popular digital technologies such as smartphones, tablets, gaming devices, and social media, teachers' classroom behavior regarding technology differed depending on the race of students. White students' use of technology such as smartphones during in-class educational activities was encouraged, while Asian and Latinos students' exact same behavior was policed and/or reprimanded. Rafalow explains that "Whether the stereotypes applied are negative or positive, their application exacts real costs for children's educational development" because they "may set real limits on their potential."[18]

The teachers Rafalow studied had no intentions of negatively impacting their students. To the contrary, their conscious motive was to be helpful. Regarding Latino students, for example, Rafalow's interviews with teachers revealed that:

[T]eachers saw themselves not unlike White missionaries helping the underprivileged. As part of the shared stereotype of their students as "hardworking immigrants" from "broken homes," they assumed that the cultural knowledge and styles that students brought to school were worthless to learning and achievement. In their minds, to truly help these kids they had to teach basic skills needed for a factory shop floor.[19]

When Rafalow asked the teachers about their in-class behaviors, they revealed no conscious malicious intent to treat students better or worse based on race. Rafalow writes that teachers "described themselves as being on 'auto-pilot,' often owing to the mixture of stress, time management, and student management as they desperately attempted to get through their lesson plans."[20] When he would quote a teacher something he or she had said, Rafalow found that teachers "had a hard time even remembering the things they would say (racist or otherwise) when trying to teach their lessons."[21] Drawing on psychological concepts of cognitive processing load, he explains that teachers were "less aware of the racist beliefs they hold and express as they are teaching in the classroom because they are expending the bulk of their mental energy on meeting the explicit workplace demands."[22] Nonetheless, teachers' lack of conscious, deliberate, mens rea does not change the fact that their actions and words contribute to racial disparities. Rafalow concludes that "Despite teachers' good intentions, [racist stereotyping] was a profoundly focused tunnel vision that guided their working-class Latinx youth to working-class jobs before they even had an opportunity to aspire to other paths."[23]

Even before looking ahead to labor market outcomes, though, there are negative educational impacts on students that can be seen in the moment when racist stereotypes are applied in the classroom. In my own classes, I've witnessed students' jaws drop or faces fall when someone makes a racist or homophobic comment. Once while observing another professor's lecture, she made a poorly phrased comment that gave the impression that she was dismissing hate crimes against Black US Americans. I know for sure that was not her intent; nonetheless, that is how the comment came across. In that moment, I saw the only two Black men students in the large lecture literally deflate (slumped in chair, leaned back, shoulders dropped), stop taking notes as they had been doing, and just stare at their laptops silently for the rest of the period. As one of a small

handful of Black professors on campus, every semester I am contacted by students following incidents like these in their classes,
advising meetings, or study groups. Though they appreciate when
someone (the professor, themselves, classmates, etc.) addresses it
in the moment, they also confirm that casual stereotyping interrupts one's ability to concentrate, sometimes for the whole rest of
the day.[24]

According to US law, however, teachers' or schools' disparate
impact or outcomes alone are not racial discrimination. In the
mid-twentieth century, *Brown* backlash institutionalized the Mens
Rea Fallacy by establishing the need for racist harm to have been
committed intentionally by school districts in order for civil rights
protections to apply. Legal scholar Tanya K. Hernández explains
that US "case law decisions have limited the Constitution to the
prohibition of only 'intentional' discrimination."[25] In practice,
what this does is impose "unrealistic demands for evidence of
explicit statements regarding [a school's, employer's, etc.] intent
to discriminate" on victims in order to achieve any redress under
federal Civil Rights' protections.[26] Thus, even in cases in which a
minority student has documentation of being disparately treated,
even harassed, Hernández notes that the institutionalization of the
Mens Rea Fallacy means that "Title VI only provides for legal relief
for school racial harassment where the school districts have been
'*deliberately* indifferent' in poorly responding to student reports of
harassment."[27] In other words, ignorance (real or feigned), ineptitude, inefficient actions, etc., are all "Get Out Of Protecting Minority
Students' Civil Rights Free" cards. The Mens Rea Fallacy thus functions to uphold White supremacy not just cognitively but in active
practice. It not only normalizes but enshrines into law the perception that redressing harm against racial minorities – individually
or as a group – is less important than the thoughts of the (majority
White) perpetrators of that harm.

The Search for Mens Rea in Everyday Life

In my research on the experiences of mixed-race people in the US
and UK, two-thirds of the cis gender/heterosexual and nearly all of
the queer mixed-people I have interviewed over the years told me
stories of others asking them, "What are you?" "Where are you

really from?" and other microaggressive questions. These experiences were described by the vast majority of interviewees on a spectrum from "annoying" to "ruin my whole day." Yet a small few did not mind the inquiries. Smith (UK, White/Asian, 25 in 2011) said that being asked his race does not bother him because "no one's ever asked me maliciously what I was." Jennifer (US, Black/White, 34 in 2012) likewise answers strangers' questions about her race because "I've never been in a situation where it seemed rude or sort of intrusive to me." The other interviewees who were not bothered by the questions chalk them up to others' benign "curiosity."

Research has demonstrated that microaggressions can be harmful, in fact physically taxing in some cases.[28] Speculating that it was not done on purpose to discriminate does nothing to explain the harm that was caused, nothing to help victims heal from it, and nothing to prevent others suffering the same fate. The Mens Rea Fallacy, though, would have us center White perspectives and experiences rather than focus on the harm their unsolicited questions cause the majority of mixed-race people.

In addition to microaggressions, the Mens Rea Fallacy also comes into play with respect to perceptions of mass violence. Media attention in the wake of domestic terrorism, for instance, has been criticized for being more interested in discussing the alleged aggressors than honoring his victims. Moreover, media is often remiss to label domestic mass violence as "terrorism." The Nashville Christmas bombing offers an example. On Christmas Day 2020, a bomb exploded in downtown Nashville, Tennessee. It caused damage to communication infrastructure that resulted in telephone and internet outages for people across the state as well as in neighboring states for upwards of a week. However, this bombing was not called a terrorist attack at first because the "motives were unknown."

This repeated pattern is even more frustrating when one realizes *why* media have to look so hard for motives. Unlike the FBI definition of international terrorism, the domestic terrorism definition includes intentionality. To be domestic terrorism, the motive of the violence must be "to further ideological goals."[29] In other words, the US defines international terrorism simply based on the perpetrators' *affiliation* ("individuals and/or groups who are inspired by, or associated with, designated foreign terrorist organizations or nations (state-sponsored)"); but it defines domestic terrorism based on mens rea. The fact that international violence against the US has been carried out by non-citizens who, in recent years, have been non-White while domestic mass violence is disproportionally committed by straight White Christian US-born men should not be lost on us. Like all the fallacies, the Mens Rea Fallacy is an ends-based tool used to maintain White domination.

Legal scholar Michelle Alexander writes that "The widespread and mistaken belief that racial animus is necessary for the creation and maintenance of racialized systems of social control is the most important reason that we, as a nation, have remained in deep denial" about the nature of racism.[30] The bomber's mens rea or lack thereof does not change the fact that part of Nashville's iconic 2nd Avenue was destroyed, or that people across the mid-south region had no telephone or internet service for days, or that people across the nation were horrified on one of many of their most holy days. As the various examples in this chapter have shown, outcomes do not rely on mens rea. But maintaining denial about racism and White privilege, that is, reproducing the epistemology of ignorance that support it, does.

Finally, many racially unequal daily experiences with technology are due to racism that lacks mens rea. Social scientists define algorithmic bias/oppression as the ways in which humans' social biases are encoded into technologies.[31] General anti-Black biases, for example, can explain why online anti-cheating software, which uses laptop webcams to confirm that students doing online tests remain at their laptop during the test, has a more difficult time detecting dark-skinned people than White/light-skinned people. Algorithmic bias/oppression also explains why early cameras' designs made them unable to photograph dark-skinned people as nicely as White/light-skinned people and why early automatic hand driers and soap dispensers would not turn on when dark-skinned hands were placed under them.

In her chapter "The physics of melanin," theoretical physicist Chanda Prescod-Weinstein identifies the coders' biases as the origin of the technology's biases:

> It had not occurred to the technologists behind the infrared detector and the [soap] dispenser that because darker skin has a broader spectrum of [light] absorption, the skin would absorb the infrared light rather than reflect it back to the sensor. The dark skin was invisible, not because it wasn't there, but because the detector hadn't been designed with dark skin in mind.[32]

That said, though, African American Studies professor Ruha Benjamin notes that even when an individual programmer is aware of racial biases, the person may not have the power to effectively intervene. In her book *Race After Technology* (2019), she explains that focusing on individuals is "overlooking the norms and structures of the tech industry."[33] It is programmers as a group and the industry as a whole that will need to address tacit racism, not simply single individual employees.

From the beginning, facial scanning and recognition technology was quickly found to be encoded with racist bias and immediately functioned to perpetuate systemic racism. For example, in January 2020, the wrong Black man in Michigan was arrested after police detectives used facial recognition software on video footage of a robbery incident. "I hope you don't think all Black people look alike," the man is said to have told police.[34] However, this is exactly what the artificial intelligence (AI) the detectives used "thought," and it is not an anomaly. Regarding facial recognition technology, research shows that false positives occur substantially more often for US racial minorities than for White people.[35] In other words, AIs think all minorities look alike.

But the Michigan detectives who used facial scanning and recognition technology in that 2020 case did not have mens rea. Likewise, there was no one out in Silicon Valley sitting around a vision board years before saying: "I know, let's make no-touch hand driers but, like, only for White people, muahahaha!" Despite the lack of conscious malicious intent all around, though, when humans create and program technology, they can only do so from the limitations of their own knowledge and logic. Thus, the Silicon Valley workforce of disproportionately White and Asian (and men) coders create and program new technology that functions – not via a "neutral" logic – but via the logic that its creators input into it. Eurocentrism and anti-Blackness are dominant perceptions. Benjamin reiterates that programmers' "'lack of intention' to harm is not a viable alibi."[36] However, for many, lack of conscious intention to harm is an alibi; and that lack of mens rea is used to maintain that racism never occurred.

Conclusion

The root of the Mens Rea Fallacy is a Eurocentric epistemology of ignorance. Epistemic White privilege makes it difficult for many people to understand how racism can exist absent a White person's intention for it to happen. This perception centers Whiteness, even and perhaps most especially in matters concerning racial inequality, and thus functions as an ends-based means to uphold the status quo of White domination.

Focusing primarily on intentions reinforces assumptions of White innocence and reinforces subordination of non-White concerns. Viewing racism as only malicious intent is a "Get Out of Racism Free" card for all accidental, that is tacit, instances of racism. It narrows racism only to the most egregious examples, thereby legitimizing and even legalizing the mundane ways that White domination is maintained. Rather than focusing on the harm and ways to ameliorate it or prevent its reoccurrence, society has "instead wholeheartedly embraced the view that intent matters more than historical context or impact."[37] A primary focus on perpetrators' intentions is not only "dehumanizing because it means victims' feelings always come in second,"[38] but it functions to maintain White supremacy by re-centering Whiteness.

In sum, scholars across disciplines agree that whether a harm stems from intentional or tacit actions is not what is most important. Ultimately, unintentional racism still has "spin-off effects and consequences that are exactly the same as if the motivation had been racist."[39] That outcome is harm to minorities; and as sociologist Simone Kolysh writes of the everyday street catcalling that many refuse to see as racist, sexist, or homophobic because so often "He meant it as a compliment": "When initiators [of violence] are centered, it is hard to see the harm and the oppression involved."[40] That is exactly the function of the Mens Rea Fallacy.

6

The Innuendo Fallacy

Philosopher Charles Wade Mills describes the majority of US history as a time that, rhetorically, "had the great virtue of social transparency: white supremacy was *openly* proclaimed."[1] In other words, until recently, "One didn't have to look for a *sub*text [of racism], because it was there in the text itself."[2] In the US Declaration of Independence, for example, Thomas Jefferson called the Native Americans who resisted Euro-American colonizers' attempts to steal their land and kill them "merciless Indian savages." The first state to secede from the union, South Carolina, wrote about slavery explicitly in their secession declaration, saying that the "increasing hostility on the part of the non-slaveholding States to the institution of slavery" plus the election of Abraham Lincoln, a man "whose opinions and purposes are hostile to slavery," were the principal reasons they were forming their own nation.[3] The Chinese Exclusion Act of 1882, by its name, made clear which group of people were being barred from entry to the US simply due to their race.

This transparency continued into the twentieth century. When my grandparents and parents were coming of age in the 1930s and 1960s, respectively, typical speech was very clear that it was rooted in White supremacist thinking. In the South where the majority of my family lived, signs saying "Whites Only" and "Colored" (with the former placed in the nicer of the two accommodations despite the claim of separate but equal) openly communicated White domination. Black adult men being called boy, minority adults being called their first name not Mr. or Mrs. TheirLastName, and of course racial and ethnic slurs were clear manifestations of White supremacist communication.

At the same time, though, coded language has always existed too. Slavery was sometimes referred to as the "peculiar institution." In the late nineteenth century, during the post reconstruction era of open racial and ethnic terrorism, newspapers printed codes like "come ready for action" to mean "come we're forming a lynch mob." The latter, implicit meaning, though, was well understood.[4] Into the twentieth century, there was no confusion when Japanese Americans, but not German or Italian Americans, were imprisoned in the 1940s. US citizens were put in internment camps during World War II because of their ethnonationality, even though the Executive Order that made that possible used the code word "alien enemies" rather than race-specific language.[5]

In response to the Civil Rights Movements exposing the US's hypocrisy for promoting democracy abroad while practicing colonialism and apartheid at home, racial equality replaced open White supremacy as the publicly asserted national value. As such, overtly bigoted language became taboo and sanctionable; so, codes took their place as the new dominant linguistic norm. To be clear, it was not thinking, feeling, or supporting bigotry that was newly stigmatized; just *plain-facedly saying* it. Psychology professor Cyndi Kernahan explains that presently "[b]ehaving in racist ways or expressing racist stereotypes that are not coded or cloaked in other more neutral terms is perceived as wrong."[6] Or, as Hermione, in the movie *Harry Potter and the Chamber of Secrets*, explains of the British Wizarding World's magical racial slur, race-explicit racist language is "not a term one usually hears in civilized conversation." Thus, as dominant thinking increasingly situated racism as a relic of a barbaric and fully bygone era (see chapter 10), racist codes increased in prominence in order to facilitate expression of unchanged White supremacist views and negative stereotypes about minorities without running afoul of new norms of public multicultural respectability.

The epistemology of ignorance, though, compels otherwise logically thinking people to deny that racist codes exist. I call the thinking that language must overtly use race-specific language in order to be considered racist the Innuendo Fallacy. Innuendos are readily accepted as normative communication with respect to non-race matters. For example, if a kid goes up to another on the playground, cracks their knuckles, and says, "Did you bring any lunch money?" that would be recognizable as bullying (or attempted robbery). Even though the perpetrator did not overtly spell out that he would beat up the other child unless he gave him his cash, the behavior (cracking knuckles as one asks about money) is an innuendo that is understood to be a threat of physical violence. The bully does not need to say, "Give me your lunch money!" In that context, his meaning is understood.

Innuendos are also an accepted part of sexual communication too. With regard to text messages, for instance, asking what someone is doing at 11:30pm sends a completely different implied meaning than asking at 7:30am. Emojis too carry sexual innuendos. Savvy users of emojis know what the eggplant emoji "really" means. Urban Dictionary spells it out, though: "It means a penis. Or just a normal eggplant. But mostly a guy's penis."[7]

Racist innuendos function similarly. Both in politics and in everyday life, whether in-person or online, there are codes that communicate racist messages. These are just as clear as a knuckle-cracking kid inquiring about a classmate's lunch money or a midnight text asking if you want to come over for eggplant. Regardless of location or topic, the function of innuendos is to discuss a topic without having to do so explicitly. Racist innuendos allow the expression of White supremacist views while protecting the speaker from looking "bad" for violating contemporary norms to outwardly value racial equality. In other words, racist innuendos function to allow the status quo of White linguistic domination to continue to operate. Given that codes are understood and accepted when considering other topics such as bullying and sexual encounters, denying the existence of racist innuendos is a cognitive practice that is rooted in the epistemology of ignorance.

The Theoretical Root of Innuendos

In *Two-Faced Racism: Whites in the Backstage and Frontstage* (2007), sociologists Leslie Houts Picca and Joe R. Feagin explain that in the latter half of the twentieth century many "blatantly racist performances moved to the backstage" while front stage performances "became more racially polite."[8] The concepts of thinking of social settings as stages comes from sociologist Erving Goffman's dramaturgical analysis.[9] Goffman theorizes that members of society perform social roles, complete with costumes, props, etc., much like actors in a performance. The stage on which social actors give their performance for the public audience in Goffman's metaphor is the front stage. The actors-only private places, such as green rooms and dressing rooms, where actors can "drop face," is called the backstage.

From content analysis of qualitative diaries of college students, Picca and Feagin find that White students present different versions of themselves when around other White people (backstage) versus when around people of color (front stage).[10] The backstage is "safe" from contemporary social expectations to be "polite" on "racial matters."[11] Here, Picca and Feagin found that "openly racist comments and jokes are not out of the ordinary" and that they are tolerated, encouraged, and in some cases expected.[12]

In his book, *The Souls of White Jokes: How Racist Humor Fuels White Supremacy* (2022), sociologist Raúl Pérez explains how humor that utilizes "racial ridicule, harassment, and dehumanization" is "generally intended to reify a racial ideology and hierarchy of white superiority and dominance."[13] The "new stigma of racism," he explains, makes public versions of racist humor, such as nineteenth-century blackface minstrelsy, no longer acceptable.[14] Thus the "forbidden pleasure" of racist humor is primarily (though not exclusively) expressed in private, homogeneously White – i.e., in backstage – regions.

Front stage settings, by contrast, are often multiracial.[15] Picca and Feagin's students' writings revealed that in front stage regions many of them were concerned with not appearing racist. They report that numerous students described behaving with over-the-top extreme politeness in interactions with people of color. In *Nice Racism* (2021), educator Robin DiAngelo discusses this practice. She says that "niceness" is "fleeting, hollow, performative, and requires no further action. Niceness is not the same as authenticity."[16] One example she discusses is over-smiling at people of a different race than oneself, which Black colleagues of hers told her that White people do to them. DiAngelo critiques this front stage performance of inauthentic, over-the-top politeness bitingly, saying: "Over-smiling allows white people to mask an anti-Blackness that is foundational to our very existence as white."[17] Far from showing how not-racist a person is, DiAngelo sees performative extreme niceness toward someone of a different race than oneself as stemming from at best a good intended desire to avoid offending them and at worst a passive aggressive attempt to mask one's deep-seated racial resentment and ill-feeling.

The Rise of Political Innuendos

Talk about race cannot only be confined to the backstage, however; sometimes it is necessary to mention race in public. This is where innuendos come in, and it is easily seen in politics. Rare are the days when elected officials give speeches declaring explicitly racist sentiments like, "Segregation now! Segregation tomorrow! Segregation forever!" Sociologists use the concept of "implicit racial appeals," anthropologists use the term "covert linguistic racism," and legal scholars use the concept of "dog whistle politics" to describe the form of contemporary coded racist speech.[18] All of these academic concepts refer to "coded racial appeals that carefully manipulate hostility toward nonwhites."[19] Law professor Ian Haney López explains that codes are needed because "the substance of the appeal runs counter to national values supporting equality and opposing racism."[20] Linguistic anthropologist Paul Kroskrity adds that coded language is "not viewed as offensive by most whites" and as such it functions socially to "promote misrecognition of the structural violence it propagates as an inevitable expression of a natural order."[21]

Haney López offers examples from the US in the 1960s to early 2000s, chief among them Reagan's use of "criminals and welfare queens" to mean Blacks, and Clinton's and Bush's talk of "illegal aliens" and "terrorists" to refer to Latinos and Middle Easterners, respectively. In Canada, "tax-payer" is a code for White people and "foreign" is code for Asian. Using these codes allows politicians to communicate racist messages just as openly as their predecessors while appearing on the surface to adhere to post civil rights values of racial equality. Apropos to the Mens Rea Fallacy discussed in the previous chapter, dog whistles also lend a politician plausible deniability that negatively targeting a specific racial group was their intent. Thus, when policies are enacted based on these dog whistles, they (re)produce not only racist perceptions but in many cases material inequality as well. The US slashing direct aid to low-income citizens because of so-called "welfare queens" supposedly abusing the system literally took food off of poor people's plates. Because coded (versus race-specific) language was used, however, to many people the changes to welfare, and the entrenchment of racial and class disparities in income and food insecurity that accompanied it, are unrecognizable as a product of racism.

When politicians are accused of dog whistling, one common response is to pretend that the innuendos were not about race. This ostrich-like move does not stop the innuendos from doing their ideological work of maintaining racial inequality, though. The 2006 US Senate race from my home state of Tennessee offers a classic case study. The contest was between State Congressman Harold Ford, Jr., a Black man from the city of Memphis who was a centrist Democrat, and Chattanooga Mayor Bob Corker, a White man who was a party-line Republican. Ford attempted to run a race-neutral campaign; for example, he did not highlight the fact that if elected he would be the first Black man from a southern state in the US Senate since Reconstruction and the first ever to be elected since those nineteenth-century Black Senators were appointed.

After attempts to cast Ford as an irresponsible bachelor vis-à-vis Corker the family man did not alter his slight lead in the polls, the Republican National Convention (RNC) made Ford's Blackness a key issue in the contest. They released an attack ad featuring:

- a black-haired Black woman saying, "Harold Ford looks nice, isn't that enough?"
- a black-haired White woman saying, "Terrorists need their privacy"
- a gray-haired White man (with a silent White woman standing by him) saying, "When I die, Harold Ford will let me pay taxes again"
- a camo-clad White man saying, "Harold is right, I do have too many guns"
- a blonde White woman saying, "I met Harold at a Playboy Party"
- a red-haired White woman saying, "I'd love to pay higher marriage taxes"
- another gray-haired White man (with a silent White woman standing by him) saying, "Canada can take care of North Korea"
- a black-haired White man laughing as he says, "So he took money from porn movie producers, I mean who hasn't?"

The screen goes black as white text displays "Harold Ford. He's just not right" and the voice-over states that the RNC sponsored the ad. The 20-second ad ends with the blonde White woman winking, holding her hand up to her ear as a phone, and saying, "Harold, call me."

As a born and bred Tennessean, I instantly recognized the misrepresentation of Ford's political stances. As a Congressman, he was a centrist, not a liberal, on issues like taxes; and he was actually conservative on other issues not mentioned in the ad, such as his opposition to gay marriage. More to the point, though, it did not take my skills gained from working on a Masters in Sociology at the time to hear the racist dog whistle that was associating him with a sexy blonde White woman. Political scientists Richard T. Middleton, IV and Sekou M. Franklin would later write that the inclusion of the blonde "Bimbo" in the ad was "clearly designed to prime embedded racial stereotypes, and convince white voters that a Ford victory would violate the South's traditional customs regulating relations between black men and white women."[22] Likely not part of the RNC's calculation was the additional fact that there were rumors among Black people in Memphis (where one side of my family is from) that Ford dated White women.[23] The White woman in the ad therefore served the latent function of stroking Black women's anger at the sexual racism that devalues us and then misdirecting that anger away from its White patriarchal roots and onto Ford as an individual. Despite a half dozen other characters in the ad, the blonde woman was the only one that people of any race in my social circle at that time talked about.

For his part, by contrast, Ford refused to acknowledge that the increasingly racist RNC ads were, in fact, racist. His first ad after the "Call me" ad featured him chuckling saying that if he had a dog, then Republicans would attack it too. Rather than acknowledging the racist innuendos, he denounced the ad in race-neutral terms: as his opponents attacking his moral character, which he counter-claimed they were the ones lacking given "their efforts to hide the scandal involving Congressman Mark Foley, the Florida Republican who made sexual advances to underage, male congressional pages."[24] When asked directly about the racist turn of his opponent's attack ads, Ford "refused to call the ad racist and said about Republicans, 'You have to ask them about race. I don't focus on those things.'"[25] This was not just for the camera either. Some of my family members worked as volunteers for the Ford campaign, and even in meetings with no news cameras he did not discuss racism.

Ford would ultimately lose the Senate race. Middleton and Franklin's analysis of political polls of the time shows that

> voter attitudes shifted after the first airing of the "Bimbo" advertisement. Six weeks before the election, Ford had a six-point lead over Corker, although a sizeable number of voters had neither favorable nor unfavorable views of the two candidates. By mid-October, the race was a virtual dead heat, yet after the ad was aired, Corker's favorability rating over Ford increased by eight percentage points.[26]

While every political contest is multifaceted and so no one ad is solely responsible for the outcome, nonetheless we see in the Ford/Corker race and other races analyzed by sociologists and political scientists that politicians can "secure whites' support by 'playing the race card'" so long as they do so through implicit racial appeals, covert linguistic racism, and dog whistles.[27] What is more, voters "need not be outspoken racists for racial appeals to resonate with them."[28] Kroskrity and other linguistic anthropologists explain that innuendos can "do their ideological work 'while passing unnoticed.'"[29] This is especially true for people, mostly but not exclusively White, whose uncritical perception stems from the dominant, culture-serving epistemology. Ford shows us that denying that the innuendos are about race does not deracialize them; but that denial *does* allow racist ideas to continue to permeate public discourse and have concrete social impacts.

Trickle-Down Dog Whistles

Former US President Ronald Reagan may have been wrong about financial resources "trickling down" to the masses from the wealthy to whom he gave tax cuts, but his and other politicians' use of racist innuendos did trickle down to the public. Sociologist Eduardo Bonilla-Silva explains that avoiding race-specific language in public has become a hallmark of contemporary talk. Regarding political talk, whereas in the 1960s segregationists openly chanted "Two, one, four, three, we hate Kennedy!"[30] their grandchildren now use codes to express displeasure in a "liberal" president. This was demonstrated in fall 2021 when the phrase "Let's go Brandon" emerged as code to mean "Fuck Joe Biden." *The Washington Post* reported that the saying started due to a reporter at a NASCAR race mistaking the latter for the former, likely owing to the fact that a driver named Brandon had just won. This phrase quickly morphed from an inside joke among some conservatives to virtually an unofficial motto of the Republican Party. Driving around Alabama, for instance, I saw bumper stickers supporting Brandon. In true coded fashion, the phrase was a way to insult the administration, voice anger about its tenure, and signal irritation with the media – all in language designed to conceal an expletive and, to the unknowing, to not be about race.[31]

Public use of coded language has spread beyond just politics as well. In the 1990s, a large employment agency was revealed to be facilitating racist discrimination via "signal[ing] that an applicant was black by reversing the initials of the placement counselor."[32] A decade later, in the early 2000s when I was working in chain restaurants to make money for university, I ran into a similar practice. I occasionally overheard White servers request that hosts not seat any "Canadians" at their tables. Not understanding the US system, it was claimed, made the US's neighbors to the North "poor tippers." The idea that international diners are poor tippers was so common that it was featured in the movie *Waiting*, an early 2000s comedy about young adults' life working in a restaurant. In the movie, a table full of Asian businessmen leave a small tip. Speaking among themselves in a non-English language as they exit, English subtitles reveal to viewers that they are laughing about how US Americans think they don't know to tip better.

But my White coworkers saying no Canadians was not to avoid the poor tip (accidental or otherwise) of international visitors. I found out from a White friend that Canadians was code for Black people. The code functioned to allow White servers to publicly express their racist stereotypes about Black diners as low-income and rude. It was a way for restaurant workers to communicate their racist biases in such a way that shielded them from sanctions from Human Resources. If overheard by management, for example, their comments would not be seen as racially prejudiced but as simply legitimate frustration that the US underpaying its servers was so different than in other countries that travelers didn't know to tip more.

This practice also allowed White servers to not have to think about their own anti-Blackness. On the surface, their request was in response to the financial hardship caused to them by others' intercultural incompetence regarding tipping. This allows them to not have to think about the possibility that maybe they, given their anti-Blackness, did not provide the same level of customer service to Black diners and that *that* was why Black diners (allegedly) tipped less.

Mistreatment from a restaurant server is the first overt act of racism that I recall experiencing and understanding as a child. Once while at my favorite restaurant, our waitress rolled her eyes and sighed while taking my family's order, brought us bowls of nothing but lettuce as "salads," then ignored us completely when a White couple was seated shortly after us. My family left, and on the way out my dad spoke to the manager about the waitress's behavior. The White couple who stayed surely tipped her more than the $0 we left despite her (reluctantly) bringing us drinks and "salads." But it was not our income, rudeness, or Blackness that was the cause: Her racism was.

Sociologist Adia Harvey Wingfield's book *Flatlining: Race, Work, and Health Care in the New Economy* (2019) reveals that health care workers, too, use racially coded language to be able to openly communicate racist messages undetected. One physician's assistant she interviewed recounted a story of a coworker who commented that he "hated Mondays." Like me, the interviewee would later learn that his coworkers were using Monday as a racist code. As Wingfield explains: "The term Mondays is a pretty common, recently developed derogatory meaning 'black people.' The thinking behind this is that no one likes Mondays, hence they are comparable to black people."[33] She concludes that in using a code that only certain (mainly but not exclusively White) people in the organization were clued into, a worker could express bigoted views like "I hate Black people" in the presence of others, including members of the group being disparaged, without repercussion.

Sociologists have also found that innuendos are used within the social institution of education. In *Digital Divisions: How Schools Create Inequality in the Tech Era* (2020), Matthew Rafalow writes that: "[White] parents I spoke with at school events rarely named the racial groups they were referring to, and instead used 'bad neighborhoods,' 'bullies,' and 'drug dealers' and euphemisms to allude to poor Latinx youth whom they perceived to be threats to their child's proper development."[34] In discussing her kids making friends in their increasingly Latino but still supermajority White and wealthy community, one mom told him that "You just have to hope that, with all we've taught them, that they will seek out other normal kids and not be influenced by the bad ones."[35] Rafalow concludes that despite parents claiming to have sent their children to the wealthy White school that was part of his three-cited ethnography, "to provide a 'safe' environment," that their underlying intention, as revealed by their other comments, was to "[separate] them from the growing population of poor people of color in their community."[36]

In sum, innuendos and codes are used not only in politics but also in employment sectors and social institutions. When they are pregnant with not only racial meaning but racist stereotypes, they allow people to communicate racist messages in public and to avoid considering how racism, their own or others', is the actual cause of the thing they are discussing in code. As Picca and Feagin's research revealed, speakers are principally concerned with not *appearing* racist, not with actually avoiding saying or doing things that could be harmful. Thus, denying the racist meaning behind codes is transparently disingenuous.

The denial aspect is what makes the Innuendo Fallacy both a fallacy and makes it pertain only to codes for racial minorities. Even though there also exists coded language about the White majority, it differs from codes about minorities in two ways. First, these codes are not used by those in power to support material domination. Codes for Black women like Welfare Queen are used to make detrimental policy decisions such as to cut aid to low-income people of all races. Codes for White women, like Karen or Becky, by contrast, are not used by those in power to materially harm large, multi-racial segments of the population. Second, codes for White people are openly acknowledged as race-based codes. It is no secret that Chad is a code for an obnoxious straight White man. By contrast, codes for minorities are supposed to remain a secret.

Innuendos Gone Wild

By definition, innuendos are not supposed to be explicit. When "the quiet part is said out loud" or when out-group members learn of their hidden meaning, though, the spell is broken and critique ensues. Perhaps the most infamous misuser of racist innuendos is former US President Donald Trump. From the 2016 campaign trail onward, Trump used so many cliché dog whistles and barely concealable racist innuendos that nearly every comment of his was discussed and critiqued in the mainstream media. In summer 2020, Trump tweeted an especially noteworthy innuendo:

> The "suburban housewife" will be voting for me. They want safety & are thrilled that I ended the long running program where low-income housing would invade their neighborhood. Biden would reinstall it, in a bigger form, with Cory Booker in charge![37]

The tweet exemplifies multiple of the characteristics of the linguistic style of contemporary racist discourse, just they were overdone so as to be more readily identifiable than usual. Regarding the characteristics of "avoidance of direct racial language,"[38] Trump put "suburban housewife" in quotation marks, identifying it as a transparent code for White women. Given the racial convents and discrimination in the 1950s and 1960s, the US was suburbanized racially unequally, with Whites leaving urban centers for the newly created suburbs and non-Whites facing barriers not only to relocation to the suburbs but also to home ownership in general.[39] Yet even without this historical knowledge of how suburbs came to be majority White, US Americans are familiar with the archetypal suburban White housewife from TV shows like *Leave It to Beaver* (1957–1963), *The Brady Bunch* (1969–1974), *Married with Children* (1987–1997), *Family Guy* (1999 to present), and more.[40]

To be sure, there are TV shows about families of color, like *Sandford and Son* (1972–1977), *Family Matters* (1989–1997), *That's So Raven* (2003–2007), and *Fresh off the Boat* (2015–2020). However, first, in more minority TV families the mother works; and second, people of color are associated with urbanism. In fact, urbanism has long been a code specifically for Black people. An episode of the TV show *Black-ish* (2014–2022) addresses this when the father on the show, Dre, gets a promotion at his advertising agency to be head of "urban" advertising. The new job focus is ironic because Dre and his family are archetypally suburbanites in all ways except that they are Black.

Trump's tweet also contained other by now readily identifiable dog whistles. He claimed that "low-income housing" would "invade their neighborhood." Given that housing is not sentient and thus cannot invade anything, it is clear that it is a code. The "long-running program" he vaguely referred to in this tweet was explicitly identified in another tweet as "an Obama-era fair housing regulation that aimed to combat segregation in suburbs by conditioning federal funding on local governments providing low-incoming housing and preventing racial bias."[41] Unlike eras past when White homeowners' racist fears were stroked with race-specific language naming Black people as the undesirable new residents set to move in,[42] it is taboo now to fearmonger with race-specific language. Thus, we have the non-sentient "low-income housing" launching an invasion since contemporary styles of speech frown upon naming the racial group assumed to live in low-income housing.

Finally, Trump ended the tweet claiming that if elected his challenger Joe Biden would not only reinstate the program but put Cory Booker over it. Booker is a Black man and outspoken US Senator. Using his name was a transparent "linguistic move" to say "scary Black man" without saying "scary Black man."

Unlike the debates over the 2006 RNC "Call me" ad, Trump's 2020 tweet drew widespread condemnation. Demonstrating how some academic concepts have become mainstreamed, a *New York Times* opinion piece was literally titled "Trump is dog-whistling. Are 'suburban housewives' listening?"[43] Trump's tweet was condemned by many, but it is important to note that he was not actually all that wrong. He was correct that the majority of White women would in fact vote for him. Moreover, research has found that White people, from realtors to house hunters, do in fact want all-White neighborhoods and do not want minorities, who are assumed to be low-income, moving in.[44] As Rafalow's research shows, White people say they want "safety" and consider the presence of minorities antithetical to that.[45] In other words, with the exception speculating about Cory Booker, the content of Trump's tweet has been shown to be shared by many White people. His tweet drew condemnation, therefore, because it was so overt and overdone. He said the quiet part too loud.

In sum, the fact that racial innuendos are used in public front stage regions even though explicitly racist language is normal in backstage regions lays bare what makes the Innuendo Fallacy an ends-based tool of White supremacy. Refusing to acknowledge racist innuendos *as* racist, unless they are overdone and very explicit, is disingenuous since ideas *can* be communicated indirectly. The perception that this truism does not apply to racism functions to allow bigoted views to flow freely and without sanction in public discourse.

Conclusion

In Sociology, we define language as a system of symbols used to communicate. Considering the fact that Hello, Hola, As-salamu alaikum, Bonjour, Kon'nichiwa, Nnọọ, Osiyo, and hundreds more words all mean the same thing, clearly *what* language people use matters less than the fact that others *understand* its *meaning*. In the US, most folks know that "inner city" refers to non-Whites, mainly Black, and that "suburban" or "country" implies White. "Immigrant" is associated with Latinos and Asians despite people of all races but Native Americans being voluntary or involuntary immigrants. In the UK, "take back our country," like the US version "make America great again," are "racist nostalgia," i.e., a desire for a return to when White-majority countries were, first, superma- jority White and, second, could un-obstructively benefit from the exploitation of Black and Brown people at home and in colonies.[46]

The past was also a time when race-specific bigoted language could be uttered in mixed company in public with no consequence. For the last half century, though, speaking covertly via codes, dog whistles, and innuendos has been the dominant linguistic form. This norm is revealed most clearly when it is broken, that is when it is done in an over-the-top fashion. The perception that codes are any less racist than openly race-based language serves to obscure contemporary racism and thereby assist in maintaining it. Both "Stand back and stand by" and its nineteenth-century counterpart "Come ready for action" were followed by White mob violence. Such White supremacist violence is made possible in part by the Innuendo Fallacy denying that racist language can exist in code.

7

The Recognition Fallacy

"What are you?" "Where are you from?" "Where are you *really* from?" My interview research with mixed-race people in the United States and United Kingdom has found that both children and adults are asked these questions frequently. Other researchers have documented the fact that US/UK racial minorities who do not identify as mixed-race also face demands to explain their presence in the nation, a perception phenomenon Mia Tuan called being seen as a "forever foreigner."[1] One difference between the accounts of experiences with questioning in the US and UK, though, is that in the former it is more often reported to be the first question a person receives at the start of a conversation. A second difference is that in the US the query is typically "What are you?" whereas in the UK it is "Where are you from?" Sophie, a 22-year-old Black/White Londoner who I interviewed in summer 2012, explains these two dynamics saying that in the UK "[race] is probably on their mind from the beginning, but people [are] quite sensitive nowadays. They're not gonna wanna just say 'Oh hi, you're Sophie! Where you from?'"

Ten years later, however, at a December 2022 event at Buckingham Palace, that exact scenario played out. The BBC reported that "Ngozi Fulani was questioned about her background by Lady Susan Hussey."[2] Hussey, who is White and was lady-in-waiting to Queen Elizabeth II as well as Prince William's godmother, "made a beeline" to Fulani, who is Black and the founder and CEO of a local charity organization, and peppered her with questions like, "Where are you from? Where are your people from?"[3] Fulani's answer that she and her family were British was not accepted.

Hussey continued to "interrogate" Fulani "repeatedly to explain where she was from."[4]

Fulani shared the frustratingly common experience on social media, resulting in much support as well as the Palace making a statement that "described the remarks as 'unacceptable and deeply regrettable.'"[5] Hussey also resigned from her symbolic post as lady-in-waiting to the by-that-time deceased Queen. Within a month, though, Fulani's charity, Sistah Space, an organization that provides services to Black women who have suffered domestic and sexual abuse, announced that it had to "temporarily cease many of our operations to ensure the safety of our service users and our team."[6] Sistah Space halted operations because they were receiving "vitriolic abuse on social media."[7] In addition, the organization was suddenly faced with an "official probe into its finances" by the Charity Commission.[8] By March 2023, so much violence was being directed at Fulani that she stepped down as CEO of her charity in an attempt to protect it from the continued abuse.[9]

It has been said so many times that I don't even know who to attribute it to: In a racist society, minorities naming racism is perceived as worse than racial inequality itself. This is because within a White-dominated society, claiming the existence of phenomena that the dominant group's epistemology of ignorance obscures is undesirable. In the Introduction to How To Be Less Stupid About Race (2018), sociologist Crystal Fleming called the imposing of White's views of racism on others and acting like theirs is the only legitimate perspective on the matter the Gaslighting Fallacy. At the time of her book's publication, I was teaching about the culture-serving perspective that racism only exists when and how members of the dominant group recognize it as the Perception Fallacy; but I've since rebranded it the Recognition Fallacy.

My conceptualization of this perspective is rooted in Karl Marx's famous assertion that the ideas of the ruling class are the "ruling ideas" of the society. Antonio Gramsci further explained that the ruling ideas are not recognized as the ruling class's ideas, though. His concept of hegemony describes the phenomenon of something being dominant, and dominating, and yet being perceived as neutral. Reflecting on economic inequality in Europe, he wrote that the unquestioned seemingly neutral ideas (as well as values, attitudes, beliefs, norms, etc.) served the bourgeoisie's interests and oppressed the proletariat. He also explained that one function of both socialization and formal education is to teach people to accept the ruling ideas as legitimate, thereby granting "spontaneous consent" and validity to their own oppression.[10]

Within an unequal society, perceptions will also be given more or less validity depending on the status of the social group with which they are associated. In other words, patterns of perception associated with higher status groups are deemed valid while the perceptions of lower status groups are at best invalid and at worst rage-inducing. In my scholarship and teaching, I have observed that the Recognition Fallacy manifests in two ways. First, it appears as umbrage that a given manner of treatment of minorities is called racist. Second, it also appears as retaliatory sanctioning of those who recognize racism as being the "real" racists themselves. Given that the very same group who usually engage with this fallacy ironically frame their own perceived mistreatment as racism, the Recognition Fallacy is revealed to be an ends-based perception that functions to reassert the dominance of a White supremacist worldview.

"Shut Up and Play"

Philosopher Charles Wade Mills explained that people "take for granted the appropriateness of concepts *legitimizing* the racial order."[11] By contrast, concepts like discrimination or micro-aggressions that *de*legitimize the racial order draw umbrage. The backlash abuse Sistah Space received for Fulani calling attention to Hussey's racism is but one example in the long history of the Recognition Fallacy. In sports, from Mohammed Ali resisting being drafted into the army to go to war to Colin Kaepernick taking a knee at football games, Black male athletes are told to "shut up and play" when they critique agents of the state for their systematic violent treatment of Black people and other Western minorities. BBC sports reporter and highest-paid presenter Gary Lineker was not simply *told* to "shut up" but was temporarily forced to when he was "taken off air over a tweet criticizing the government's new asylum policy."[12]

Singers, too, are told "shut up and sing or [your] life will be over," as The (Dixie) Chicks crooned in their song *Not Ready to Make Nice*. The group wrote the song in 2006 in response to receiving death threats after group member Natalie Maines said she was ashamed that then US President George W. Bush, who had invaded Iraq in 2003, was a fellow Texan. A decade later, Beyoncé came under fire from those whose thinking aligns with the Recognition Fallacy when systemic racism against Black Americans was highlighted in her *Formation* video and 2016 Super Bowl Halftime performance. In short, there is a vocal segment of society for whom recognizing that racist inequality exists and asserting that it is undesirable is completely unacceptable.

The perception that recognizing racism is wrong extends to non-celebrities as well, as the following example from women of color professors demonstrates. For quick background, research during the Covid-19 pandemic shows that "student demands for special favors," in particular those requiring emotional labor, were disproportionately directed at women, especially women of color. By contrast, "the status shield afforded white cisgender men by their race and gender protected them from student demands."[13] In short, women professors are viewed by some as "modern mammies," that is as the middle-class office versions of the traditional Black woman domestic workers. No longer predominantly working in White people's home, the "new version of mammification" attempts to press women of color into the same role just in a different building: Modern mammies are expected to take "care of the personal needs of the destitute and the weak" within White-dominated middle-class professions.[14]

Returning to higher education specifically, many students, colleagues, and administrators expect women of color to untiringly fulfill their every request. This situation would be overwhelming but understandable if the reason for the disproportionately large number of requests was that people valued our expertise and skills; but unfortunately, that is not typically the case. For example, a White woman who had not taken any of my classes nonetheless requested to meet with me to discuss me potentially advising her research project. After she told me her ideas and interests, I realized they more closely aligned with a White man colleague's research than mine; so I told her that he would be a more appropriate person than me to advise her project. She responded: "I know. I've taken his class. But he's really busy." She seemed to truly not realize that she had just plainly admitted, to my face, that she respected a White man's time more than she respected mine.

I shared this experience one day on #AcademicTwitter in response to an Asian woman professor posting that she had just gone through something similar. A second Asian woman professor replied too, and she and I offered the first woman solidarity and affirmation in her feelings. Then, an uninvited White woman professor commented[15] to say that what we experienced was not offensive. Annoyed at her attempt to erase racism by fiat, I replied snarkily that only folks with low self-image would not be offended by someone admitting to their face that they don't value their time. To this, she attempted to delegitimize our recognition of sexism/racism by using an arsenal of White supremacist tools in a now-deleted or restricted tweet:

> I have no problem with self-image. I guess that's why I'm not angry at the world playing the victim while pretending that I live in a teen fiction novel series.

Before we jump in, let me just say that if anyone out there would kindly write a "teen fiction novel series" featuring Black and Asian teenage protagonists with PhDs who are navigating academic research and teaching as well as heart-breaking love triangles involving scholars in multiple disciplines, I would forever be grateful. To my nerd heart, that sounds like it would go great with wine, my college track sweat suit, my couch, my fireplace, and a rainy day. In all seriousness, though, of course there was literally nothing *teen* in our discussing our working in the *professorate*. Infantilizing adults as "teens" is the grown-up equivalent of playground children taunting someone by calling them a "baby." Basically, it is a weak attempt to insult and demean by positioning a person as less mature than you.

In addition, calling us "angry" for discussing an experience we found problematic is so cliché that it makes me tired to even write about it. Our discussion group included two Asian women and only one Black woman; and yet the Angry Black Woman stereotype nonetheless reared its head. It is actually not even a stereotype but a "controlling image," which is Black feminist sociologist Patricia Hill Collins' term for racist distortions that are used to attempt to control minorities' behaviors.[16] Negatively characterizing women of color as "angry" when we critique racism/sexism is meant to sanction us for that behavior and dissuade others from following suit.

Finally, the White woman professor's description of our naming our experience as undesirable as us "playing victim" is a feeble and overly-worn White attempt to position the disrespect people of color describe as legitimate and thus "not offensive," as she said in her first uninvited response. In her view, we are not real victims of racism or sexism in higher education; we are angry children who are playing make-believe.

The hold that the Recognition Fallacy can have over people's thinking is clear. This common perception resulted in a random White woman professor being so disturbed by three non-White professors who were chatting in public about a shared experience they considered racist/sexist that she could not just scroll by. She spontaneously vomited cliché ad hominins to strangers all because we recognized an instance of racism in our own lives.

Many academics receive backlash for what we say in public, sometimes even from our own families. Sociologist Shantel Buggs' autoethnographic work on mixed-race Black people's online interactions with their White family offers an example. After making a Facebook post sharing a blog by a Native American author who critiqued Hollywood's practice of casting White actors like Johnny Depp to play Native characters, Buggs' White family berated her publicly via their comments on the post. Like the White woman who jumped into my Twitter conversation, some of Buggs' Facebook friends and family rejected her recognition of racism and declared that it was not racist for White actors to play Native characters. One commenting on the post asked, "Why is a black person getting upset that Depp is portraying an Indian in a movie? Thats ridiculous!"[17] This person, a "childhood or college" friend, added that "to say it's another instance of whites 'eliminating people of color' is absurd. Period."[18] Here we see the heart of the Recognition Fallacy: the perceptual refusal to acknowledge the validity of any viewpoint other than one that upholds White domination. Buggs writes that "Here, their white innocence – the belief that society is fair and equal regardless of race – transitions to white arrogance."[19]

The title of Buggs' article "Your momma is day-glow white," comes from a relative who clearly felt that Buggs having a White mother and White ancestry should stop her from questioning the validity of White people's actions, in this case, of them playing Native Americans in movies. Buggs analysis demonstrates that her friends and family expected her to show *loyalty* to White supremacy, but to *eschew recognizing and naming it.*[20]

The backlash Buggs experienced on Facebook is an example of what Mills meant when he observed that those oppressed by White supremacy are socialized to accept the epistemologies of ignorance that support it. Quoting Fredrick Douglass' comments on enslavers' efforts to make sure the enslaved "be able to detect no inconsistencies in slavery; he must be made to feel that slavery is right,"[21] Mills reminds his readers that "[r]acism as an ideology needs to be understood as aiming at the minds of nonwhites as well as whites, inculcating subjugation . . . nonwhite self-loathing and racial deference to white citizens."[22] In other words, both Whites and non-Whites face "White racial obligation" to not recognize racism;[23] and there are social sanctions for those who refuse.

Offline, professors who discuss race in their lectures can face backlash for recognizing that racism exists. While I was teaching Race/Ethnicity as a graduate student lecturer in Wisconsin, a Black woman in neighboring Minnesota was teaching Communications as a full-time adjunct instructor. I heard about her in the news when she was reprimanded for violating the civil rights of two white male students . . . for talking about racism in class. Although upon further investigation the university "rescinded her reprimand and removed it from her file,"[24] the incident showed how strongly some White people are against even so much as hearing about the existence of the unequal system their ancestors created and their contemporaries and accomplices work to maintain.

The academy also does the reverse as well, that is it rewards people, especially minorities, who comply with the racial contract and participate in the epistemology of ignorance by not mentioning racism. Sociologist Ted Thornhill's research reveals that Black college applicants who do not mention race or racism as topics they would like to study in college are preferred by college admissions personnel compared to Black college applications who do mention those topics.[25] Mills reminds us that those who "claim not to recognize [structural racism], are only continuing the epistemology of ignorance required by the original Racial Contract."[26] Society allocating desirable goods like college admissions and sanctions such as reprimands at work based on whether one adheres to the Recognition Fallacy or challenges it is how White supremacist ideology and material conditions are justified and maintained.

"The Worst Type of Racist"

The second way I have seen the Recognition Fallacy manifest is as stigmatizing those who call out racism as the "real ones" doing something "wrong," and in turn attacking them rather than investigating and holding accountable the person or institution that was identified as problematic. Social scientists argue that "projection is part of our normal equipment to defend ourselves" and that racist projection like "They are the racist ones" functions "as a way of avoiding responsibility and feeling good about [oneself]."[27]

Sometimes this is done subtly via appeal to norms of politeness. For example, theoretical physicist Chanda Prescod-Weinstein recalls that she once "witnessed a white man tell an Indigenous Canadian scientist that it was rude to call anti-Native Hawaiian comments what they were – racist and colonialist – during a contentious conversation about occupied Indigenous land."[28] Upon the death of Queen Elizabeth II, many people, disproportionately but not exclusively people of color, refused to join in glorifying the late monarch on the grounds that, as head of the British Empire, she was responsible for the violent atrocities committed by that regime in her name. In addition to some people having their account locked for a time period as a sanction by Twitter for expressing these sentiments, the perspective in general was seen as "disrespectful" to the dead and inappropriately timed. In short, making anti-Indigenous and pro-colonial comments is normal but recognizing racism and making anti-colonialist comments is rude and disrespectful. One need only ask oneself "rude and disrespectful to whom" to begin to see the status quo supporting function at play.

Other scholars have noticed that recognizing racism is also stigmatized as "complaining."[29] In her book *Complaint!* (2021), sociologist Sara Ahmed explains that complaints are considered negative speech. "To hear someone as complaining," writes Ahmed, "is an effective way of dismissing someone. You do not have to listen to the content of what she is saying if she is just complaining or always complaining."[30] With respect to inequality, complaining is also "a killjoy genre." Drawing on Ahmed's work, mixed-race essayist Samira K. Mehta explains that pointing out sexism or racism – and, more importantly, communicating that one is upset by it – creates tension in social situations because it reveals that others were perfectly willing to allow that inequality to exist unchallenged.[31] Thus,

Ahmed and Mehta continue, for the action of exposing others' complicity in injustice, recognition of inequality is dismissed as invalid "whining" and "complaining."

At the root of labeling the recognition of racism as being "rude," "disrespectful," or "complaining" is the perception that there exists nothing problematic that legitimately deserves acknowledgment and rejection. Drawing on Patricia Hill Collins, Ahmed describes how the pervasiveness of the empirically unsubstantiated view that sexist and racist discrimination no longer occurs sets the mental stage for people, especially women of color, who point out instances of discrimination to "easily be dismissed as complainers who want special, unearned favors."[32] However, this dismissal is only tenable from a perspective that either ignores the mountains of empirical evidence of racial discrimination or from a perspective that acknowledges disparities but attributes them as the valid outcome of White men's innate superiority/others' innate inferiority. In other words, White supremacist-serving patterns of thinking lie beneath stigmatizing those who recognize racism.

It is an ironic twist, therefore, that the recognition of Whites' actions as racist often is labeled as a "racist" act itself, that is as "reverse racism" against White people. Sociologist Miri Song explains that present "understandings and conceptualizations of racism are highly imprecise, broad, and readily used to describe a wide range of racialized phenomena."[33] The problem with this "culture of racial equivalence," as she calls it, is that the word racist is thrown around "without enough consideration of how and why particular interactions and practices constitute racism as such," which thus "denudes the idea of racism of its historical basis, severity and power."[34] One such example occurred after the incident at Buckingham Palace in which Hussey verbally harassed Fulani. Black Studies professor Kehinde Andrews was invited to speak about the incident on *Good Morning Britain*. As he, and many others including myself, have explained on UK media previously in response to other incidents, the British Royal Family "is an institution that is deeply embedded in institutional racism."[35] Andrews also restated his well-known, not even fringe, position that the monarchy should be abolished.

Thereafter, it was reported that viewers "slammed the show" for giving a platform to a "hate spreader" like Andrews.[36] Comments online included "Kehinde Andrews is the worst type of racist."[37] In a nation that enslaved, colonized, and/or attempted genocide in a part of every continent on earth, the "worst" type of racist is . . . someone who points out the racism in that society? The "worst" type of racist is someone who wants to end the outdated institution that has been responsible for countless violent atrocities? By this line of thinking, abusing non-Whites is not "racist"; it is only labeling systemic abuse of non-Whites as racist that is "racist." To quote Inigo Montoya, the skilled swordsman from the movie *The Princess Bride*: "You keep using that word. I do not think it means what you think it means."

Across the pond in the US, sociologist Saida Grundy inadvertently revealed that recognizing the flip side of non-White oppression – White privilege – is also taboo. Grundy once tweeted asking: "why is white America so reluctant to identify white college males as a problem population?"[38] Backlash was swift, with some people calling for Grundy to lose her job. Sociologist Tressie McMillan Cottom explained the backlash as the situation of an expert "using 'inside' language in an 'outside' context."[39] Academics know, for instance, statistics like that the majority of college campus rapes are perpetrated by White men; but the average non-expert likely does not. Regardless of the reason for the backlash against Grundy, though, the *form* it took is illuminating. Like Andrews, Grundy was called "racist" for recognizing the existence of racial inequality.[40] In both nations, then, we see how the now stigmatized figure of The Racist is "increasingly used as a means of delegitimizing the [public racism] claims of others."[41]

Both Andrews and Grundy were commenting on institutionalized racism, which we remember from chapter 1 is bias rooted in policies, laws, and institutions. Beyond labeling individuals as racist for recognizing it, though, White nationalists also reveal the ends-based nature of the Recognition Fallacy in that they too use the language of institutional racism to describe their own (alleged) social experiences. Sociologist Marcus Brooks' analysis of White nationalist vlogers (video bloggers) found that their content included a victimized White consciousness and claims of systemic anti-White racism within social institutions like schools.[42] One vlogger, for example, discussed the negative psychological impact on White children of "institutionalized anti-whiteness" such as schools and television "constantly" telling them "they are bad because of slavery."[43] The fact that no schools or television programs actually do this is irrelevant for the moment. The points to note are that such claims demonstrate, first, the general ability to understand and, second, the acceptance of public recognition of institutional bias. White nationalists vlogging about institutional anti-Whiteness shows that the Individualistic Fallacy from chapter 1 and the Recognition Fallacy of this chapter are both White supremacist-serving in that only racial minorities' perception of structural inequity is intolerable.

"What a Piece of Racist Trash": Beyond Individual Recognition

Groups, not just individuals, who recognize racism have also been called racist. A staff member at the University of North Texas was accused of engaging in racism for offering White accountability groups. Given that White people are often "scared" to "say the wrong thing" in conversations about race in public and in classrooms,[44] the White accountability groups were a space for White people (or anyone) to "start broaching sensitive topics in settings where they feel more confident."[45] In response, Turning Point USA, a conservative non-profit organization in the US that works to promote "freedom" in education, released a statement saying that by "singling out white people and holding them 'accountable' for discrimination, the event 'promotes legitimately racist ideas.'"[46]

Turning Point USA took issue with the fact that White people were "singled out"; but apropos to the intention of the groups – to provide a safe space to discuss and learn about racism – there is empirical support for the idea that White people *do need* to be "singled out." A National Public Radio poll of parents found that race is a topic they "rarely, if ever" discuss with their children.[47] Research on childhood socialization has documented racial differences in this phenomenon, however. While Black and other Western racial minorities often discuss race and racism with their children (e.g. "The Talk"),[48] White parents in general do not.[49] Sociologist Maggie Hagerman conducted interviews and ethnographic observations with multiple White families to study how White children are socialized around race. Her book *White Kids: Growing Up with Privilege in a Racially Divided America* (2018) reveals that while many White parents sent subtle messages to their children about race, for instance by referring to things associated with Black culture as "ghetto," most did not have open, frank conversations about race, be it other races or their own Whiteness. Turning Point USA taking issue with an attempt to offer White people an alternative to the silence around race that characterizes so much of their education is thus an attempt to legitimate and maintain the racial ignorance that such silence produces.

Second, the point of the White accountability groups was not to hold White people accountable for discrimination. But if, just for the sake of argument, the point *were* to hold White people accountable, one can only take umbrage with that if one thinks White people have nothing to be held accountable for. To be sure, no White person alive is responsible for the Trail of Tears, or slavery, or the Asian Exclusion Act. However, with respect to contemporary discrimination, it is an uncomfortable fact for many that it is widely perpetrated by White people. It is majority White employers and school officials in the US and UK who make dress code policies that ban natural textured African hairstyles.[50] It is White men, as many researchers have pointed out, who commit the vast majority of mass shootings, including racist attacks on Black Churches, Sikh Temples, and Asian-owned businesses. It was a White woman who accosted a Black woman in Buckingham Palace. So if a group were to be formed with the intent to hold White people accountable for discrimination, one could only take issue with it if one refuses to recognize the literal facts of who does what to whom *disproportionately* in society.

In White settler nations, though, the dominant cognitive framework is not built to accommodate such recognition. Sociologist Joe Feagin described the dominate cognitive framework, which can influence the perception of people of all races, as perceiving the status quo of White domination as normal and neutral, not as unjust or "racist." He calls this the "White racial frame." When this seemingly normal and neutral state of affairs is characterized as "racist," therefore, those ensconced in the framework experience cognitive dissonance, confusion, disbelief. Because of this, many people "experience genuine cognitive difficulties in recognizing certain behavior patterns as racist."[51]

In his book *Backlash: What happens When We Talk Honestly about Racism in America* (2018), philosopher George Yancy reflects on reactions by those within the White racial frame to an op-ed he wrote.

In his op-ed, he invited White readers to recognize "the subtle ways in which so many white people go about their daily lives oblivious to the gravity and violence of white racism in this country and the ways in which they simultaneously benefit from and contribute to that racism."[52] In other words, he characterized the nation as racist versus neutral and identified White people as a group who typically does not recognize that. Per the Recognition Fallacy, Yancy was immediately assaulted with a violent backlash (hence the name of his subsequent book). He writes that he received

> foul and nasty voice messages, sickening email messages, vulgar letters mailed to my university, comments on many conservative and white supremacist websites in which I was lambasted and called everything but a Child of God . . . There were white threats of physical violence, talk of putting a meat hook in parts of my body, threats of knocking my "fucking head off" (their words), of beating me and leaving me half dead, and vile demands that I kill myself immediately.[53]

As if he and others might miss the fact that this rage was coming from people who were committed to the ideology and practice of White superiority, many of the messages contained gratuitous use of the N-word.

Like social media posts and newspaper op-eds, the publication of social scientific research that recognizes racism draws vitriol as well. In the 1990s, sociologist James Loewen published *Lies My Teacher Told Me*, a 400+ page painstakingly researched volume on the empirical inaccuracies printed in US History textbooks. The now classic book drew similar rage from White (Loewen assumed) readers.[54] In the time just before mass use of email, letters and postcards arrived calling Loewen a Socialist, Marxist, hippie, anti-American,[55] and anti-Christian.[56]

One postcard Loewen received sheds further light on why calling attention to racism is so offensive. The anonymous postcard read, "What a piece of racist trash . . . Take your sour mind to Africa."[57] A quarter century later, George Yancy would similarly be told that "planes leave every day for Africa" so he "should fuck off to Africa if he doesn't like living in a white country."[58] Another person who was angry at Yancy's op-ed wrote that "Africa is calling you!" and yet another threatened that "There are two ways you can return to Africa: On a passenger ship, or in a coffin freighter.

Choose quickly."[59] While Loewen characterized these as "a white response," looking deeper it is clear that they are specifically *anti-Black* responses. The invocation of Africa, not only to a man of actual African descent (Yancy) but to a man of European descent too (Loewen), like the application of a stereotype of Black women to my Twitter discussion trio that was majority Asian, suggests that *maintaining the legitimacy of anti-Blackness specifically* is often what underpins the Recognition Fallacy.

Loewen's anonymous postcard writer as well as many letters received by Yancy also, predictably, called the men and their work "racist," which just gives themselves away as believing that publishing work that states that White people did "bad" things is unfair to them. The double standard is clear, though, when one considers the ease with which White society stomachs mentions of and publishes work on the supposed bad deeds of others: No one is told to take their "sour mind" to a different continent for claiming that Mexicans are rapists. Mainstream thinking does not consider it "Socialist" to talk about "Black on Black crime" the way many object to discussing White police officers' abuse and murder of Black people. Stigmatized labels like "racist" are not applied when Muslim States are characterized as violent even though they came swiftly when the late Queen was described as the head of a violent nation.

Of US American history, which we can extend to White settler colonial history more broadly, Loewen said that "anything bad" is to be understood as having "happened anonymously."[60] But more specifically, the Recognition Fallacy is that anything "bad" in Western history or the present that was/is done by *White people* must either be not recognized or, if it is, must be talked about as if it was/is done anonymously. The Recognition Fallacy seeks to compel us to talk about an invisible hand of colonization, slavery, and contemporary aggression. The fact that the majority of those hands are clearly White is not supposed to be recognized.

This compulsion is not just at the individual angry letter writer level; it is institutionalized in some cases. In journalism, there is a "balanced" reporting norm, based on the "bothsidesism" perspective that views positioning opposing "sides" as equally legitimate as being "neutral" and thus "fair." During the lead up to the 2016 US Presidential Election, though, this meant that many news outlets gave air time/print space to the empirically inaccurate information

Donald Trump's campaign put out *without* labeling it as disinformation. Recognizing that claims that Mexicans are rapists and are bringing drugs is not only empirically inaccurate but also racist, would have risked being labeled as "biased" versus "balanced" reporting. Despite a campaign and administration full of these types of comments, the Recognition Fallacy and the stigmatization as being "racist" if one violated it meant that the mainstream media refrained from recognizing many racist statements from Trump and his administration *as* racism. By the time this bothsidesism was finally broken under the weight of the "Big Lie" that Trump had won the 2020 election, the US had lost three points on the Democracy Index calculated each year by Freedom House.[61] This was in part due to the reduced score on the "Are there free and independent media?" criteria.

The media pick and choose what topics get bothsidesism treatment, though. Whenever an eclipse occurs, there are no reputable news sources reporting that it is a warning of an angry God. Everyone reports the scientifically valid fact that that is what happens when various celestial bodies line up in certain ways. Meanwhile, though we have literal numbers that plain as day tell us that right-wing extremists commit exponentially more violence than left, the Recognition Fallacy protects White supremacy from justifiable criticism and denouncement by falsely claiming that it is people who point out statistics on White supremacist violence, not those who perpetuate that violence, who are "divisive" and "racist."

In Millsian terms, the maligning of those who recognize racism stems from their rejecting the epistemology of ignorance that is necessary to maintain White supremacy. That this backlash occurs so often over social media, the newest of society's public spheres, is evidence of Mills' observation that "in frontier situations, where official White authority is distant or unreliable, individual whites may be regarded as endowed with the authority to enforce the Racial Contract themselves."[62] Regardless of the location of backlash against recognizing racism, though, the function of the Recognition Fallacy is to maintain as the dominant pattern of thinking the idea that "the status quo of differential racial entitlement [is] normatively legitimate, and not to be investigated further."[63]

Conclusion

Sociologists Nathanial Chapman and David Brunsma have explained that "Far from 'name calling' and/or calling out all 'white people' as immediately to blame, sociologists of race and ethnicity are 'system calling' and ask us to understand the system of whiteness under white supremacy."[64] Nonetheless, many people balk when mistreatment against minorities is recognized, even when that recognition implicates impersonal social structures not any one individual's personal "fault." Since White nationalists deploy the concepts of systemic and institutionalized racial bias to describe their own alleged experiences in society, though, the perception that minorities doing so is wrong or racist exists to legitimize White supremacy. This cultivated racial ignorance supports the continuation of racism because it is harder to challenge that which you cannot recognize.

That said, another reason that the recognition of racism elicits such extreme responses is that many White people "take their racial privilege so much for granted that they do not even see it as political, as a form of domination."[65] This goes for non-Whites who see White privilege as neutral versus as domination, too. As we will see in the next chapter, the perception that a society in which Whites are on top is a legitimate, fair, and orderly system means that attempts to *change* the system are perceived as perverse threats to the very survival of the society; and as such, they are seen as deserving of even more than hate mail.

8

The Self-Defense Fallacy

If the dominant patterns of thinking lead to revolt at the mere recognition of racism, active attempts to defend and protect minorities incites both incredulity ("How dare they!") and vindictive rage ("They will pay for this!"). As thinkers from Fredrick Douglass to Carter G. Woodson to Charles Wade Mills and more have noted, White supremacy seeks to compel not only White allegiance but also the allegiance of its non-White victims. Mills explains that White supremacy "prescribes nonwhite self-loathing and racial deference to white citizens."[1] In other words, within the dominant White supremacist cognitive framework, minorities are supposed to accept subordinate status by perceiving Whites' treatment of them as most White people do, that is as legitimate and unproblematic. Such non-White acceptance is needed in order to maintain the delusion that White supremacy is not doing anything wrong since even the so-called victims themselves have no complaints.

When non-Whites *do* perceive their treatment in particular, or the status quo in general, as illegitimate and unequal and go beyond merely recognizing that as we saw in the last chapter to actually *doing* something to stop or prevent it, the White power structure uses the Self-Defense Fallacy to reassert White supremacy. This fallacy is the White supremacist culture-serving perspective that actions to defend or protect people from biased individuals, organizations, and social institutions are "just as bad," or even worse, than White domination.[2] As literary historian Koritha Mitchell explained, "disrespecting you is built into the culture."[3] Thus, challenging, or worse trying to prevent, that disrespect is to behave in a countercultural manner.

For example, in the eighteenth century, US White men claimed to have a natural entitlement, given by God, to resist a tyrannical foreign government; and yet in a document declaring just that, they called Native Americans "merciless" and "savage" for doing the same thing, that is for resisting the tyrannical foreign government they were trying to establish. Centuries later, Native Americans were met with rubber bullets for protesting the oil pipeline that was to be run through their land because White people had protested the original plan to run it near theirs. Native Americans were painted as paranoid for fearing the pipeline would leak and ruin the water while it was White residents of Bismarck's exact same concern that resulted in rerouting the pipeline away from them and onto Native land in the first place.

Resistance to anti-Black racism has even been medicalized. Doctors in the nineteenth century claimed that runaway slaves were mentally ill, in particular suffering from a condition called drapetomania.[4] History books in the US paint White men who fought against slavery as insane fanatics.[5] In the twentieth century, Black men who fought for their civil rights were perceived as schizophrenic.[6] Black Studies professor Kehinde Andrews writes of the medical concept of psychosis that it "is a label that has been put on us from wanting to be free; trying to resist; and existing in ways that go against an established White norm."[7] According to the dominant patterns of thinking, then, Black subordination, up to and including the brutality of slavery, is supposedly so normal and acceptable that only people suffering from severe mental illness would object to it.

We need not even speculate as to why dominant thinking perceives minorities' rejection of White supremacist treatment as unacceptable for we have empirical evidence to give us insight. In their study of the violent comments and actions that women and LGBTQ people are subjected to in public in New York City, sociologist Simone Kolysh interviewed not only victims of street harassment but also the perpetrators. Regarding an Asian woman who told the White man who catcalled her with sexually racist comments that his behavior was inappropriate, he replied that "It's my right to express myself the way I want to."[8] Given that the way this man chose to "express" himself was by harassing a stranger, his explanation is thus saying that he has a right to harass women of color. It is only within a White supremacist frame of mind that one can think themselves to have a "right" to harm others and dismiss the legitimacy of complaints thereto.

This is an old stance, though. Citing the nineteenth-century French scholar Alexis de Tocqueville's description of antebellum White southerners' expectation "of ruling without resistance," philosopher José Medina explains that "An important part of this 'ruling without resistance' is not being called into question in one's opinions, that is, having an undisputed cognitive authority."[9] Though it has been nearly 200 years since de Tocqueville was in the US, Medina explains that the "epistemic arrogance" he observed among White Southerners still exists among many today. To be clear, as noted in chapter 2, some White people break the racial contract and call out individual or institutionalized racism, too, while some people of color collude with it. As we saw in that chapter and others, though, whoever rejects White supremacy will find themselves on the receiving end of backlash, too.

I have seen the Self-Defense Fallacy manifesting in two main ways: as umbrage that minorities responded to White supremacist aggression with self-defensive maneuvers; and as labeling minorities' and allies' offensive protective maneuvers as problematic. Before discussing examples of each and demonstrating how they function to uphold White domination, though, I will first describe in more detail the epistemic and social conditions that set the stage for the two manifestations of this fallacy.

The Epistemological and Social Foundations of the Self-Defense Fallacy

Philosophers consider the phenomenon of being closed off to the mere possibility that one's own understanding of a situation is one-sided, incomplete, or even empirically inaccurate *epistemic vices.*[10] Noting that epistemic vices "are not incidental and transitory, *but structural and systemic,*"[11] Medina outlines three specific vices: *epistemic arrogance* (narcissistically viewing oneself/one's group as the sole cognitive authority on all matters), *epistemic laziness* (a pathological lack of intellectual curiosity that results in avoiding expending even bare minimal effort to learn anything new), and *epistemic closed-mindedness* (refusing to entertain alternative views even in the face of empirical evidentiary support). He says that these three and other cognitive habits thwart the ability (mainly of members of privileged groups) to make sense of perspectives other than their own. What is more, Medina says this state of mind "does not result from *a decision or conscious effort to ignore*, but from a *socialization* that leads one to be insensitive to certain things and immune to certain considerations."[12]

Sociologist James Loewen would agree with Medina's analysis. His now famous book *Lies My Teacher Told Me*, which is based on a comprehensive content analysis of US History textbooks, found that these widely used materials utterly fail to recognize past injustices perpetrated by White Westerners. They also portray historic anti-racism efforts negatively. For example, White people like John Brown who led an anti-slavery raid on Harper's Ferry in 1859 are portrayed in many textbooks as "crazy."[13] Other textbooks sidestep the question of Brown's mental state and simply portray his raid – *which freed enslaved people* – in line with how it was perceived at the time: As a treasonous offence for which he was hung.[14] Like Medina, Loewen reminds his readers that it is this type of epistemically arrogant, lazy, and narrow-minded socialization that results in adults who lack the humility, will, or even cognitive ability to perceive social phenomena outside of the hegemonic racist frame. This sets the stage for mass incomprehension of defensive and protective actions on the parts of minorities. Thus, as Loewen explained, a history education that presents past defensive actions like slave revolts as "crazy" functions to ensure that contemporary defensive actions like Black Lives Matter (BLM), Missing and Murdered Indigenous Women (MMIW), Stop Asian Hate, etc., are "incomprehensible" to many people as well.[15] This design feature of education leaves people "unable to understand why others are upset with [the mainstream US]."[16]

Regarding this line of reasoning, that socialization into epistemic vices "blind" people (mainly but not only members of privileged groups) to others' experiences, I am uneasy with its conclusion that particular types of unjust actions thus stem from socialized epistemic vices rather than from a "decision or conscious effort to ignore" certain types of knowledge. For example, both Medina and fellow philosopher Miranda Fricker under-acknowledge the role of *social desirability* in actions. Both discuss the trial of Tom Robinson in Harper Lee's 1960 novel *To Kill a Mockingbird* to explain how the epistemic vices of the White prosecutor and jury result in Tom's conviction. Briefly, both scholars point out that the epistemic arrogance, laziness, and closed-mindedness of White men in 1930s Alabama is why they found Tom guilty of assaulting a young White woman, Mayella Ewell, despite the physical evidence of his innocence. During the trial, Ewell's injuries were discussed and it was established that she was beaten by a left-handed person; but Tom's left arm is paralyzed. Medina and Fricker both conclude that *critical openness* to imagining alternatives (a White woman made sexual advances to a Black man) beyond one's default habits of thinking (Black men are sexual predators) is "what is most needed for attaining justice in the trial of Tom Robinson."[17]

And yet, social science research reveals that people act in ways that are contrary to the facts, not because they *cannot cognitively process* the facts but to *avoid the social consequences* of violating social norms. Social psychologist Solomon Ashe's classic line experiments vividly demonstrated that people will deny crystal clear reality in order to go along with their group. Ashe would show a group of men two cards, one with one line on it and a second card that had three lines of different lengths. The task, he told them, was to identify which line on the card with three was the same length as the line on the card with one. Only one man in each group was a real research participant, though. All the others were working for the researchers and were told to say wrong answers sometimes. Ashe famously found that research participants often agreed with wrong answers, even though in debriefing interviews afterwards they admitted they knew that the answers they gave were wrong. Ashe, like other social psychologists of the time, concluded that social groups exert a powerful influence over individuals' behaviors.

In more recent sociological research, sociologist Jonathan Metzl studied White US American's views on guns. While conducting participant observation in a support group in Missouri for people who had lost loved ones to gun suicides, Metzl gently asked if they thought stricter gun laws would have prevented their loved ones' deaths. A unanimous "no" was the reply, along with reminders that he was in "gun country." An even bigger gut punch, at least for me as someone who has lost a friend to gun suicide, came at the end of the section. Ready to depart, Metzl got into the car with the participant who had invited him and she revealed that she actually *is* in favor of "some kind of middle ground" with regard to gun regulation. The chapter ends with her telling Metzl that she "would never say that" in front of the other (White) people in her group.[18]

Even before the twist ending of Metzl's gun chapter, I knew that White people's comments were sometimes a lie to maintain public White solidarity. I knew this from my mother's experience in the 1970s in a local Miss South Carolina feeder pageant. There was a delay in announcing the winner because upon tallying the scores, my mother, a Black woman, had won. The lone White woman judge sat resolutely shaking her head "no" as the other two judges, both White men, attempted to coerce her to change her scoring, i.e., to deny the evidence of my mother's excellence that day, in favor of upholding the fiction of White supremacy. She refused. Ultimately, my mother was given all of the first place awards but was not allowed to compete in the Miss South Carolina pageant (and by extension, was not allowed to have a chance at maybe going on to Miss America). The White runner-up was given the runner-up prizes and was sent to the state pageant.[19]

Despite Medina noting that *Mayella Ewell* was "clearly coerced to lie" during the trial, neither he nor Fricker discuss the possibility that the White *prosecutor* or *jury* were coerced to lie too. Like Mayella Ewell and Metzl's study participant, others could be making the conscious though admittedly pressured decision to lie in order to go along with a racist system that advantages them. They lack the *epistemic courage* of people like the White woman judge at my mother's pageant to refuse to deny evidence, even when it inconveniently challenges White supremacist sensibilities.

Invalidating Self-Defense

Whether due to suffering from genuine epistemological arrogance, laziness, and/or narrow-mindedness or due to a calculated decision to deny one's true views to avoid angering peers, one way that the Self-Defense Fallacy manifests is as the common perception that minorities responding to White supremacist aggression with self-defense is invalid behavior. This culture-serving perception considers resisting oppression "just as bad" as the actions that lead to that resistance because the first actions are not seen as (or not acknowledged as) oppression in the first place.

The invalidation of oppressed groups' self-defense can be observed within the most intimate spheres of social interaction. As discussed in chapter 3, research with mixed-race people frequently documents the racism that people of color experience from White partners or families. I heard examples of this phenomenon from some of the mixed-race people I interviewed when they would talk about how other people responded quite angrily, not only at them recognizing racism, but taking an action to protect themselves from it. A pansexual Asian/White non-binary femme named Janette (24 in 2019) told the following story of their White Latino ex-partner's family's response to her hurt feelings over a racist remark:

> And their family, the issue there was with their family. Because their family was actually super racist and didn't want to admit it. At one point, I was at their house for Easter and they were Skyping in my ex's brother who was in Alaska, he was in the military. And he was asking about a Thai restaurant. He was asking what it was called. And then my ex's mom went into like Chinglish, like these words that aren't actual words, but just derogatory ways of thinking about Asian language as a homogeneous thing. And I went upstairs because I was upset and I was trying to sort of isolate myself and calm down. When my ex came to see what was up and I told them why I was angry and they went downstairs and they told their family why I was angry. And the mom threw a fit. Slamming cabinet doors, crying, screaming that I thought she was a racist. And then my ex's dad yelled for me to come downstairs to talk about what was wrong. And he was like, I thought you would know us better than this. We're not racist. I can't believe you would – Like it was this half assed apology of like I'm sorry you think that what we said was racist but it wasn't racist.

Despite allegations that "political correctness" now has a choke-hold on Western discourse, research shows that Janette's experience is all too common. As discussed in chapter 4, "jokingly" mocking Asian languages is a form of racist humor. In his book *The Souls of White Jokes: How Racist Humor Fuels White Supremacy* (2022), sociologist Raúl Pérez coins the term "amused racial contempt" to describe the "pleasurable and enjoyable feeling and practice that regards racial-ized 'others' as inferior, worthless, and beneath consideration."[20] He notes that "From private gatherings among friends to the politi-cal arena, racist joking continues to play an important role in main-taining a 'white racial framing' of US society."[21]

Pérez reminds us that "Philosophers – such as Plato, Aristotle, and Thomas Hobbes – long ago observed that feelings of superiority, and the viewing of others as inferior, can be pleasurable and amusing."[22] He then extends this general observation of the existence of "schadenfreude" to note that the shared emotional state of *white racist schadenfreude*, which he reminds us Gunnar Myrdal observed among White US Americans over 200 years ago, specifically has social functions. As in the days of minstrel shows and human zoos, contemporary mocking and misrepresenting of racial minorities, as Janette's ex's mother-in-law did, continues to be a pleasurable way for Whites to build White racial solidarity. Sociology of the family scholars have found that this expectation to share in White racist perspectives extends to non-White family members too.[23] Importantly, Pérez reminds us that racist humor is used "not only by white people but also by non-whites who aspire towards the social power of whiteness and its class privilege."[24]

In sum, while on the surface it may seem easy to dismiss my interviewee's White ex's parents as exhibiting classic White fragility, or just to call them unhinged, both explanations are too simplistic to capture what was going on that Easter Day. The main function of racist jokes, that is, what they *do*, is maintain and reinforce White domination by perpetuating misrepresentations of racial minorities, in this case Asians. Pérez says, "Part of what makes racist humor so powerful and insidious is that it appears as something other than it is – harmless and delightful rather than socially destructive."[25]

But Janette was hurt by her White ex-mother-in-law's mockery of Asian language, and so she went upstairs to protect herself ("I was trying to sort of isolate myself and calm down"). Both being hurt and trying to do self-care were seen as unacceptable and rage-inducing to her former in-laws. The ex-father-in-law in particular displayed epistemic arrogance with his "half assed apology" that asserted the epistemic supremacy of their view that the joke "wasn't racist." He and the ex-mother-in-law both displayed epistemic laziness in that they did not even bother to be curious about and seek to learn more about why Janette viewed the comment so differently than them. The only thing that mattered was that Janette *cease self-care* and instead allow them to *reassert their perspective* that mocking Asian languages is acceptable versus racist.

Another interviewee, 41-year-old Jen, a bisexual Asian/White cis woman who had also dealt with racism from ex-partners, explained the root of the Self-Defense Fallacy when I interviewed her a few months after Janette. She said such behaviors stem from the fact that "people think of themselves as more liberal than they really are." When I asked her if she thought potential (White) partners were lying to her or to themselves when they asserted their commitment to racial equality, she reflected that "Probably they're lying to themselves. I mean, no one likes to think of themselves as a racist. And no one identifies as that really, I mean, you know, unless you're extreme." The challenge to Whites' positive self-image that Jen discussed offers insight into the "fit" of "[s]lamming cabinet doors, crying, screaming" that followed a mixed-race woman privately soothing her hurt feelings. The White couple who respond in this manner were upset at the idea that someone does not view them the same way they view themselves. They were more upset at that than at the incomprehensible idea that their words upset a member of the family.

Such responses occur not just in families but in workplaces as well. In academia, for instance, racial minority scholars who seek to defend ourselves against racism are often met with derision. For example, theoretical physicist Chanda Prescod-Weinstein reported the experiences of Indigenous students who received a racist email and responded that it was inappropriate: They were told that "their anti-racist stance was embarrassing to the community."[26] It is no wonder, then, that some members of oppressed populations have learned (been compelled) to prioritize the perspectives and feelings of those who harm them over their own and other victimized people's perspectives and feelings.

Prioritizing aggressors includes using a gentle hand in response to racism, even violent racism. This is the only type of response that is supposedly approved of. Sociologist David G. Embrick has noted that calls for "peaceful protests and the calls for civility are often used by whites (and their supporters) to quell public unrest."[27] Embrick continues that this expectation that self-defense "should" be peaceful and that responses to oppression should be "civil" represents "an acknowledgement that some lives are worth more than others." In other words, despite a White policeman torturing a Black man to death for nine minutes in broad daylight, and another White policeman shooting an unarmed Black child on sight on a playground, the Black community (and our supporters) "should" nonetheless respond in ways that do not harm or offend the sensibilities of our murderers.

In the West, the notions of "fire should be met with fire" or "stand your ground (and shoot to kill)" are only imaginable for Whites. When expressed by racial minorities, especially Black people, it is considered wholly inappropriate. For waging a long bloody war against the colonizing English, the United States' forefathers are practically sanctified. For doing *the exact same thing* against their French colonizers, though, the people of Haiti were punished financially and socially by the other late eighteenth/early nineteenth-century nations. White nationalists call themselves patriots and claim they are defending the nation, but non-White attempts to defend ourselves are considered anti-White and "reverse racism." The White supremacist-serving nature of the Self-Defense Fallacy is clear: White self-defense is glorified, but self-defense by racial minorities is unacceptable.

Minorities' self-defense is often met with White calls for minorities to "protest peacefully" and "be civil." But these are easily revealed to be a bad-faith ploy to delegitimize self-defense because these responses are not actually accepted when they *do* occur. My interviewee Janette quietly stepping away to calm down, only for her ex-in-laws to still get upset at her, is one example. On the national scale, people today love to point to Dr. Martin Luther King, Jr. and the (southern Christian part of) the Civil Rights Movement as what is acceptable protesting; but that is because people today are remembering the boycotts and sit-ins of the mid-twentieth century through rose-tinted glasses. Gallup polls on public opinion of Black US Americans' sit-ins and other non-violent actions show that the majority of those polled at the time *disapproved*. Moreover, the police of today violently responding with water hoses and attack dogs to peaceful protesters are evidence that objectively "peaceful" and "civil" protests are not actually an acceptable form of self-defense either.

In a Christmas 2014 statement, then Nashville, Tennessee, Police Chief Steve Anderson explained this state of affairs. He was responding to requests from some Nashvillians for him to order police to stop the peaceful Black Lives Matters demonstrations that had been occurring around the city. He wrote:

> It is readily apparent that their thought processes are driven, not by what has occurred during the demonstration, but more by the social positions taken by the demonstrators. Clearly, they are more angry at the thoughts expressed by the demonstrators than how the demonstrations are being conducted.[28]

Former Chief Anderson was talking about traffic disruptions in the city, but his analysis applies to other peaceful protests around the country. From basketball players wearing "I can't breathe" warm-up T-shirts, to Colin Kaepernick quietly kneeling during the national anthem, to actors calmly addressing an elected official who put his hand on a Bible and swore to represent We The People, the dominant mode of thinking is that minorities' self-defense against racism is inappropriate in *any* form. Someone once asked on Twitter when do White people think it is a good time for minorities to defend themselves against racism; and someone else replied "Neveruary 32nd."[29]

Invalidating Offense

If reacting to defend oneself *after* having experienced a "racially charged" event is unintelligible to common perception, then the *offensive* efforts of minorities and accomplices to *preemptively protect* minorities from racism in the first place is characterized as even worse. Preemptive protective action denies White supremacy the "right" to treat non-Whites how it wants. Moreover, as an offense move, it also lays naked the fact that mistreatment of non-Whites is so normative and routine that offense is necessary. Given the deep commitment to the epistemology of ignorance, that is to denying that racism occurs, offensive maneuvers are not seen as protection. They are seen as unprovoked attacks.

An experience I had with student evaluations offers an institutional example. At the conclusion of each semester, students complete evaluations of their instructors. Research has consistently shown that these evaluations are biased against women and racial minorities; and dozens of professional organizations have gone on record asserting that "student feedback should not be used alone as a measure of teaching quality."[30] In my early evaluations, one thing I noticed was that students wrote things about me and my class that were objectively, measurably, and documented to be untrue. For example, one semester a student wrote that everyone failed the first paper and that this was a sign that I was a poor instructor. Only the average score for that paper had actually been a B.

I had explained the math to the student early in the semester when he came to my office to discuss "everyone" failing. There were a few students in the class who only needed to pass; and so upon seeing that the first paper was worth just 15 percent of the final grade, they decided to skip it. Taking a zero on it meant the highest score they could earn in the class was an 85, which is a B and thus well above the D they needed to pass. Those zeros pulled down the numeric class average (mean) yes, but the most frequent grade (mode) for those who submitted the paper was a B. Despite this, the student (or perhaps another who did not come to my office to talk) wrote on their evaluation of me that the whole class failed the paper and that I was a poor instructor. In the United States, students' evaluations of instructors are used in decisions regarding tenure, promotion, awards, and pay raises. This means that the documented racism, sexism, homophobia, fatphobia, ableism, nativism, and other biases literally bake inequality into the evaluation process. And then we wonder why so few Black women are tenured professors.

Attempting to protect myself from the impact of this institutionalized inequality, I annotated my evaluations that year before submitting them as a part of my annual review dossier. By the comment that everyone failed the first paper, I wrote out the actual grade distribution that showed that the modal score was a B. By the comment that I "was not clear on what not to do on assignments," I made a note directing my reviewers to my assignment prompts, which showed that I did in fact provide detailed information on expectations. By the comment that I talked about inequality too much, I explained for reviewers outside my discipline that inequality is a major topic of focus in Sociology. In short, I provided counter-information to the misrepresentations that students write about women of color professors in evaluations.

I was told to cease and desist. My end of the year review commented that I took "keen interest" in "defending myself" against "negative" comments. The fact that my defenses were against literal, numeric *falsehoods*, not just "negative" comments, was not acknowledged. For correcting lies that could impact my career and income, I was called too sensitive and antagonistic. I was told that I should approach student comments more graciously and learn to adjust my teaching in response to student input. How to adjust to mathematically inaccurate accusations was not offered. Alternative ways than annotation to protect myself from inaccuracies and the documented bias in student evaluations so that it did not negatively influence my employee reviews were not offered either.

The message was loud and clear: Do not protect yourself. I was to "trust" that the predominantly White and predominantly male administrators who reviewed my file would understand that students don't always perceive women of color professors objectively. Meanwhile, on the other side of campus, the same administrators I was supposed to have trusted to understand that evaluations contain bias, believed the "negative" things students wrote about another Black woman professor (also the only Black woman in her academic unit). She had not annotated her evaluations to correct the record. Despite other evidence of her teaching effectiveness, such as students from her classes scoring higher than others on standardized disciplinary assessments, she was not reviewed favorably with regard to teaching because of her lower than average student evaluations.

Years later, after I gained tenure and began serving as a reviewer on others' tenure and promotion committees, I discovered why. Despite giving lip service to the known biases in them, committees nonetheless give a lot of weight to student evaluations, sometimes to the point of them being the only teaching effectiveness document a committee member seems to care about despite others (e.g., peer evaluations, unsolicited thank you notes from former students, etc.) being in the dossier as well. Thus, the case of my annotating my student evaluations reveals that the objection at the root of the Self-Defense Fallacy is the interruption of the smooth functioning of institutionalized racism/sexism.

If one Black woman's offensive move was unacceptable for an organization, it goes without saying that institutionalized mechanisms to protect minorities will be even less favorable. While not an issue at my workplace, other workplaces in Alabama have dress codes that ban natural Black hairstyles like braids and locks. These hairstyles have been worn for protection by people of African descent for millennia.[31] In their book *Sister Style: The Politics of Appearance for Black Women Political Elites* (2021), political scientists

Nadia Brown and Danielle Lemi explain, "For kinkier Afro-textured hair, braiding is more than a fashion statement. Braids protect natural hair from humidity and damage."[32] In addition, head wraps are often worn to protect hair. Bans on these types of styles and headgear, therefore, are quite literally forbidding racial minorities from protecting their body.

Representing an institutionalization of the Self-Defense Fallacy, Brown and Lemi explain that the 1981 US Court case "*Rogers v. American Airlines* upheld that the airline could ban its employees from wearing braids because this style can be easily changed and is not specifically tied to race, and as such, it did not fall under the protection of Title VII."[33] Nearly 40 years later, the *EEOC v. Catastrophe Management Solutions* case again upheld an employer's legal right to discriminate against Black protective hairstyles, this time locks. Schools, too, in both the US and UK, have dress code policies that ban protective hairstyles.[34] Nonetheless, recent legislation outlawing hair discrimination is finally starting to spread across the US. The fact that legal action is something needed simply to allow a racial minority group to protect their physical body at work and school, though, speaks volumes about the ambient hostility in society to a minority's ability to engage in self-protection.

Conclusion

Protecting oneself is a normal reaction to harm; but for any system based on inequality to endure, it must develop ways to stave off this response. The stigmatizing of defending or offensively protecting minorities against racism, the Self-Defense Fallacy, functions to naturalize a mythical resistance-free White domination. It helps to maintain the culture-serving perspective that we all should respect and protect White people's "freedom" to act as they wish and we should not consider their actions to be harmful to the rest of us. By extension, this epistemic orientation means that the rest of us do not deserve a life free from harm, which is of course the aim of White domination.

The fact is, though, that White people do not have any natural or God-given right to colonize, enslave, rape, war against, incarcerate, mock, catcall, lie about, or even just stare at anyone else. Straight White men wrote laws (see next chapter) to justify them committing violent as well as microaggressive actions against the populace; and patterns of thinking like the Self-Defense Fallacy developed and continue to have hold over the population's perception in order to maintain the delusion that that status quo is natural and normal.

But opposing slavery was *not* as bad as slavery. Opposing Native American removal was *not* as bad and sending adults and children on the Trail of Tears. Black Lives Matter protesters are not as violent as the Proud Boys. The bleat of "There's bad guys on both sides," when one side is defending themselves against attacks from the other, is just the Self-Defense Fallacy trying to maintain the epistemic arrogance, laziness, and narrow-mindedness needed to view White domination as legitimate. Social pressures and risk of social consequences exist to coerce those who do understand multiple perspectives to nonetheless outwardly conform to the racist status quo.

From the perception of the Self-Defense Fallacy, non-White protection is wrong, unfair to Whites, and inexcusable. This is so because it not only seeks to interrupt the functioning of the present order but also because it reveals that White supremacy's most cherished premises – that Whites are superior to non-Whites – is not true. Mills notes that the defenders of the status quo have a "readiness to employ massively disproportionate retaliatory violence" when non-Whites fight back against dominant forces of oppression.

The Self-Defense Fallacy is not saying that, in fighting back against oppressors, the former do not ever "hurt" the latter. In explaining how women and LGBTQ people who are harassed in public respond, Kolysh reveals that receivers of everyday gender/sexual violence often reach for classist or racist comments as their retort. Kolysh cautions against interpreting that as "just as bad," however, because the different groups "do not hold the same amount of power."[35] As such, while the harm arrow may "go both ways," the *first* as well as "the *larger* arrow is drawn from initiators to recipients."[36] Because of that, as Malcolm X said, oppressed people can resist "By any means necessary"; and only the Self-Defense Fallacy views that as rude, embarrassing, not "respectable," or "as wrong as" the violence against which we are defending ourselves.

Section III
Macro-Level Fallacies

The broadest approach to social analysis focuses on "the structures, composition, and processes of society" as a whole as well as "long-term processes of change."[1] This is a macro-level approach, and it is key for understanding not only the overall nature of the society but also for identifying the forces that shape, constrain, or facilitate micro- and meso-level social phenomena.[2]

Within the study of race and racism, macro-level analysis focuses on structural and systemic racism. Since the social structure is the durable patterns of social life within the various areas of a society, structural racism is the "interinstitutional interactions across time and space that reproduce racial inequality."[3] Sociologist Tanya Maria Golash-Boza offers the example of how enduring patterns of "racial inequality in housing leads to racial inequality in schooling, which in turn leads to racial inequality in the labor market."[4] Systemic racism is the "diverse assortment of racist practices" within the structure of society.[5] Sociologist Eduardo Bonilla-Silva argues that "we all participate in systemic racism (no one can be outside systemic racism much like no one can be outside capitalism or patriarchy)."[6] He continues that this "normative participation" in the macro level "racial structures of everyday life" is even more important to "the reproduction of racial order" than the individual actions of openly bigoted individuals.[7]

The four chapters in this section are all Macro-Level Fallacies, that is they focus on common perspectives of society that relate to multiple institutions, locations, and/or time periods. Chapter 9 examines the location-based perspective that removing overt inequality from one area of society (the law) automatically removes it from others. Chapter 10 focuses on the temporal perspective that racism is a phenomenon of the past, and chapter 11 focuses on the temporal perspective that that past has no impact on the present. Chapter 12 debunks the perspective that structural and systemic inequality will resolve itself if the victims of such systems, but not members of the dominant group, cease bringing attention to them.

9

The Legalistic Fallacy

As described in chapter 1, the Individualistic Fallacy is viewing racism as only individual thoughts and behaviors. This perspective not only limits what is perceived as racism but it also limits the solutions proposed to address it. Most common solutions to racism are individual-level suggestions, like donating and being "nice." A common structural solution I often hear, though, is for governments to make more anti-discrimination laws.

Historically, settler colonial countries' laws were designed to support the White colonial project. Laws about racial groups' legal status within the nation, for example, at best defined non-Whites as second-class citizens and at worst considered them sub-humans who had no legal or human rights anyone was bound to respect. In this context, eradicating such laws was a key goal of social activists. Outlawing slavery and legally defining Black people as a whole human, not three-fifths of one, for example, was a goal of abolitionist movements. However, we must be careful not to assume "that abolishing racist laws (racism in principle) automatically leads to the abolition of racism in everyday life (racism in practice)."[1]

In their textbook *Race in America* (2020 [2010]), sociologists Matthew Desmond and Mustafa Emirbayer call this thinking the Legalistic Fallacy. Expanding on Desmond and Emirbayer, I see the Legalistic Fallacy also manifest as thinking that overlooks two key facts about racism and the law. First, laws are written by those in power; thus, rarely will they outlaw the behavior of those in power. Second, laws on the books are purely symbolic if there are no accompanying mechanisms of enforcement. The Legalistic Fallacy therefore can be understood as a pattern of thinking that sees the law as a silver bullet solution to racism as well as obscures the limitations of the law that would contradict that perspective.

"Except for as Punishment for a Crime": When Lions Write the Rules of the Hunt

Even the briefest review of past laws in any settler colonial state makes it easy to spot laws that legalized harm against those positioned as non-White. Colonization stole land from Native Americans writ large. For example, the 1830s Indian Removal Acts were specific US policies that legalized the theft of land from a recognized sovereign nation (the Cherokee). During slavery and Jim Crow, it was not a crime for a White man to rape a Black girl or woman. In fact, the notion that White men forcing Black girls and women into sexual activity was something that should be outlawed was nonexistent as a legal concept into the middle of the twentieth century. The First Violence Against Women Act passed in the 1990s had loopholes that effectively made the rape of Native women by non-Native men when perpetrated on a reservation unpunishable by law.[2] Regarding murder, beginning with attempted genocide of Native Americans, for the majority of Western history killing non-White people was commonplace. Regarding its legality, settler colonial nations have a "long history of vigilantism and lynching at which the white officialdom basically connived, insomuch as hardly anybody was ever punished, though the perpetrators were well known and on occasion photographs were even available."[3]

Violent land theft, slavery, rape, and murder are now illegal.[4] But *illegal* does not mean it *does not happen*. Desmond and Emirbayer demonstrate how the perspective that simply making laws against racism will ensure it ceases "begins to crumble after a few moments of critical reflection."[5] Their textbook gives the example that "laws against theft do not mean that one's car never will be stolen."[6] Another ready example is underage drinking. The legal drinking age in the US is 21. Nonetheless, one does not need peer-reviewed empirical research to know that people under the age of 21 drink alcohol. Regarding the culture of US colleges, despite more than half of traditional college aged students (18–22) being underaged, drinking is practically synonymous with college life.[7]

Thinking that racism cannot exist if it is outlawed directly contradicts knowledge regarding the nature of other outlawed behaviors. The Legalistic Fallacy also manifests, though, as thinking that racism cannot exist unless it *is* officially proscribed in the law, a perspective that directly contradicts the Individualistic Fallacy (chapter 1), thereby revealing both fallacies to be illogical mental gymnastics used to deny racism. For example, at the 2021 conference for the Mid-South Sociological Association, sociologist Stephen Berrey gave a talk on his and his late collaborator James Loewen's research on Sundown Towns. Sundown Towns are cities where historically people of color could not live or be in after dark. These towns allowed racial minorities to shop or pass through during the day, but ordinances, signs, or word-of-mouth established them as "Whites Only After Dark." Loewen and Berrey's website contains a list of known Sundown Towns and encourages visitors to do research into their own towns' potential histories with the practice. During his conference presentation, Berrey told the audience that a frequent comment they get from website visitors is that their town was not a Sundown Town because they never had official city ordinances specifying that racial minorities could not be there at night. Even when these commenters acknowledged that their towns were not the most welcoming to non-Whites, they apparently still insisted that the lack of explicit laws meant their town did not engage in the racist sundown practice.[8]

A perspective like this that appeals to the law as the ultimate standard for the existence of racism is problematic for a number of reasons. First, it ignores all of the ways that social life operates without explicit laws demanding it. There are plenty of common social behaviors for which there are no official laws. There are no laws saying that diners must eat entrées before desserts, for instance, and yet the vast majority of restaurant patrons do. There are also no laws mandating that we send relatives birthday cards. Yet Hallmark, ShoeBox, Mahogany and many other card companies would not be in business if sending birthday cards were not a dominant social practice. Denying that racism, too, can exist as a social practice despite no official policy spelling it out runs counter to how other social practices are experienced and understood.

Second, appealing to the law to establish if racism exists or not ignores that it is the powerful in society, who are disproportionately though not exclusively from the dominant racial group, who write those laws. In settler colonial societies, it is a case of the lions writing the rules of the hunt. It is illogical to believe that lions would write any laws that would result in them losing the upper hand against the gazelles.

History tells us that even when laws are written that on the surface benefit minority groups, closer examination of them often reveals careful wording or flagrant loopholes meant to maintain White domination. The Violence Against Women Act mentioned above is one such example. The 13th Amendment to the US Constitution is another. The 13th Amendment outlawed slavery "except for as punishment for a crime." Labeling Black and Brown men as criminals meant that Whites could continue to profit off of their labor on chain gangs and in prison camps long after slave plantations were outlawed.

Anti-Law Laws: The Irony of "CRT" Bans

Explicating the ways in which the powerful have built racial inequality into the law is Critical Race Theory (CRT) in a nutshell.[9] Apropos to the Recognition Fallacy (chapter 7), however, acknowledging that laws create inequality is one of conservatives' most hated actions. It is ironic, then, that in recent years US Republican politicians have launched a crusade to rid schools of CRT. In short, they want to use the law to outlaw teaching about how the law is used.

To be clear, CRT is not being widely taught in US schools. In my state of Alabama, a review found that there was one class on the topic: an elective at a law school. What conservatives call "CRT" is really just honest history about formerly legalized racism. More to the point, though, is how disingenuous the moral panic over teaching this history is because just two generations ago, i.e., when many politicians were students, formal education made it a *point* to teach that White supremacy was the law of the land.

Award-winning Alabama journalist Kyle Whitmire has written about this. He explains that until the middle of the twentieth century, Alabama openly declared White supremacy in the law. For instance, the State's Democratic Party, which was the right-wing conservative party at the time, had "White Supremacy, For the Right" as their motto until the late 1960s.[10] By the time Whitmire was a student in the 1980s, though, explicit racism of this nature had been replaced by the codes and innuendos discussed in chapter 6; and history lessons were scrubbed of references to legalized racism. Whitmire writes of his history education as a child that "No one taught us that the foundational law of our state had been written with the explicit purpose of 'White Supremacy by Law.'"[11] With respect to the anti-"CRT" bills sweeping his nation, he said "there's something very Southern about awkwardly hiding from one generation something that had been plastered on seemingly every flat surface a few decades before."[12]

"Awkwardly hiding" the legalized racism that was proudly proclaimed just a few decades before is not unique to the southern US, though. In a piece for *The Guardian*, British writer Maya Goodfellow explained that "The national curriculum says young people are supposed to learn about 'how Britain has influenced, and been influenced by the wider world'" but that with respect to colonization "there can be near silence."[13] Black Studies professor Kehinde Andrews remembers the silence well, writing that "It is utterly mind-bending that I went through *every* level of education in Britain and never once heard the word empire uttered in a classroom."[14] This silence on colonization and the British Empire, when its existence is within *living memory*, is the same awkward hiding of previously proudly proclaimed legalized racism that Whitmire identified in the US.

The fact that politicians in the US have now turned to the law to legalize the awkward hiding of past legalized racism reveals, to quote sociologist Simone Kolysh, that "the law is not neutral . . . [it is] a violent arm of the state."[15] Just like the historical laws that anti-"CRT" bills want to cover up, the *anti-"CRT" laws themselves* are an example of the law being used to institutionalize White domination. Moreover, when it became apparent that this attempt at censorship might fail due to educational institutions' accrediting bodies requiring history and social science classes, status quo defenders turned their sights to changing the laws regarding accreditation.[16] In 2023, Florida Governor Ron DeSantis vowed that accreditation would be changed from "You only get accreditation if you do DEI" to "We will not accredit you if you do DEI."[17] DEI stands for diversity, equity, and inclusion; and apropos to the White supremacist-serving epistemology of ignorance that is at the root of accreditation attacks, the head of one of the US accreditation agencies clarified that "Nobody has lost accreditation for failing to meet a standard under DEI . . . It's another one of these myths – just a trigger to make someone the evil party."[18]

In the context of a nation's leaders making laws to prevent education about the role of laws in racism, the law alone cannot logically be seen as cure for racism. As Black feminist Audre Lorde reminds us: The master's tools will never dismantle the master's house. Asserting that they can is at best naïve; and at worst demonstrates commitment to the White supremacist-serving epistemology of ignorance that upholds racial inequality.

The "Sad Duty" of Law Enforcement

The fact that anti-"CRT" and anti-DEI laws may potentially be enforced speaks volumes about the role of the law vis-à-vis racism. In 2021, in my home state of Tennessee, a group of mainly White parents referenced the anti-"CRT" bans in their complaint about desegregation being taught in history lessons in public schools.[19] The next year, *The Washington Post* reported that confusion and fear over the new laws led to teachers in other states to preemptively remove content from their lesson plans and even led one school administrator to rename a student group that was originally called "Black and Proud" all just in case.[20]

The fear that anti-"CRT" and anti-DEI laws will be enforced stands in stark contrast to the demonstrated unwillingness of many authorities to enforce equality when legally mandated to do so. The Legalistic Fallacy, however, manifests as a perspective that ignores the differential enforcement of racist and anti-racist laws, principally the historical lack of desire to enforce the latter. A historic moment from my current state of Alabama offers a case study.

Since the 1954 *Brown v. Board of Education* decision had ruled against segregation in education, Alabama Governor George Wallace was committing an illegal action in 1963 when he stood in a building doorway at the University of Alabama to prevent two Black students from going inside to register for classes. In a brilliant display of why appeals to the law with regard to racism are faulty, Wallace gave a statement that inverted the direction of the law. He alleged that the Federal Government was the one committing "unlawful" action by attempting to force his state to comply with *Brown*. He positioned his action, as he was Governor, as legal and as doing his duty to protect Alabama.

When then President John F. Kennedy federalized the national guard and ordered them to remove Wallace from the building, the head of the guard greeted him and announced that it was his "sad duty" to remove him. His *sad* duty. Despite the laws changing and minorities (women, people of color, LGBTQIA people, and more) gaining equal rights on paper, in the 1960s there were a great many people in law enforcement, mainly but not exclusively White, who found enforcing minorities' civil and human rights a "sad duty." Wallace and the head of the guard were at the level of the state, but even national-level law enforcement was not on board with equal protection. At that time, civil rights workers were being arrested, shot, and murdered by White supremacists; and yet the Federal Bureau of Investigation (FBI) repeatedly claimed that "protecting civil rights workers from violence was not its job."[21]

Presently, the court system continues this practice of finding it a "sad duty" to enforce compliance with anti-racist laws. Despite evidence from audit studies showing the pervasiveness of racial discrimination in employment,[22] race-based job-discrimination claimants have a significantly lower win rate compared to other types of civil cases.[23] Even prior to former US president Donald Trump appointing numerous conservative and right-wing judges, legal scholars in the US had already identified "the growing hostility with which courts approach allegations of discrimination" and how they "seemingly believe that the passage of civil rights laws alone has wrought a post racial society in which instances of discrimination are rare."[24]

Those who view making more anti-discrimination laws as a structural solution to racism cannot be faulted for not knowing these somber facts about discrimination prosecution. Their not knowing is a dual product of the general epistemology of ignorance and of clickbait media. Presently, the mainstream news media focuses on extremes, from weather to inequality, to the neglect of the more normative aspects of life. Social media, for its part, has been critiqued for giving inaccurately lavish and positive views of others' social life. Distorted images and other negative aspects of social media prompted the US Surgeon General Dr. Vivek Murthy to declare that too much social media use is a danger to adolescents' mental health.[25] Within this context, people are sure to hear about successful high-profile lawsuits brought by minorities alleging disparate and/or illegal treatment, such as Meghan Markle winning in court against the newspapers who published her private letters. They are less likely, though, to hear about the outcome of the vast majority of minorities' lawsuits: They rarely ever even reach a jury.[26] Thus, the present state of multiple forms of media contribute to the Legalistic Fallacy via cultivating an epistemology of ignorance with regard to the efficacy of anti-racist laws.

Rather than courts, though, it is police officers who are the branch of the criminal justice system with whom most people interact; and many in this group, too, feel it a sad duty to uphold the legal rights of minorities. Beyond the frequent headlines of US police killing unarmed people, disproportionately racial minorities, research shows that a culture of racism, specifically anti-Blackness, permeates many police departments. In his book *The Souls of White Jokes: How Racist Humor Fuels White Supremacy* (2022), sociologist Raúl Pérez devotes a chapter to "Blue humor: The racist insults and injuries of the police." He explains that police use humor in the workplace

> for the same reason that people in other organizations and settings use humor . . . as a form of fun and amusement against occupational boredom, to strengthen collegial bonds and enhance social and group cohesion, to release work-related stress, and to increase positive group affect and collective pleasure.[27]

With regard to racist and sexist humor, this type of humor is rooted in the racist and sexist culture of many police departments and moves outside of it via police actions toward minorities. Pérez offers the example of nurses' reports that White police officers joked and laughed about beating the unarmed Black man they had brought to the hospital. He writes that police rarely face any sanction for such joking about violence against minorities, which reveals that both individual prejudice and systemic racism are accepted parts of the institution.

Beyond just harboring biased sentiments, historically members of law enforcement have had a heavy hand in law breaking. Writing during the height of Jim Crow lynching in the US, investigative journalist Ida B. Wells dared to point out that "those who commit the murders write the reports."[28] Enforcement of anti-discrimination laws, therefore, cannot be assumed when those in charge of enforcing the laws are members of the population who are committing the harms in question. I remember watching live coverage of the US Capitol being attacked on January 6, 2021, and seeing people tweet "Where are the police?" Replies referring to the fact that one never saw Disney character Miley Stewart and Hannah Montana in the same place were much needed comic relief on that otherwise deadly serious day.

For those unfamiliar with the Disney TV show *Hannah Montana*, country music singer Miley Cyrus plays a teenage girl named Miley Stewart whose big secret is that she is a pop superstar named Hannah Montana. The show and subsequent movie center on Miley's attempts to "have the best of both worlds," meaning to be a normal girl who goes to school and the mall with her friends while also topping the pop charts and rocking out to sold-out concerts. Akin to Clark Kent changing clothes and becoming Superman, brunette Miley puts on a blonde wig and makeup to become Hannah. The references on January 6 to never seeing them together, therefore, was highlighting the suspicion that many of the rioters, i.e., the "patriots" who wanted to overturn the 2020 election, were off-duty police officers and other city, state, and national law enforcement. What the Hannah/Miley tweets were pointing out, then, is that the people who break the law and the people who are supposed to prosecute people for breaking the law are from the same set of people. This is not to say they are always the exact same individuals like Hannah/Miley, but research does suggest that White supremacists and White nationalists make up a not insignificant portion of law enforcement.

In sum, philosopher Charles Wade Mills explains that even when laws are in place to protect minorities, they are often not enforced because "the Racial Contract manifests itself in white resistance to anything more than the formal extension of the terms of the abstract social contract (and often to that also)."[29] Mills explains "the police, the penal system, the army – need to be seen as part of the enforcers *of* the Racial Contract."[30] He continued that indeed these "coercive arms of the state . . .[are] working both to keep the peace and prevent crime among white citizens, and to maintain the racial order and detect and destroy challenges to it."[31] In other words, to quote Kolysh, then and now "the police protect moneyed white people while harming everyone else."[32]

Conclusion

From analysis of students' papers, sociologist Jennifer Mueller iden-tified an "epistemological maneuver" that she called "mystified solutions."[33] This occurred when 15 percent of her sample learned and "embraced the veracity of racism ... but followed with state-ments indicating broad sometimes personal confusion and doubt about what could be done to alter such patterns."[34] I recognized the same confusion in my students, which is why I started asking them to brainstorm structural solutions. While many still reach for individual solutions like donating, a few are able to go beyond that to brainstorm structural-level changes. The most common one, though, is to add more anti-discrimination laws. While a legal appeal is at least demonstrating that one is thinking structurally, given the way laws have been and still are used by the powerful in society, and the fact that without enforcement they are purely symbolic, this solution nonetheless represents continued entangle-ment in the epistemology of ignorance.

Philosophers talk of the hypothetical "state of nature" that humans were in prior to coming together to form societies; and regarding ethics, they have noted that "it is wrong to steal, rape, kill in the state of nature even if there are no human laws written down saying it is wrong."[35] Indeed, from this philosophical view, "[r]eliance on rules would be rather the mark of someone who had not yet achieved full virtue, being still in the imitative phase."[36] And yet, reliance on rules when perceiving what is or is not racist is a common pattern of thinking. Given recent attempts to use the law to ensure that the next generation does not learn how the law was and still is implicated in racial inequality, the perception that simply making new laws can end racism is rooted in the epistemol-ogy of ignorance and functions to maintain the status quo of White domination.

10

The Fixed Fallacy

The anti-"CRT" and anti-DEI legislation mentioned in the last chapter are ironic in that they are attempts to make new laws to stop dissemination of information about past laws and are attempts to resist complying with present anti-discrimination laws. These bills are ironic for a second reason as well: In addition to there being a common perception that the law is neutral or good, the reverse perspective – that past laws represent the epitome of racism – also exists. The Fixed Fallacy is the perspective that acknowledges racism – even the systematic and legalized oppression that the Individualistic Fallacy denies and the Legalistic Fallacy has a love–hate relationship with – but *only* with regard to the *past*. Sociologists Matthew Desmond and Mustafa Emirbayer define this fallacy in their textbook *Race in America* (2020 [2010]) as perspectives that "assume that racism is fixed, that it is immutable, constant across time and space."[1]

The Fixed Fallacy manifests in a number of ways. First, it considers past forms of racism to be the only type of racism. Second, though, the specific past form of racism is US-centric. In other words, racism becomes conflated with what it looked like and how it manifested in the United States, particularly in the South prior to the 1960s. Other countries' manifestations of racism get interpreted through a US-centric lens and at best only are understood through that specific framework and at worst are considered not racist or "not that bad" for occurring differently. All manifestations of fixed thinking, though, function as an attempt to define contemporary phenomena as not racist and thus as not in need of changing.

It Is Not Over: On the Evolution of Racism

If you had to guess how I physically wrote this book, you would probably not say that I did so on parchment with an inked quill. My use of a typewriter to type these chapters would also likely not be a frequent first guess. Venturing that I typed on a laptop would be the logical (and correct) answer given the time period. However, just because authors today do not write the same way as authors did centuries ago does not mean that literature and scholarship no longer exist. It would be illogical to perceive typing on a laptop as not "writing" just because the process does not involve the same tools or hand movements as writing did in the past. This can also be said of other social phenomena, such as transportation (cars are transportation despite not being horses) and dance (hip-hop is dance despite not being ballet).

Like other social phenomena, racism evolves with the times. Race scholar Alana Lentin explains how a "frozen" view of racism ignores this fact and supports White supremacy: "by freezing so-called 'real racism' in historical time, we allow discrimination and abuse to continue polyvalently."[2] By polyvalently, she means that the many forms of discrimination and abuse (i.e., explicit and tacit, micro and macro, etc.) are allowed to exist and they are afforded immunity from de-legitimation as "racist" due to the common perspective that "real racism" is a historical phenomenon. In other words, fixed or frozen perspectives on racism see racism against Blacks as only enslavement, lynching, and segregation laws. Racism against Native Americans is only smallpox blankets, the Trail of Tears, and government-sponsored massacres. Racism against Asians is only vigilante violence, immigration restrictions, and internment. Such perspectives allow contemporary racism against Western racial minorities to continue unencumbered by stigmatization as racist and thus not be perceived as in need of changing.

I once saw an image that demonstrates the adaptive nature of anti-Black racism specifically. It is a picture of a Black man that shows slave shackles on the left side of his neck, a lynching rope around his neck in the middle, and bloody bullet holes on the right side of his body. The picture powerfully conveys the different ways that White power has abused Black people over the last three centuries and lays bare the illogic of a fixed perspective.

Because the Fixed Fallacy acknowledges that the past was racist, connecting the contemporary situation of US Black Americans to past situations is frequently met with dismissiveness. The present cannot be said to be similar to the past, lest the present have to be acknowledged as containing racism, too. Responses to alleging that there is racism in sports illustrates this. *New York Times'* columnist William C. Rhoden's book *Forty Million Dollar Slaves: The Rise, Fall, and Redemption of the Black Athlete* (2006) and Health and Human Performance professor Billy Hawkins' book *The New Plantation: Black Athletes, College Sports, and Predominantly White NCAA Institutions* (2010) both point out that, like slavery, sports is an institution in which Black men do physical labor for the financial benefit of White men. While players sometimes get a college degree and a few professional athletes get rich, the predominantly White coaches and owners are the ones making the most profit, just like the slave masters of yore. There are also similarities in language – "owners" in both cases – and in acquisition processes – slave auctions and the Draft.

My students have not been nearly as interested in these parallels as I'd naïvely assumed folks in states with big football cultures would be. Some could not even entertain the similarities at all and instead instantly reached for the Fixed Fallacy to assert that the past was racist not the present. Rebuttals like "But athletes are paid, slaves were not!" do not demonstrate critical thinking skills, for that observation is vapid and self-evident. Such knee jerk rebuttals show the quickness with which the racism of the past is reached for, not to understand or contextualize the present, but as a *tool* to use to *avoid thinking* about it.

With regard to racism against Native Americans, Sioux scholar-activist Vine Deloria Jr. observed that the dominant White colonial perspective views Native Americans with a fixed mindset, what he calls primitive purity. Within this perspective, past mistreatment of Native Americans can be acknowledged as racist. The children's book *Who was . . . Andrew Jackson*, for example, acknowledges that Indian Removal was an "illegal" and "shameful act" of "white Americans" just wanting to take Indigenous land. It is more contentious, though, when contemporary theft of Native peoples' land is called out as racist.

Theoretical physicist Chanda Prescod-Weinstein has written of how Native Hawaiians to this day are still protesting White people taking their land. In her book *The Disordered Cosmos: A Journey into Dark Matter, Spacetime, & Dreams Deferred* (2021), she discusses a particular mountain that a White-owned company wanted to use as a location for a scientific observatory and the Indigenous protests that met the proposal. Building a science lab is of course different than the past ways that White settlers took over Indigenous land; but both actions stem from the same colonial ideas of the idle Indians who are not "adding value" to the land or "using it properly."[3] Recall Prescod-Weinstein's example, in chapter 7, of an exchange in which she "witnessed a white man tell an Indigenous Canadian scientist that it was rude to call anti-Native Hawaiian comments what they were – racist and colonialist – during a conversation about occupied Indigenous land."[4] She continues noting that the fact that "No such pushback was offered to the colonialist commentators" speaks volumes.[5] Both contemporary and historical actions of land occupation and theft are examples of White domination, i.e., racism. The epistemology of ignorance, however, justifies contemporary occurrences like bulldozing over Indigenous people's lands via the lie that modern behavior is not racist.

On a global scale, colonization proper may be over, but neocolonialism has taken its place. In his book *The New Age of Empire: How Racism and Colonialism Still Rule the World* (2021), Black Studies professor Kehinde Andrews explains why contemporary global processes are racist, too:

> Western imperialism did not end after the Second World War, it merely evolved ... The UN [United Nations], IMF [International Monetary Fund], and World Bank pose as friends to the underdeveloped world, all whilst creating a framework that continues to allow the West to leach from the Rest.[6]

Andrews also cautions against combining the Token Fallacy and Fixed Fallacy to assume that contemporary Western imperialism is not racist simply because a few of its powerful agents are now people of color. Of China's rising global influence in particular he writes that:

> The fact that there are non-White faces at the head of the latest version of empire does not mean that the system has changed. It is perfectly possible to maintain racism whilst diversifying those in charge of dispensing it ... a collection of crazy rich Asians does not alter reality for the majority of people on the continent ... There have always been some who were better off

than others, even under the brutally violent version of Western imperialism.[7]

In short, Andrews' *The New Age of Empire* highlights the heart of the Fixed Fallacy. While in the past it was independent Euro-American nation-states – e.g., Great Britain, France, Spain, the United States – who exploited non-Europeans at home and abroad, today it is international organizations including a few based in Asian nations who perpetuate global racism. A perspective that refuses to consider the ways in which contemporary world powers (re)produce global racial inequality, simply because it does not look like it did one hundred or more years ago, is a perspective caught up in the epistemology of ignorance. It is a view that accepts a distortion of contemporary social processes and it functions to maintain the legitimacy of them.

The increasing global power of China, India, and a few other Asian countries, coupled with the removal of barriers for Asians to immigrate to the West, offers the alluring mirage that anti-Asian racism in the West is a thing of the past. In the US, the epistemology of ignorance was hard at work in the late twentieth and early twenty-first centuries inducing US Americans of all races to defocus on empirical examples of anti-Asian racism, such as the brutal murder of Vincent Chin, and instead homogenize Asians as "model minorities" who face no racism in the contemporary era. The outbreak of Covid-19 shattered this illusion in the US as the Trump Administration openly blamed China for the virus and created new racist slurs like "Kung Flu" and "China Virus." Reports poured in to news stations of anti-Asian harassment and violence, including young and old Asian Americans being yelled at, shot while at work, or pushed to their deaths in front of a train. Perhaps because the Covid surge of anti-Asian hate crimes were so reminiscent of historical violence against Asian-American communities, these crimes were covered in the mainstream media as stemming from racism. This recognition further reveals the folly of the Fixed Fallacy: How can racism be only historical abuses when the exact same *types* of abuses are often what is literally occurring today?

US-centered Thinking about Racism

Of his theory of the Racial Contract, philosopher Charles Wade Mills writes that not only does it change within a given nation due to being "continually rewritten to create different forms of the racial polity," but that it exists and changes on an international scale as well.[8] The Fixed Fallacy denies this and instead perceives racism only as specific narrow ideal types. Ideal types are sociologist Max Weber's term for the archetypes found in typologies against which real examples of phenomenon are compared. The conditions in the US, especially in the South prior to the 1960s, represent a key ideal type of racism.[9] However, first, racism outside of the US often manifests the same as in the US; and, second, when racism in non-US locations is in fact different, it is still harmful to a group of people based on assumed racial group membership, i.e., so it still meets a typical lay definition of racism.

From my research with mixed-race people in the United States and United Kingdom, I have heard first-hand accounts that demonstrate that US-centrism dominates fixed thinking about racism. In the US and UK, the perspective that racism in the latter is not as bad as in the former is common. The US is racist, people say; and while the UK has class problems, there are no race problems like in the US. One point of supposed difference between the two nations that supposedly demonstrates how the US is racist but the UK is not is the fact that the US had a legalized one-drop rule while the UK never did. The "one-drop rule" in the US were laws stating that a person was classified as Black if they had so much as "one drop" of Black blood, i.e., any known ancestors who were Black. Apropos to the Legalistic Fallacy of the last chapter, the fact that the British Parliament never wrote this down the way the US government did does not mean that the notion of Black hypodescent, and the anti-Black racism that accompanies it, do not exist in the UK.

The stories of being called the N word versus mixed-race slurs that my Black mixed-race interviewees in both nations told offers evidence that the one-drop rule exists in both the US and UK. Judy (US, Black/White, 30 in 2012) recalls how as a child living in the Southern state of Tennessee "the N word was hurled around endlessly." Anthony (US, Black/White, 34 in 2018), also from the US south, shared that in high school his White friends "endearingly" called him "the nigger Nazi queer" as homage to all three of his identities: Black mixed-race, German-American, and gay. Contrary to ideal type fixed perspectives, anti-Black slurs do not only occur in the US South. Joy (US, Black/White, 27 in 2012) grew up in the Western states of Wyoming, South Dakota, and Colorado and she was called the N word, too. Regarding the North, Sydney (US, Black/White, 39 in 2012) recalls "another little boy said the N word to me" in upstate New York.

My Black mixed-race interviewees in the UK had similar experiences. Sara (UK, Black/White, 38 in 2011) grew up in a country area on the southwest coast of England where she was "called nigger all the time" and told to "go back to Africa." Dave (UK, Black/White, 30 in 2011) was born and raised in the north in Yorkshire and was called "nigger, coon, wogg, golliwog, Brillo Pad head, microphone head." Brillo pad head and microphone head are insults to afro-textured hair, a specific type of anti-Black microaggression that J.P. (UK, Black/White, 30 in 2021) and many Black mixed-race interviewees in the US all also experienced.

Dave explained that these are all slurs against Black people, not mixed-race people. He spoke for the majority of Black mixed-race interviewees saying that he has "never knowingly been called a zebra or a half breed" or any other specific mixed-race slur. Despite this, Dave still perceived the US, not UK, to be the place where there is a one-drop rule. He said of the US that he imagined it as a place where Black mixed-race people are "kinda essentially being seen as black, just light skin." Dean (UK, Black/White, 27 in 2012) also saw the US as the place where there was a one-drop rule. He explained explicitly saying: "like America because of like the history and that and the one drop thing, like black is black you know? Like Mariah Carey is black so [laugh]. We don't have that here you know."

Further evidence that the UK actually *does* have a one-drop rule can be seen in how mixed-race people are maligned in the media in both nations. At barely two days old, Archie Mountbatten, the Black/White mixed-race son of Meghan Markle and Prince Harry, was portrayed in the media as a monkey. Analyzing monkey caricatures in his book *The Souls of White Jokes: How Racist Humor Fuels White Supremacy* (2022), sociologist Raúl Pérez explains that it has a long history, is dehumanizing, and functions to reify the colonial idea that Black people are innately inferior to White people. In a chapter titled "President Chimp," Pérez analyses the portrayals of former US President Barack Obama as a monkey. Like Archie,

Obama is Black/White mixed. The fact that both nations reach for anti-black *not* anti-mixed-race slurs and images in their microaggressions against Black mixed-race people suggests that the one-drop rule, despite not being written in law, is nonetheless written in the psyche of the population of the UK not just the US.

In sum, the daily racism experienced by Black mixed-race people in the US and UK is not identical but is also much too similar to maintain that one nation has a racist notion of hypodescent (one-drop rule) and the other does not. The scale is certainly different given the difference in the two nations' populations; but the form is similar. The Fixed Fallacy, however, overlooks this in a rush to deny contemporary racism in the UK. This denial allows people in the UK, even those like Dean at risk of being targeted, to maintain the White innocence of the nation by perceiving real racism as something that "we don't have here." So strong is this perspective that "despite decades of campaigning around police violence" in Britain it was "George Floyd's murder thousands of miles away [that] finally brought mainstream awareness of the problem [in the UK.]"[10] The US-centric manifestation of the Fixed Fallacy, then, is revealed to be an ends-based tool to facilitate the uninterrupted functioning of localized White domination.

There are of course differences in how racial oppression manifests outside the US. In previous work, for instance, I have discussed the difference in phrasing of questions to mixed-race people, most often as "what are you?" in the US versus "where are you from?" in the UK.[11] Nonetheless, anti-Black racism against mixed-race people stemming from the one-drop rule is not uniquely US American. Perceiving that the mistreatment of minorities does not occur in a given place or is not "as bad as" in the US is a perspective rooted in the epistemology of ignorance that functions to legitimize the specific form of inequality that exists locally.

Conclusion

The Fixed Fallacy justifies and (re)produces contemporary White domination by preventing recognition of contemporary forms of racism as racism. Lentin reminds us that "by seeing racism only in these examples from the past about whose horror there is universal consensus, we have been left unable to speak about race."[12]

The Fixed Fallacy encourages us to not perceive or label contemporary forms of racism as "racism." It also encourages us to consider racism to be a feature of certain locations, not just time periods. The fact that such a perspective can hold even among those whose personal experiences reveal it to be a myth is a testament to the strength of this fallacy.

The Fixed Fallacy principally betrays itself as supporting White supremacy because it violates the very first fallacy covered in this book, Individualism. If historic actions such as slavery, colonialism, Jim Crow laws, and Nazism – that is, racist *systems* – are what was "really" racist, then in one's haste to delegitimize claims of contemporary racism one betrays the understanding that systemic racism *can* in fact exist. Attempts to ban teaching about past systemic racism further underscores that pointing to the past to delegitimize the present is an ends-based maneuver to maintain an epistemology of ignorance about both time periods.

Recall, too, from chapter 7 that critics of Kehinde Andrews' anti-royalist comments called him "the worst type of racist." How, logically, can Andrews be racist if, as the Fixed Fallacy asserts, "real" racism is the historical actions of the US not modern actions like an academic's comments on *Good Morning Britain*. The short of it is that he cannot. The co-existence of such contradictory stances reveals the lengths the dominant perspective will go to to try to maintain the legitimacy of White supremacy.

11

The Ahistorical Fallacy

In *Black Reconstruction* (1964 [1935]), sociologist W. E. B. DuBois expressed astonishment "in the idea that evil must be forgotten, distorted, skimmed over." He lamented that "history loses its value as an incentive and example" when it only "paints perfect men and noble nations, but it does not tell the truth."[1] With respect to racism, US Americans are formally taught that the past was both not racist (Legalistic Fallacy of chapter 9) and that it represents the only manifestation of racism (Fixed Fallacy of chapter 10). The result of this contradictory education is evident in the fact that most US Americans, especially White people, don't perceive contemporary social patterns to be rooted in historical processes.

The authors of *Race in America* (2020 [2010]), sociologists Matthew Desmond and Mustafa Emirbayer, used the term Ahistorical Fallacy to describe the common perception that history has not constructed the present. They define it as thinking that "most U.S. history – namely, the extended period of time during which this country did not extend basic rights to people of color (let alone classify then as fully human) – is inconsequential today."[2] Desmond and Emirbayer grant that "a soft version of the ahistorical fallacy might admit that events in the 'recent past' (such as the time since the Civil Rights Movement or the attacks on September 11, 2001) matter, but things in the 'distant past' (such as slavery or the colonization of Mexico) have little consequence."[3]

This fallacy manifests with regard to thinking about contemporary domestic and global racial inequality. In both cases, it represents a cultivated ignorance, that is a critical thinking deficit given to us by state-sanctioned education systems. Recent "anti-woke" initiatives in the US and the limited coverage of colonialism in UK curriculums are attempts to maintain this deficit and with it the illusion of natural White superiority. One result of this cultivated ahistorical perspective is that contemporary circumstances are easily seen as a result of recent and equal actions by "both sides." The stranglehold that "bothsidesism" has on common perception is both a concrete result of the ahistorical perspective as well as an example of how this fallacy functions to legitimate the status quo.

Domestic and International Non-History

An artist I follow on Instagram has a picture of two anthropomorphized cell phones running toward a rotary phone. The speech bubbles indicate that the cell phones are excitedly running to "Grandma!" The image cutely conveys how the technologies we have today have their origins in the technologies of the past. Likewise, regarding social conditions today, sociologists write that "If there is a 'settled science' about legacies of racial violence, it is that our violent national history remains relevant to contemporary social relations and outcomes."[4] The Ahistorical Fallacy denies this, though, by making perceiving the role of history on the present difficult.

In Wisconsin, struggle with the Ahistorical Fallacy often manifested as comments like, "MY family didn't own slaves, so I have not benefited from racism." Wisconsin did not have chattel slavery, and the White population are mainly descendants of twentieth-century immigrants. However, as economist Sandy Darity has explained, one's family having immigrated to the US in the twentieth century "isn't absolution" from being a White beneficiary of historical White supremacy. Regarding the assertion that one's family came over after slavery had ended, Darity points out, first, that descendants of immigrants could also have ancestors who participated in slavery, for instance due to immigrants' marriage to US-born White people or due to their pre-immigration engagement with companies in their home countries that were involved in and thriving from the slave trade. Second, Native American removal occurred not just in the South but in places like Wisconsin, too; and the post-Reconstruction creation of the Jim Crow social structure was practically nationwide. Thus, concludes Darity, if one's great-great-grandparents "got a Homestead Act land patent, took Black property after a massacre, and/or bought a home under the GI Bill you've benefited materially from American racism."[5]

Looking at US history, lots more can be added: Who bought the houses and businesses that Japanese Americans were forced to liquidate in order to go to internment camps? Whose great-great-grandparents immigrated to the US between 1924 and 1965, i.e., during a time when – by law – one had to be classified as White to enter? Who can watch old Hollywood movies and see people who look and talk like them represented in a wide variety of roles, versus just see yourself reflected at best as criminals and at worst not at all? Who has centuries-old blood diamonds, pearls, gold, or silver family heirlooms to treasure, or to pawn/sell when money is needed? Who can boast that their family business was begun in the 1800s, i.e., at a time when most business loans were For Whites Only? Whose family business, begun decades ago, is also still flourishing because it was not burned or bombed since its success didn't threaten the myth of White superiority? In short, from material possession to entertainment to employment, many people today, mainly but not exclusively White, have benefited materially from historical racism whether or not their blood relatives were active in perpetuating it.

But also, for the sake of argument, let's entertain the idea that one's blood relatives need to have been active participants in, not just the passive recipients of the spoils of, key historical racist events to acknowledge their influence on conditions today. Even in this case, a non-zero number of people who bleat that their family didn't have anything to do with racism of the past would still be mistaken because the family history people are told is not always true, as a student of mine learned by accident while researching for a class paper.

The class was called Sociology of Diversity, and in order to help students vividly see how experiences of diversity have changed across time, one assignment was to talk with someone over 60 years old about the state of race, ethnicity, class, gender, and sexuality in their youth and what they remember about the key historical events of the twentieth century. One student, a White man in his 20s, talked with his great uncle (then in his 70s, so born in the 1940s). The great uncle took the talk as an opportunity to reveal what his grandfather (born about the late 1890s) had told him on his deathbed: Their family were not actually twentieth-century European immigrants. The family were really from the US South and had been slaveholders. After losing everything in the Civil War, the family moved north to Wisconsin where they began a new life claiming they were members of the hardworking industrious immigrants who were arriving in huge numbers from the 1880s to the 1920s. The family's origin as US-born enslavers who fought – and lost – to carry on brutal racist domination was concealed from subsequent generations. It became a family secret only to be revealed to selected others near the end of one's life.

The fact that many US southerners left the region after the war, not only to go north or west in the US but some internationally to Brazil to continue their peculiar institution for another generation, is one of the many present-relevant facts about slavery that are not widely taught. The largest recent challenge to the ahistorical perspective regarding slavery is award-winning journalist Nikole Hannah-Jones's *1619 Project*. It is on how slavery contributed to the foundational development of the US and how current conditions are a result of it. Apropos to the Recognition Fallacy (chapter 7), there has been White backlash to it. Former US President Donald Trump even countered it by attempting to re-center Whiteness in the nation's origins by creating a 1776 Commission. This counter-move reveals that the Ahistorical Fallacy is not a perspective that ignores the role of *all* history on the present. It is one that seeks to ignore the role of past *racism* on the present.

This ignoring is a global affair. Of the UK, Black Studies professor Kehinde Andrews explains:

> We urgently need to destroy the myth that the West was founded on the three great revolutions of science, industry, and politics. Instead we need to trace how genocide, slavery and colonialism are the key foundation stones upon which the West was built. The legacies of each of these remain present today, shaping both wealth and inequality in the hierarchy of White supremacy.[6]

Public rhetoric that "they" (Arabs, Muslims, and people in Middle Eastern/Western Asian nations) hate "our" (US/Western Europe) "freedom" offers a contemporary exemplar of the distorted perceptions of global affairs that flow from the Ahistorical Fallacy. I am just barely old enough to vaguely remember Iran-Contra in the 1980s. As child, I heard words like "Iran," "Iraq," "weapons," and "embargo" as my parents listened to the news and I asked them what it meant.[7] Likewise, the first US war I am old enough to remember is the Gulf War in the 1990s, the name Operation Desert Storm standing out particularly in my memory. A bit older by then, I understood that Iraq had invaded Kuwait and so the US and other nations were fighting to help Kuwait. Fast-forward to the early 2000s, to September 11, 2001, and to me this seemed like a continuation of the decades-long bloody power struggle between nations on opposite sides of the world to control natural resources. In spring 2003 when the US prepared to invade Iraq, hearing people say that "they" hated "our" freedoms and that "they" had "attacked us for no reason" made no sense to me.

The Ahistorical Fallacy, however, makes it make sense. Neither Iran-Contra nor the Gulf War were taught in any history class I ever took. I learned about the US/UK orchestrated coup in Iran in the 1950s and the overthrow of the US-aligned Shah in the 1970s much later in life, in college and graduate school. As documented by sociological research, my middle and high school history was US-centric and devoid of information on any international misdeeds committed by my nation.[8]

Since teaching that the US was involved in deposing a democratically elected leader and installing a puppet king would make the nation look bad, such information is almost never included in US history textbooks.[9] The outcome of this sanitized education is that when that puppet king is overthrown by his people and the region around them becomes "destabilized," US formal education has – by design – prevented the majority of people from being able to see how the present is a result of past racist actions. Dominant understanding of why "they" are "always fighting" are thus based on "massive historical amnesia and factual misrepresentation."[10] In other words, the culpability of White supremacy in general, and US imperialism in this example in particular, is obscured in service to maintaining the false perception that Whites/the West are civilized and "they" are violent, warring, and jealous of "our" (totally legitimately secured and equally shared) "freedoms."

"Life in Timbuktu Today": The Culture-Serving Nature of Ahistorical Education

A main reason that the Ahistorical Fallacy so freely operates in society is that history education not only *skips content* or *whitewashes it* but also does not teach the *analytic utility* of history. Sociologist James Loewen explains that people cannot be blamed from coming away from their K-12 history education thinking that "Nothing ever causes anything." History education at the primary and secondary level focuses on herofication of a few people, disproportionately White and male. In this pursuit, those men's racist, sexist, imperialist, and genocidal actions are either completely omitted, are perversely presented as noble, or are presented as done only under duress.

A primary school history book series offers an illustration. Penguin books has a *Who Was . . .* series of biographies for children. I was browsing them one day while looking for readings to supplement my daughter's social studies lessons. The book for Confederate General Robert E. Lee described him as "a man of honor." His waging war on the United States was portrayed as him having "no other choice" but to make the "hard" decision to "defend his homeland," i.e., the slave state of Virginia. The fact that Lee and others left the union so they could enslave people without "interference" was nowhere to be found. Not all *Who Was . . .* books so blatantly praise violent White supremacists. Recall from the last chapter that the *Who was . . . Andrew Jackson* book rightfully called Indian Removal an "illegal" and "shameful act." But content analysis of history books shows that more take the first approach than the second.[11]

The reason I was in the store looking for children's history books in the first place was because I was frustrated at the history lessons in my daughter's third-grade social studies textbook. The textbook's chapter 1 on communities is illustrative. Lesson 1 focused on one's own community (city), Lesson 2 looked at three different cities across the US, and Lesson 3 looked at one international city. Each lesson gave a short summary of the city's geography and history and discussed how those elements influenced the way people "live, work, and have fun together" in that community.

The international city was Timbuktu, Mali. The lesson opens in the 1400s discussing how during the fifteenth, sixteenth, and seventeenth centuries the city was a "very wealthy" business hub. Other "supporting details" in the history paragraph are that there was a "huge university" in the city and that "many thousands" of people lived there at that time. The next paragraph on "Life in Timbuktu Today" opens with the remark that "Fewer people now live in Timbuktu than in earlier times." Later in the paragraph it mentions that the languages spoken are Bambara and French and that "There are few good roads." The "Critical Thinking" questions at the bottom of the page then ask students, "How is the community of Timbuktu today like your community? How is it different?"

Neither of these are questions that require *critical thinking*; they require nothing more than listing *decontextualized facts* side-by-side. My daughter could have answered: "Huntsville has a lot of people while Timbuktu has fewer people," "We speak English and Spanish here and kids in Timbuktu speak Bambara and French," and "We have good roads but Timbuktu does not." A *real* critical thinking question, one within a history lesson aimed at teaching history as a tool to be used to understand the events that came after it, would ask the reader to brainstorm what events in the past may have influenced the conditions of the present. "Why did Timbuktu's population decline over the last 400 years," and "Why do people in an African country speak a European language?" and "Why aren't there good roads in Timbuktu?" would be such questions.

By design, those questions cannot be asked or answered because the "History" section skipped from 1600 to the present. It skipped 400 years and does nothing to encourage curiosity about what may have happened during them. What happened, though, was that the slave trade depopulated the whole region. In fact, the King of the Congo sent a letter to the King of Portugal decrying it.[12] Lacking knowledge of the events of the skipped 400 years? young readers have no idea that Europeans' racist commerce in human beings is why the population in African cities like Timbuktu declined so dramatically. Skipping that specific 400 years also deprives children of knowledge of how the French language came to the area: France invaded and colonized the land that is now Mali. Not at all mentioning that Mali only just liberated themselves from official French rule when their grandparents were their age means students have no reason to realize that parts of a country don't have "good roads" because it takes most countries, including their own, longer than 60 years to make good roads across an entire nation. Not discussing the exact centuries during which the wealth of White colonial countries like the US, UK, France, and Spain was built on the exploitation of places like Timbuktu means that one never learns the origins of the good roads and other things they enjoy.

Using the analytical exemplar of herself, the United States, and Puerto Rico, philosopher Shannon Sullivan writes that White people's ignorance of settler colonial nations' exploitative international relationships points to "the intimate relationship between power, knowledge, and ignorance, and the relationship of all three to processes of racialized colonization."[13] Skipping the 400 years of Europeans' colonization and enslavement ensures that young people come away from school with only "ancient" historical information, not any more recent information that would illuminate contemporary conditions, such as present population size, language, or quality of national infrastructure.

To be clear, in teaching children to think ahistorically, textbooks are functioning to uphold not only an epistemology of ignorance but also material White domination. A populace who understands the slave control roots of the present system of policing would be a populace less willing to perceive police brutality as one "Bad Apple" year after year after year. A populace who learned how the 1930s New Deal was implemented at the state level as a "Devil's Bargain" so that Southern states would have the "states' rights" to implement it within their White supremacist frameworks would be a populace that looks much more critically when those same states engage in contemporary actions like refusing federal health care expansions. How people perceive the present is related to how they understand the past, which is why there are struggles over what parts of the past are institutionalized to be remembered, how, and by whom.[14]

In sum, the Ahistorical Fallacy that racist events in history have no bearing on present conditions upholds White supremacy by normalizing viewing them as independent phenomena that are unconnected to anything else in society. This view protects the White supremacist structure from "blame," which maintains the myth of "White innocence." It also is a perspective that upholds White domination, both ideologically and materially, because "[w]ithout causal historical analysis, these racial disparities are impossible to explain" outside of a victim-blaming framework.[15]

Ahistorical "Bothsidesism"

Multiple sociology books have back-to-back chapters demonstrating "the complicity of liberals and conservatives in maintaining white supremacy."[16] Nonetheless, acknowledging that members of both majority US parties have contributed to the status quo becomes an ahistorical tool to maintain the status quo when lack of historical knowledge leads people to conclude that that means that "both sides" are responsible for any and all "racist" events.

A high-school classmate of mine fell into this common perspective following the January 6, 2021 Capitol Riot. He took to Facebook to post that both sides, i.e., Democrats and Republicans, were responsible for the January 6 attack. This is an ahistorical hot take, for to reach this bothsides-based conclusion, my classmate had to ignore the previous 12 years (all years that we were old enough to vote). He had to ignore that 12 years before, it was one side, not two, racistly portraying the first Black president as a non-citizen (and non-human with respect to monkey depictions). He had to ignore that eight years before, it was one side, not two, refusing to compromise on any legislation proposed by the then president. He had to ignore that during the four years before January 6, it was one party boldly admitting to inventing "alternative facts" and one party whose leader told them to stand by and stand ready should the majority of the nation choose to vote for the other party. Thus, while it is correct that both parties have been complicit in White supremacy, my high-school classmate using that fact to perceive that "both sides" are at fault for the specific actions of that day turns a historical truism into a culture-serving ahistorical perspective.

Conclusion

Analyzing ahistoricism at the international level, Andrews states that "Across the globe White people have enforced their will with a barbarity that is so X-rated [that now] we simply cannot bear to acknowledge the unspeakable truth."[17] There are consequences of failure to acknowledge that truth, though. In her book *Viral Justice: How We Grow the World We Want* (2022), African American Studies professor Ruha Benjamin writes that "adults who advocate for a white-washed version of history are engaged in a kind of theft –

intellectual and spiritual – robbing the next generation of an essential understanding of how we got here, how it could have been otherwise, and how they can be protagonists of a different kind of future that does not repeat the failures of the past."[18] Preventing remedying the problems of White domination, though, is exactly why the Ahistorical Fallacy exists. The epistemology of ignorance obscures understanding of the past, which decreases people's ability to effectively address racism in the present.

We can see the Ahistorical Fallacy manifest not only in textbooks but in legislative attempts to prevent today's youth from learning about the racism of past generations. This occurs with regard to both domestic and international history. Sociologist Hajar Yazdiha explains that collective memory of history is not just about how we see the past but also how "we make sense of the present and the way we direct action toward the future."[19] She also states that "willful historical amnesia threatens and erodes American democracy."[20] Lest this seem unnecessarily alarmist, Yazdiha's book, *The Struggle for the People's King: How Politics Transforms the Memory of the Civil Rights Movement* (2023), demonstrates how rollbacks to US democracy, observable via the reduction in the nation's Democracy Index Score since 2016, were enabled by key groups using revisionist history as political weapons to discredit and detail social justice efforts. The Ahistorical Fallacy, though a perception, functions to maintain White domination materially. It effectively ensures that with respect to racism, present thinking will be filled with confusion, victim-blaming, or bothsidesism at best and will "mobilize everyday people to violent action"[21] at worst.

12

The Silence Fallacy

Previous chapters identified frequent structural suggestions to address racism, such as mandating sensitivity training or making more anti-discrimination laws. A third common macro-level solution to racism is to stop talking about it, as in not just cease conversations but also cease collecting data on it in applications and records. National surveys in the US indicate that nearly three-fourths of people express some version of this perspective.[1]

This perspective no doubt stems from the fact that in the US children are socialized early to consider even so much as mentioning race to be taboo.[2] Research by psychologists Evan P. Apfelbaum, Kristin Pauker, and colleagues has identified age ten as the turning point toward preferring to not mention race. They had 101 mostly White children, half aged 8–9 and half 10–11, complete a picture-matching task. The children were given a stack of cards with pictures of people on them, one of which matched the researcher's card that they could not see. The control condition cards differed by background color, gender, and weight; and in the experimental condition, they differed by race as well. The objective was to identify the researcher's card by asking as few yes/no questions as possible.

In the control condition, which featured people of the same race (White) on the cards, the older children identified the match with fewer questions than the younger children. This was expected given older children's developmental advantage. However, when the cards featured people of different races, younger children performed the best, i.e., asked the fewest questions to make the match. One reason why was that younger children were willing to ask about race. The authors reported that whereas one-third of 8–9-year-olds asked questions like, "Is the person Black," *none* of the 10–11-year-olds did. They conclude that "At approximately ten years of age, children's tendency to regulate the appearance of prejudice is powerful enough to undermine performance on a task rooted in basic cognitive skills."[3]

Notice that the authors said the older children were regulating the *appearance* of *prejudice*. As they summarized in the introduction to their work, "strategically avoiding" race versus "frankly acknowledging" it has become the "prevailing social and moral convention in the United States."[4] This is what sociologists refer to as colorblindness or colorblind racism.[5] Recall that prejudice is defined by sociologists as the holding of preconceived *ideas about groups' innate hierarchal differences* that are resistant to change even in the face of empirical evidence to the contrary.[6] *Thinking* that African Americans are less hardworking and intelligent than White Americans, like many US White people do, is prejudice.[7] Simply *saying* the words "African American" is not prejudiced.

The Silence Fallacy is what I call the magical thinking that ignoring a phenomenon will make it go away, i.e., that "Avoiding talk about or noticing race are all that we need to maintain [supposed racial] equality."[8] Other scholars use visual metaphors for the social process of ignoring racism, like colorblindness and White epistemic blind spots. I selected a hearing metaphor instead because my students seem to feel like *talking* about race, racism, and anti-racism is the issue. As such, their proposed solution has been no talking, in verbal or written form.

The second reason for my choice to name this fallacy with reference to hearing versus sight is because those who display the second manifestation of it use that language. Whereas my students suggested silence in their efforts to brainstorm ways to disrupt White supremacy, those who continue to circulate overt and covert racist messages in society ironically claim they are "being *silenced*" when their White colonial epistemological authority is not enthusiastically embraced.

The culture-serving nature of both manifestations of the Silence Fallacy is revealed in the hypocrisy of the coexistence of the perspective to "Ignore it and it will go away!" with "How dare I be ignored!" What closer examination reveals is that it is specifically racial minorities and anti-racists whose "silence" this common perspective claims will benefit society. Traditional White colonial messages, by contrast, are considered a form of speech that must not only be allowed to be uttered/written but must be accepted if there is to be true equality.

Ban the Box: Race Edition

In her book *White Fragility: Why It Is So Hard for White People to Talk About Racism* (2018), educator Robin DiAngelo explains that because White people are "insulated from racial stress [they become] highly fragile in conversations about race."[9] She goes as far as to say that "the smallest amount of racial stress," such as merely talking about race or racism, is "intolerable" to most White people.[10] In his book *Conceptualizing Racism* (2016), sociologist Noel Cazenave explains that language that accommodates Whites' fragility is the prevailing semantic practice. This can include a visceral response to recognition of racism as discussed in chapter 7. It also can manifest as the common perspective that talking about race or racism is the fuel that drives observed inequalities.

I first noticed this mindset in my students' inequality papers when many suggested that a structural solution to racial discrimination in employment would be for job applications to not ask for applicants' race. This answer was likely common because the course textbooks reference economists Marianne Bertrand and Sendhil Mullainathan's 2004 study "Are Emily and Greg more employable than Lakisha and Jamal?" In short, the answer is yes; so it is easy to see how one might reach the conclusion that not asking for names and race on applications would prevent discrimination.

The parking situation at many universities offers a useful way to explain the folly of this perspective, though. Parking lots at my university are designated as for faculty/staff, commuter students, or residential students; and there are also a few spaces in each lot for visitors. While we faculty/staff have an easy go of it to find parking, and while residential students simply park near their dorms, commuter students face a daily challenge of finding parking. Sheer numbers wise, there are not enough spaces on campus for all commuter students. As our enrollment grew, the number of parking spaces did not keep pace. For this reason, commuter students must often circle full parking lots, like hungry vultures waiting for prey to expire, hoping to get a space. Some commuter students have even ended up missing class and having to just go home when they were unable to find parking in time to make it to class within a reasonable late period.

The parking situation is one of structural inequality. There are enough parking spaces for faculty/staff and enough for residential students; but there are not enough spaces for commuter students. In recent years, the university has built a new parking deck and has experimented with re-zoning existing parking lots; but neither has solved the problem yet.

My fall 2021 Honors Introduction to Sociology class loved this example. Not only did it resonate with their lived experiences but many of them animatedly recalled an episode of the TV show *The Office* that included it as a plot point.[11] In the show, another company housed in the same building as the main characters is doing renovations, and the construction crew's vehicles are taking up their parking spaces in the parking lot closest to the building. While some of the employees have to park in and walk from a satellite parking lot, the boss has an assigned parking space so is unaffected by the construction disruptions. When two employees tell him of the situation and ask for help, he declines. He does take a moment to "try to think about what it would be like" to not have a close, unaffected parking space; and after a few moments of reflection he concludes, "Okay yes that would be bad." Despite this understanding, he says he "can't, well can but won't" help the others.

After their boss's unwillingness to assist them, the employees on *The Office* resolve their parking issue another way. As a thought experiment, though, what would likely happen if they had just . . . stopped talking about parking? What if my university's student records database did not collect information about students' resident or commuter status? What if campus planning surveys did not ever ask about parking? Or what if we stopped labeling parking lots or spots by who could park there?

At first this might seem great because then anyone could park anywhere and commuter students could stop "complaining" about being late to class because of full lots. But further thought reveals that the silence that is ditching group labels does not solve the problem. For even without labels, full-time faculty/staff and residential students would still enjoy the bulk of parking spaces because those are groups who arrive earliest to and live on campus, respectively. Even without personal or lot labels, commuter students and part-time faculty/staff who arrive later in the day would still be circling by-then already full lots because the issue is not the *labels*, it is the inadequate *structure*, i.e., the number of parking spaces. Refusal to use labels does not alter that structure. Moreover, using the labels, such as me identifying students as residents or commuters or myself as faculty, has no bearing on the structure, either.

If colleges are silent regarding parking, then individual solutions like "just leave home earlier" can flourish. This would further harm commuter students, though, such as the grocery store employee I had one semester, who work in the mornings and come to campus for afternoon classes. Such students cannot simply come to campus earlier to find parking. Stopping talking about the parking situation or stopping labeling people or lots as faculty/staff, resident, or commuter will not help him or any other commuter student.

Verbal and written silence would only benefit those whom the structure already privileges: faculty/staff mainly. Stopping discussion of parking means no more emails from students asking, "Did I miss anything important?" when they leave because they never found parking in time to attend class. Removing lot labels would benefit us too in that we'd be relieved of the twinge of guilt that accompanies pulling into our lot, parking easily, and walking into the building while students in the next lot over circle and circle. In sum, silence would benefit the already privileged. It would not end the structural inequality that is negatively affecting others.

Likewise, naming races and/or discussing racial inequality no more causes unequal social experiences than discussing parking is what makes it easy for me to park but hard for commuter students. In her book *Why Race Still Matters* (2020), race scholar Alana Lentin explains that "not speaking about race does nothing to serve those who are targeted by racism. But it does benefit those who are not."[12] Silence ensures that language that accommodates Whites' fragility is not just normative but is in fact mandated to be the prevailing verbal and written practice. Second, the perspective functions to uphold material inequality as well. As Australian singer Kasey Chambers soulfully reminds us in her song *Ignorance*: "just 'cause you don't see it, it don't mean it's gone away." Silence allows unequal conditions to remain as they are. They don't disappear just because people don't talk about them.

My students suggesting that applications and other forms remove the race question is a testament to the power of the Silence Fallacy because they suggest this *after* I had previously taken care to teach the value of collecting data on social phenomena. Since 2020, I have used the non-race example of data on Covid-19 cases to illustrate the value of categorical data. During the height of the pandemic, many universities maintained an online dashboard that reported the number of cases of the disease among faculty, staff, and students at that institution. While this was helpful information for, say, faculty and commuter students deciding to come to the campus library to work or Zoom in yet again, for residential students who lived on campus it would also be helpful to know dorm-level case counts.

Early in the fall 2021 semester, students at James Madison University asked their university for dorm-level data. After their first request was "rebuffed," subsequent inquiries led to the revelation that "the data didn't exist."[13] The school's positivity rate had hit 60 percent, and yet there was no way for residential students to know how many cases were literally next door to them. The editor-in-chief of the university's student newspaper sued the school. He explained that "Without accurate and detailed information, it's very hard for people to make informed public-health decisions for themselves, especially in the middle of the worst health crisis this country and world has seen in how long."[14]

With regard to race, France is a case study in how silence on race does not solve racism. France does not collect race data on official records such as the census. This does not mean, though, that there is not racism in France. It simply means that identifying, proving, and ending it is a Herculean task. In short, both non-race-based and race-based examples clearly demonstrate that simply keeping mute on an issue and/or not collecting data on it will not resolve it. To the contrary, silence logically allows inequality to flourish uninhibited. As the Covid-19 data example shows, silence can literally be deadly. The logic underlying suggestions to just be silent regarding race or racism, therefore, do not hold up to scrutiny. Like other examples of Abstract Liberalism, suggesting removal of the labels that employers and others have been shown to discriminate against sounds on the surface like one supports equality; but in reality, it does not.

To be clear, I am sure that those whose first line of thinking leads them down this path really think it will help end discrimination.

It takes a deeper look at the perspective to reveal it to not really be tenable for solving discrimination. In the end, though, advocating for silence stems from a perspective that is rooted in the epistemology of ignorance and it contributes to the maintenance of White supremacy.

Silent Shouting

Not all talk of race and racism is perceived as harmful to society, only talk that rejects White supremacy (such as discussion that rejects discrimination and violence against minorities) or facilitates exposing its workings (such as collecting race data to monitor for disparities). The quickness with which hate speech against minorities is defended against "censorship" – ironically by the same right-wing base that supports censoring children's books about the civil rights movement – is evidence. Moreover, the fact that White supremacist speech is considered "silenced" when it is not granted automatic and exclusive epistemological authority – that is, when not everyone buys it and loves it – is yet further evidence that common perceptions about silence vis-à-vis racism are ends-based tools to maintain inequality.

When culture-serving perspectives circulate but are not unequivocally accepted, the speakers sometimes claim that they are being "silenced." The TV show The Daily Show called attention to this practice by creating a compilation of conservatives speaking, quite audibly, about how they are being silenced. The minute-long clip starts with a man speaking on Fox News, a US television network with one of the highest viewership ratings in the nation, saying that "Republicans have no way to communicate." This is followed by more clips of people repeatedly asserting, on national television, that they are being silenced. One man mentions a book that he had written in his clip, and then the next clip is of a man claiming that conservatives are being silencing by being denied book deals. A woman looks straight at the camera and talks to millions of viewers by speaking the words: "If you are conservative you can't speak about it or talk about it." The final clip shows a woman on national television emotionally asking what avenues of communication conservatives even have available to them anymore; and a stamp marks the text "3 conservative networks, talk radio, countless websites, and most uncles" over the stilled image.[15]

While *The Daily Show* is meant to be comedy, regular news noticed the ironic trend as well. *The Washington Post* ran an article on the topic of "Republicans claim they are being *silenced as they speak to millions of viewers.*"[16] It is truly Olympic-level mental gymnastics to claim you are being silenced as you are, in that moment, speaking to a large audience. This more than anything should be clear evidence that "being silenced" does not mean "being prevented from speaking" but rather it is essentially a code word for being challenged or rejected.

The conservatives who make this claim confuse "speaking" and "positive reception." A Pew Research Center survey from the time found that in the US "34% of registered voters identify as Independents, 33% as Democrats and 29% as Republicans"; but "when the partisan leanings of Independents are taken into account, 49% of registered voters identify as Democrats or lean Democratic, while 44% affiliate with the GOP or lean Republican."[17] What these numbers suggest is that what conservatives are actually upset about is not having their messages *resonate* with the majority of Americans all the time. They appear to conflate the situation of less than a supermajority *acceptance* with "being *silenced.*"

Conclusion

The mere mention of race let alone discussions about racism or collecting data on it are not what is perpetuating racism. By normalizing this perspective though, people can purport to value and work for equality while actually accommodating White fragility and making racism harder to identify and combat. The fact that literal hate speech rallies cries for protection, and the fact that the dominant language is considered "silenced" simply because an increasing number of people reject White supremacist rhetoric, all reveal that "silence" is an ends-based tool to maintain the status quo.

In her book *Nice White Ladies: The Truth About White Supremacy, Our Role in It, and How We Can Help Dismantle it* (2022), sociologist Jessie Daniels reminds her readers of the bait and switch that is thinking silence will save us: "We think the bargain is this: be nice, channel light and love, and everything will work out. But the real bargain is actually: be nice and don't speak up because our collective silence, and specifically the silence of white women, facilitates the continued smooth operation of oppressive systems."[18]

Conclusion

Explaining student resistance to lessons on race and racism in the classroom, psychologist Cyndi Kernahan writes that "challenging the racial status quo triggers justifications and rationalizations as well as resistance towards what we are teaching."[1] This phenomenon occurs outside of the classroom as well, as described by educator Robin DiAngelo in her book *White Fragility* (2018). This resistance to information on racism often takes the form of common perceptions that may seem logical, even anti-racist, on the surface, but which closer examination reveals to be culture-serving distortions. Sociologist Jennifer Mueller has explained that these perceptions are ends-based. That is, they are functional, explains Black Studies professor Kehinde Andrews, because "White supremacy necessitates delusional thinking in order to sustain itself."[2]

I have followed other sociologists in calling these common perceptions fallacies of racism. Far from being specific ideas that people actively subscribe to in order to create racist disparities, fallacies are instead unexamined general patterns of thinking that are rooted in an epistemology of ignorance. As such, if they are not interrogated, they will function to justify and (re)produce White domination, both ideologically and materially. For this reason, I share sociologist Hajar Yazdiha's conviction that "the evasion of social reality is its own violence."[3]

The Individual, Token, and Familiarity Fallacies are micro-level culture-serving perspectives about individuals. The Individualistic Fallacy (chapter 1) is the notion that racism only exists at the individual level and accordingly solutions to racism are individual. It denies the existence of systemic or structural racism or solutions.

The Token Fallacy (chapter 2) is the idea that racism only exists if all power and resources are held by Whites and none is held by racial minorities. This is revealed to be a culture-serving perspective because only tokens who can be used to deny racism are trotted out. Tokens like successful people of color or the few White people who have been active anti-racists throughout history are attacked not lauded. The Familiarity Fallacy (chapter 3) is the perspective that familiarity with a minority, especially a Black person, is proof that an individual cannot act in a racist manner. Perspectives that look inward and attempt to delegitimize information on White racial privilege by pointing out how a person is marginalized in other ways also fall under this fallacy.

The five fallacies in the Meso-Level section all function with respect to groups, organizations, or institutions. At their root is the social umbrage with calling attention to the fact that there are other perspectives, norms, and symbols with respect to racism than those of the dominant group. Privileging what a person says over what they do is the Simon Says Fallacy (chapter 4); and privileging aggressors' intent over the harm that they cause is the Mens Rea Fallacy (chapter 5). Both of these re-center dominant groups and further marginalize already oppressed groups. The Innuendo Fallacy (chapter 6) is the view that coded language and behavior do not exist with respect to racism. Pointing out instances of coded or even overt racism draws umbrage, or stigmatization as the "real" racism, because it is a direct challenge to the epistemology of ignorance. I called this the Recognition Fallacy (chapter 7). Going beyond mere recognition to actually taking action to defend or protect oneself against racist oppression is perceived by the dominant lens as just as harmful as oppression itself. This is called the Self-Defense Fallacy (chapter 8).

The Macro-Level Fallacies in this book focused on perspectives of structural and systemic racism. The Legalistic Fallacy (chapter 9) is the perspective that having a law against racism means racism no longer exists. This is revealed to be overly naïve given understandings of other social behavior. The perspective that racism is only specific historical actions, such as those that new legislation in the US would ban teaching about, is called the Fixed Fallacy (chapter 10). The perspective that past actions did not create the present is the Ahistorical Fallacy (chapter 11), and the view that to create a brighter future those seeking social justice should stop talking and instead accept traditional conservative messages is the Silence Fallacy (chapter 12).

From Fallacies of Racism to Fallacies of Social Bias

This book has discussed fallacies of racism, but an analytic approach of focusing on what inequality is not can also illuminate non-race-based systems of inequality. It does not make for a perfect application in all cases, for there are of course differences in how inequalities are constructed; but considering fallacies of social bias is a useful way to spark critical thinking.

Regarding the micro-level fallacies, the Individualistic Fallacy is seen in common perspectives on sexism. Like racism, sexism too is often reduced to a few hateful or mentally ill men. Solutions to issues like sexual assault, accordingly, then focus only on individuals to the exclusion of considering the role of social institutions and structures. As with racism, imploring those in positions of power to just be "nice" to others does not change the system. The Token Fallacy also can apply to gender in that women, non-binary, and trans gender people making inroads into business, government, science, and more is taken as supposed proof that gender barriers have fallen.

With regard to sexual orientation, research shows that interviewees deny that their behavior, like using "gay" to mean something negative, is homophobic by asserting that "I have a gay friend."[4] In discussing this practice, gender scholar Sam de Boise explicitly draws attention to the similarities of homophobia and racism with respect to the Familiarity Fallacy, saying that the gay friend claim "must resonate with anyone who is familiar with the mantra of 'I'm not racist, I've got Black friends.'"[5]

The frequency with which society believes what Simon says versus what Simone says demonstrates that epistemic excess is given to members of the dominant group on multiple systems of inequality. Even though false accusations of rape are incredibly rare, as a society we still had to develop a slogan, #BelieveWomen, to encourage people to not automatically assume that inequality, harassment, or abuse didn't happen solely because a man denies it.

Gender and sexuality scholars also have demonstrated how conscious malicious intent is not needed for sexism or homophobia to occur. Rejecting the notion that phrases such as "That's so gay" are not harmful simply because a speaker did not intend harm, De Boise explains what I call the Mens Rea Fallacy as applied to sexual orientation:

> Even if there is often no conscious intent to subordinate or marginalize others, this is often achieved through unquestioned symbolic practices (Coles 2009; Pascoe 2005), naturalized through hegemonic representations, which stigmatize nonheterosexual-identifying individuals.[6]

The Mens Rea Fallacy is also applicable with respect to language about disability. In her book, *Black Disability Politics* (2022), Gender and Women's Studies professor Sami Schalk makes clear that "intention cannot be the sole basis for assessing ableist (or otherwise oppressive) language – harm can occur regardless of intention."[7]

Sexism, homophobia, and ableism are all also perpetuated via codes, meaning the Innuendo Fallacy applies to these systems of inequality as well. Recognizing these forms of inequality, though, is not "reverse" bias towards members of the dominant groups. The backlash received by the shaving company Gillette for making a commercial that encouraged men to not harass one another or women demonstrates that the Recognition Fallacy extends to sexism too.

One of the examples in the Gillette commercial was of street harassment, and the Self-Defense Fallacy can be seen in real catcallers' expectations that women do nothing to defend or protect themselves from that form of everyday violence. From ethnography and interviews with catcallers, sociologist Simone Kolysh learned that "Initiators [of unwanted street harassment] would say that it is rude for recipients not to respond" or that women should "smile" and respond "politely."[8] In other words, the simplest self-defensive move – to ignore harassment – is perceived as "rude." As with the framing of anti-racist actions, from small to large, as wrong or as "reverse racism" against White supremacists, framing women's resistance to sexism as rude to men seeks to ignore that the latter's behavior is oppressive. Such perspectives function to allow the sexist behavior to continue.

Kolysh emphasizes that the majority of the victims they interviewed want to see catcalling addressed in a way that does not rely on criminalization. This is because the Legalistic Fallacy applies with respect to gender and sexuality systems of oppression. There are already laws against other types of gender and sexual violence, as well as laws ostensibly in place to bring violators to justice. However, statistics on men's stalking, domestic violence, rape, and murder of women and the reluctance of the male-dominated legal and criminal justice fields to even investigate many of these crimes is a textbook example of how the perception that just outlawing behavior means it will be solved is folly. Indeed, in discussing possible solutions to catcalling, Kolysh's interviewees drew explicit comparisons to racist "Stop and Frisk" laws, noting that not only did such laws not help crime levels but they were applied unequally by race and thereby functioned to support White supremacy. Kolysh and their interviewees hypothesized that criminalization of catcalling would likewise result in Black and Latino men being more heavily policed while White men continue to engage in verbal street harassment with impunity. Thus, like racism, sexism has not and will not be eliminated simply by passing laws against it, especially when the vast majority of those in charge of creating and enforcing the laws are members of the population who are committing the harms in question.

The Fixed Fallacy would have us believe that nineteenth-century conditions for women – disenfranchisement from the vote, inability to attend certain schools, etc. – are the only social arrangements that are sexist, not any of the social phenomena of today. Relatedly, though, the Ahistorical Fallacy applied to gender would manifest as a failure to recognize how those prior sexist practices and structures created and still impact society today. With regard to addressing sexism, homophobia, ableism, and other systems of inequality, the Silence Fallacy reveals itself to be culture-serving in that it is a view that calls for social justice are problematic while traditional messaging that reify traditional oppressive perspectives should not only be expressed but accepted.

Incorporating Fallacies into Everyday Life

There is a long history of theorists debating which needs to occur first: changed conditions because changed thinking will follow, or change thinking because changed conditions will follow? I'm of the view that humans create the social structure and so out-of-the-box thinking is necessary to recreate it. As a teenager, I read my Dad's old copy of Carter G. Woodson's classic *The Mis-Education of the Negro* (1933) and have forever remembered his observation that "If you can control a man's thinking you do not have to worry about his action. When you determine what a man shall think you do not have to concern yourself about what he will do." During college and graduate school, I encountered other scholars, such as Patricia Hill Collins, Eduardo Bonilla-Silva, and Pierre Bourdieu, who likewise pointed out that social systems require acceptance of an attendant belief system that legitimizes them. Attempting to legitimate racism is the reason for the existence of the fallacies of racism covered in this book.

Addressing the fallacies is not about addressing the *content* of each individual one but about learning to recognize *culture-serving logic* at work. Fallacies are patterns of thinking that are mired in the epistemology of ignorance. They attempt to focus our attention on what racism is not. For this reason, a general openness to critically and *humbly* thinking is a first step. When I was a child, if a family member said "Wow, I didn't know that" in response to learning something, the others would reply with the cheeky little maxim that "What you don't know can make another whole world!" At the root of this retort is the reality of the vast amount of information that any given person does not know. One's limited knowledge was not brought up as a put down but rather to inspire continued learning. There is another whole world out there for us to learn about!

With regard to racism, though, too often there is no desire to learn. Sociologist Noel Cazenave has described what he calls the IPA Syndrome. He says that with respect to information about inequality, members of a nation's majority group have "the Ignorance of not knowing" about it, the "Privilege of not needing to know" about it, and the "Arrogance of not wanting to know."[9] Developing epistemic humility means breaking out of all three these mental shackles, especially the Arrogance one.

The philosophical concept of "epistemic humility" captures the state of mind of being open to the reality of all that you do not know. Philosopher José Medina calls it a state of meta-lucidity and Miranda Fricker calls it "a distinctly *reflexive* critical social awareness."[10] Of identifying tendencies to fall in line with fallacies-based thinking, Fricker says that "It takes a special feat of self-consciousness to be alert to this kind of prejudice in one's thinking, let alone to correct it."[11] Fellow philosopher George Yancy frames "reject[ing] the poisonous ideas that White America would rather we swallow" as taking courage. Of the US, he writes that there is "an appalling lack of courage, weakness of will, spinelessness, and indifference in our country that helps to sustain [White racism]."[12]

Fricker believes that people *can* overcome thinking solely within dominant epistemic practices, though. She said we should adopt the working hypothesis that if we cannot understand something described by a member of an oppressed group then the reason is that we do not understand. She suggests humility, saying: "learn and internalize how to resist the temptation to jump to ... attractive conclusions [based on] insufficient evidence."[13] DiAngelo advises that we recognize that often we reach first to *disagree* when really what is happening is that we don't *understand*.[14] An alternative response when we are tempted to reach for one of the fallacies in these situations is to "seek out further evidence" or temporarily "suspend judgement altogether."[15] This does not mean one can never disagree with or challenge a given perspective on racism; but it does mean that if challenge is always one's *first* response, then we should ask ourself why we are so quick to reject non-dominant perspectives.

I like Fricker's suggestions for overcoming the epistemic inequality that fallacies represent because they demonstrate that (at some point past childhood) how we think about things is a *choice*. Philosopher Charles Wade Mills also charges us to see adhering to the epistemology of ignorance as a choice. This is why the first actionable step is to embrace opportunities to learn about racism rather than resist them. Refusing to rectify one's lack of empirically accurate knowledge is not just a personal matter. As the chapters in this book have shown, mass thinking within the fallacies "makes racial domination easier to enact and defend."[16]

Mills says that rejecting an epistemology of ignorance "does not require one to leave the country but to speak out and struggle against the terms of the [Racial] Contract."[17] In our daily lives we are afforded many opportunities to do this. In conversations with family, friends, coworkers, our children, or even small talk with strangers, we can be attentive to the ways that the epistemology of ignorance guides understandings. And we can explicitly reject fallacies when they surface. Andrews reminds us of the far-reaching power of even just one person publicly rejecting the fallacies:

"Seeing someone bring some truth to these discussions can empower people to keep a grip on reality. It's useful to demonstrate the irrationality of Whiteness, to expose the faulty logic behind the verbal diahorrea [sic] we deal with."[18]

Speaking at a 2021 Zoom event, psychologist Beverly Daniel Tatum discussed the role of individual power.[19] Tatum said that we should not discount the power of one person to impact society. One person could end up being the person who signs off – or not – on a structural phenomenon that has wide-reaching and lasting impact. As a person born and raised in Tennessee, I was reminded of the one man who received a letter from one woman (his mother) that changed his planned "nay" vote on ratifying the 19th Amendment to a quiet "aye." With Tennessee's ratification, the US had the needed three-fourths of States' support to make women's right to vote the law of the land. Of course, voter suppression was and is still a thing in Tennessee and other US states. But as Tatum told the host and all of us in the Zoom audience, there is always going to be pushback following any forward movement. But neither that pushback nor even the new forms of oppression that develop to take the old form's place can change the fact that the old structure can sometimes be felled by one person's action.

While few of us will be in the position to cast deciding votes on history-making social changes, we can nonetheless take action to dismantle racism in our own corners of the world. In her book *Viral Justice: How We Grow the World We Want* (2022), African American Studies professor Ruha Benjamin explains that "small changes can add up to large ones, transforming our relationships and communities, and helping us build a more just and joyful world."[20] Considering the person-to-person method of transmission of Covid-19, she ponders whether viruses can offer a "microscopic model of what it could look like to spread justice and joy in small perceptive ways?"[21] The titular concept of her book, viral justice, is defined as "an approach to social change [that] seeks to nurture alienated species"; and by alienated species, she means "all the forms of life and living that are routinely cast out and rendered worthless in our current system."[22] Thinking and acting outside of the epistemology of ignorance is presently an alienated species in society. As multiple chapters in this book have shown, perspectives and actions that reject White domination are considered "worthless" at best and psychotic at worst. Benjamin's concept of viral justice suggests that individuals can participate in "transforming our world so that everyone has the chance to thrive" by choosing to be "vectors of justice."

In the final chapter of their textbook *Race in America* (2020 [2010]), sociologists Matthew Desmond and Mustafa Emirbayer offer that one way to spread justice is to confront expressions of racism when encountered. While people of all social categories can take up this challenge, given the research demonstrating the extent to which explicit White racism is expressed in "backstage" homogeneously White spaces,[23] it is also an explicit call for White people to "learn how to call in" other White people "when they are actively causing harm." Desmond and Emirbayer suggest asking questions, which they say are "powerful weapons against racist beliefs."[24] This does not mean "gotcha" questions, though, but critical questions that strike at the heart of the epistemology of ignorance or plain undiluted racist logic.

A family friend once did this while shopping. The store did not have the item she needed so the sales associate said, "Perhaps you should try the branch in your neighborhood." Our family friend, a Black woman, asked the store clerk, a White woman, "Where is that?" The simple question made the clerk blush because it revealed her racist assumption that Black people did not live in such a wealthy area of the town. In my experience asking simple but pointed questions, during my childhood as a student and presently as a professor and mother, I've witnessed people like my Algebra teacher learn lessons that move their thinking *and behavior* away from patterns rooted in racial ignorance. If questioning others is too daunting, though, simply saying "Hm. I see it differently" powerfully communicates that the culture-serving perspective just espoused is not universally accepted. Of course, not all interventions will result in life-long anti-racism efforts on the part of the person you spoke to. But not saying or doing anything will help even less.

In the case of teachers, doctors, nurses, lawyers, priests, and others who work directly with the public, and in the case of business owners, policy makers, social media influencers, and organizational leaders, the positive impact of rejecting fallacies can quickly multiply when one considers how many people's lives one person touches. Rejecting the Mens Rea Fallacy about the single "flesh" color crayon she grew up with, one of my daughter's elementary school teachers stocked Crayola's "Colors of the World" crayons in her classroom. That way, when the children drew self or family portraits, they could all find a color for their flesh. For another example, after admitting that his family-owned business had an unwritten policy of not hiring Black employees, a former student told me that, based on what he'd learned in class, he planned to stop that discriminatory practice and encourage his family to start hiring based on qualifications. While neither brown crayons nor one business hiring Black people will, on their own, end global White supremacy, Benjamin reminds us that all acting together in our own spheres of influence "can have exponential effects."[25] Multiplying 25–30 kids by even just a few years teaching, for instance, reveals how quickly just one person can either reify racial ignorance or spread viral justice.

In sum, cultivating epistemic humility in ourselves, even if we spread it to others, will still simply be another example of Abstract Liberalism if we do not take the next step of *acting* outside of the epistemology of ignorance as well. In *Why Race Still Matters* (2020), race scholar Alana Lentin explains the first action step when she writes that "the reason we must speak about race is to attempt to unmask it in order to undo its effects."[26] As multiple fallacies showed in different ways, speaking about race and racism is stigmatized and attacked in White settler colonial societies because that speech betrays the normative epistemology of ignorance and silence. The take home point about fallacies is not to learn them and think, "Right, well, I personally won't make *that* mistake." The point is use the knowledge gained to *speak and act* outside of the dominant White supremacist framework in the areas in which you hold *power*.

Conclusion

The fallacies described in this book function to uphold White supremacy. As academics, artists, comedians, and other social actors call attention to them, however, some of their power may be lost. In the future, other fallacies will join the Biological Essentialism Fallacy in being a periphery versus central pattern of thinking. The Fixed Fallacy reminds us, though, that racism and its structures of support are adaptive. New fallacies are constantly developing in order to maintain the ideological and resultant material status quo. In fact, we should likely expect the future appropriation of fallacies by defenders of White supremacy. Already we have seen the distortion of the legacy of Dr. Martin Luther King, Jr. to serve the aims of those working to roll back civil rights.[27] The academic language of institutional racism has been misappropriated, too. The social actors who are seeking to ban lessons on institutional racism from schools have ironically adopted that very language to characterize their experience in an equalizing society. Likewise, we should expect that it is only a matter of time before the concept of logical fallacies and/or of the epistemology of ignorance is distorted within the crucible of White supremacy into an ends-based pattern of thinking to uphold the status quo.

The reality of concept appropriation underscores how the point of this book is not the specific content of the fallacies. Learning how to debunk each and every status quo-supporting sentiment would be as fruitless as fighting the mythical Hydra by attempting to sever each regenerating head. Instead, what I hope can be taken from this book is the ability to identify not just the heads de jure but the whole beast itself.

An epistemology of ignorance that supports White domination is the beast. The dozen fallacies herein are some of its current heads, but new ones will surely develop as quickly as these present ones are rendered impotent. By cultivating and spreading epistemic habits that can recognize and reject the fallacies of racism, though, we are better equipped to recognize and resist White supremacy no matter what form it takes.

Notes

Introduction

1. Sims 2017.
2. Desmond and Emirbayer 2020 [2010]: 9.
3. Mueller 2018; 10; Mills 2007: 13.
4. Loewen 2018 [1995].
5. Ibid.: 352–3.
6. Kernahan 2019: 48; Ambrose et al. 2010: 24.
7. Mueller 2020; Hirsch and Khan 2020.
8. Desmond and Emirbayer (2020 [2010]): 6.
9. Ibid.
10. Fleming 2018: 15.
11. Desmond and Emirbayer (2020 [2010]): 6, emphasis in original.
12. There are others who contend that "the dominant understanding of the world is distorted beyond simple ignorance" (Andrews 2023: 22). I engage with this line of scholarship throughout the book as the ignorance underlying the fallacies is not "simple" but cultivated, institutionalized, and action-oriented.
13. Mills 1997: 17–18.
14. Ibid.: 18, emphasis in original.
15. Fricker 2007: 152.
16. Mills 1997: 19, emphasis in original.
17. Ibid.
18. Ibid.
19. Ibid.: 18.
20. Mueller 2020: 146.
21. Ibid.: 149.
22. For example, Korver-Glenn 2021.
23. For example, Wingfield 2019.
24. Peggy McIntosh in *Mirrors of Privilege* (documentary).
25. Mueller 2020: 152.
26. Ibid.: 154.

27. Ibid., emphasis in original.
28. Ibid.: 155.
29. Ibid.: 156.
30. Mueller 2018: 1.
31. Mueller and Washington 2022: 23, emphasis in original.
32. Mueller 2020: 148.
33. Jost 2011: 228; Kernahan 2019: 53.
34. Omi and Winant 1994.
35. Mueller and Washington 2022.
36. DiAngelo 2018: xiv.
37. Ibid.
38. Andrews 2023: 179.
39. Woodson 1933.
40. Mills 1997.
41. Fanon 1961.
42. Crenshaw 1989; Collins 2000 [1990].
43. Andrews 2023: 198.
44. Mueller 2020: 146.

Section I: Micro-Level Fallacies

1. Giddens et al. 2020 [1991].
2. Carr et al. 2021 [2018]: 39.
3. Ibid.
4. Golash-Boza 2018 [2015]: 98–9.
5. Ibid.: 99; Sue at al. 2007; Giddens et al. 2020 [1991].
6. Kernahan 2019; Loewen 2018 [1995].

Chapter 1: The Individualistic Fallacy

1. Kernahan 2019: 32.
2. Golash-Boza 2018 [2015]: 479; Giddens et al. 2020 [1991]: A13.
3. Golash-Boza 2018 [2015]: 102.
4. Loewen 2018 [1995]: 205.
5. Kernahan 2019.
6. Anderson 2020.
7. Desmond and Emirbayer 2020 [2010]: 6.
8. Ibid.
9. Fleming 2018: 16.
10. Ibid.
11. Kernahan 2019: 150.
12. Ibid.
13. Ibid.

14. Sims 2017.
15. Tim Wise in *Mirrors of Privilege* (documentary).
16. Lentin 2016.
17. Ibid.: 34.
18. Ibid.
19. Ibid.
20. Ibid.: 40.
21. Ibid.
22. Fleming 2018: 16.
23. Medina 2013.
24. Ibid.
25. Prescod-Weinstein 2021: 243.
26. Ibid.
27. Bonilla-Silva 2018 [2003].
28. Rucks-Ahidiana, unpublished manuscript.
29. Kernahan 2019: 11.
30. Golash-Boza 2018 [2015]: 106.
31. Mueller and Washington 2022: 13.
32. Ibid.
33. Hill 2022.
34. Ibid.
35. Ibid.
36. Ibid.
37. Kimmell and Mahler 2003: 1443.
38. Kernahan 2019: 11.
39. Wingfield 2019: 66; see also Govere and Govere 2016.
40. Wingfield 2019; Kalev et al. 2006.
41. Wingfield 2019: 33 and 66; Edelman et al. 2001.
42. Wingfield 2019: 92.
43. Ibid.: 70–1.
44. Bonilla-Silva 2018 [2003].
45. Chapman and Brunsma 2020: 17–18.
46. Ibid.: 17.
47. Ibid.: 100, emphasis in original.
48. Ibid.: 17.
49. Ibid.
50. Ibid.
51. Harrison in Chapman and Brunsma 2020: xiv.

Chapter 2: The Token Fallacy

1. Desmond and Emirbayer 2020 [2010]: 7.
2. Fleming 2018: 18.
3. Ibid.: 19.
4. Ibid.: 18.

5. Prescod-Weinstein 2021: 156–7. She also notes that, first, Black women physicists were told they "couldn't make it as a scientist" and only after they did make it was their achievement then recast as evidence that racism does not exist in the field of physics.
6. Prescod-Weinstein 2021: 157.
7. Ibid.: 164.
8. Kernahan 2019: 166.
9. Ibid.: 168.
10. Andrews 2023: 198.
11. Ibid.: 174.
12. Ibid.: 28.
13. Ibid.: 176.
14. Ibid.
15. Ibid.: 178, 183.
16. Ibid.: 162, 159. Andrews acknowledges that celebrities can utilize their fame to "mobilize publics and put pressure on" those with the actual power to act, but he reminds us that is not the same as having "direct access to power than can reshape people's lives."
17. Crenshaw 1991.
18. Andrews 2023: 163.
19. Ibid.: 164.
20. Collins 2000 [1990].
21. Curington et al. 2015; Robinson 2015. It should be noted, too, that much of the interest in Asian women on dating apps is often accompanied by Orientalist comments that assume the women's desire for and to submit to superior Western men.
22. Loewen 2018 [1995]: 163, 167.
23. Blumer 1958: 4.
24. Mitchell 2018: 253.
25. "1921 Tulsa Race Massacre," Tulsa Historical Society and Museum online.
26. Kernahan 2019: 166.
27. Sarkar 2023.
28. Ibid.
29. Ibid.
30. Alexander 2012 [2010]: 204–5.
31. Chapman and Brunsma 2020: 78.
32. Mills 1997: 126–7.
33. Daniels 2021: 35.
34. Mills 1997: 107.
35. Burke and Sotomayor 2018.
36. Mills 1997: 109.
37. *Ghosts of Ole Miss* (documentary) 2012.
38. Mills 1997: 37, emphasis added.

Chapter 3: The Familiarity Fallacy

1. Driscoll 2021.
2. Forsey 2020.
3. Bonilla-Silva 2018 [2003]: 81.
4. Ibid.: 81–2.
5. Ibid.: 81.
6. DiAngelo 2021: 49.
7. Associated Press 2022.
8. Ibid.
9. Ibid.
10. This deep-seated assumption was part of Barack Obama's appeal. On a more general level, political scientist Danielle Lemi's research shows that mixed-race political candidates can use invocation of their different heritages to try to connect with voters from those demographics. Compared to mono-racial candidates, though, mixed-race candidates' efforts at doing so are more often challenged and they involve more "identity labor."
11. All names of my interviewees are pseudonyms. For methodological details of the interview studies discussed in chapters 3 and 10, see the Appendix of my co-authored book *Mixed-Race in the US and UK* (Sims and Njaka 2020).
12. For example, Ali 2003.
13. Rockquemore and Laszloffy 2005: 71.
14. Mehta's essays also discuss the "cultural tension" and "authenticity policing" that she experiences from South Asian family and friends; however, she says that "because I understand racism to be deeply tied to power . . . I don't tend to name that dynamic as racism" (2023: 4).
15. Mehta 2023: 176.
16. See also Daniels 2021 and DiAngelo 2021.
17. Mehta 2023: 104.
18. Ibid.: 2.
19. Ibid.
20. Daniels 2021: 193.
21. Ibid.: 188–92; this section focuses specially on White adoptive parents since racial minority parents are most likely to adopt children of their same race (Raleigh 2012; Ishizawa et al. 2006). Raleigh (2012), for example, found that 95% of black adoptive parents adopted a black child. Speaking of the paucity of non-White parents adopting White children, Ishizawa et al. (2006) speculate that knowledge of institutional barriers due to negative stereotypes about non-White parenting and awareness of potentially being mistaken for the child's nanny due to historically racialized child care arrangements may dissuade non-Whites from seeking to adopt White children.
22. Khanna and Killian 2015: 586.
23. Daniels 2021: 188.
24. For example, Buggs 2019.
25. Robinson 2015; Acosta 2021.

26. Acosta 2021: 102.
27. Loewen 2018 [1995]: xxvi.
28. Ibid.
29. Arguably the most infamous case of White US Americans dispossessing Native Americans of their land came in the 1830s. The US Supreme Court had ruled that since the Cherokee were a sovereign nation, White US Americans in neighboring territories could not forcibly remove them to take possession of the land. With the full support of then President Andrew Jackson's Administration, though, the US Army defied the Court's ruling and instead "rounded up all sixteen thousand Cherokees and held them for months in disease-infested camps" before forcing them to walk over 1,000 miles/1,600 kilometers, from present-day Georgia, Alabama, and Tennessee to present-day Oklahoma (Marger 2015: 142). As the march took place in the middle of a harsh winter, "nearly 4,000 Cherokees and an unaccounted-for number of black slaves died" walking what became known as The Trail of Tears (Desmond and Emirbayer 2020 [2010]: 65). Since they walked through the area that had recently been colonized as the city of Huntsville, there are a number of official historical markers here that memorialize "perhaps the most devastating single action taken by the federal government in destroying Indian cultures and societies" (Marger 2015: 142).
30. Bonilla-Silva 2004.
31. Pollock 2004: 175.
32. Ibid.
33. Peggy McIntosh in *Mirrors of Privilege* (documentary).
34. Bonilla-Silva 2018 [2003]: 81.
35. Bonvillian 2019.
36. Ibid.
37. Ibid.
38. Ibid.
39. WVLT News 2019.
40. Ibid.
41. Ibid.
42. US Census: https://data.census.gov/.
43. Bonilla Silva 2018 [2003]: 77.
44. DiAngelo 2021: 58.
45. Ibid.: 59.
46. Ibid.
47. Kernahan 2019: 64–5.
48. DiAngelo 2021: 22, emphasis in original.
49. Ibid.: 136.
50. Ibid.: 92.
51. Allport 1954.
52. DiAngelo 2021: 146.
53. Ibid.: 92.
54. Ibid.: 146.

Section II: Meso-Level Fallacies

1. Carr et al. 2021 [2018]: 39.
2. Ibid.; Meghji 2022.
3. Golash-Boza 2018 [2015]: 102.
4. Meghji 2022: 90.
5. Wingfield 2019: 34.
6. Ray 2019: 26.
7. Giddens et al. 2020 [1991].
8. Bourdieu 1983.
9. Ray 2019: 46.

Chapter 4: The Simon Says Fallacy

1. Friel 2019.
2. North and Balčiauskas 2020.
3. Ibid.
4. Golash-Boza 2018 [2015]: 102.
5. In addition to the previously given examples of her portrayal as a pregnant mother, Meghan is factually not "straight out of Compton," nor is her child a monkey; and yet these are the ways that British media portrayed her.
6. Personal communication, 2023.
7. Yap 2017. Thank you to Nick Jones for introducing me to the philosophical concept of social imaginary.
8. Mills 1997.
9. Harry, The Duke of Sussex 2023: 6–7.
10. Fricker 2007: 1.
11. Ibid.
12. Ibid.
13. Ibid.
14. Ibid.: 17, emphasis in original.
15. Ibid.: 17, 90.
16. Medina 2011; Davis 2016.
17. Walsh 2021.
18. Ibid.
19. Gostanian and Ciechalski 2021.
20. Yuen 2021.
21. Hernández 2018: 79–80.
22. Ibid.: 81.
23. Ibid.
24. Ibid.
25. Walton and Gordon 2009: 239.
26. Thank you to Nick Jones for sharing Walton and Gordon's work with me and for helping me look at the logician side of this phenomenon.
27. Fricker 2007: 44.

28. Ibid.
29. Ibid., emphasis in original. Fricker notes that a secondary type of harm occurs, too. She identified these as "follow-on disadvantages, extrinsic to the primary injustice in that they are caused by it rather than being a proper part of it," and she says that these have "wide-ranging negative impact on a person's life" (ibid.: 46, 48). Examples include practical harms like disadvantage or lost opportunities, and epistemic harms such as the fact that systemic experience with testimonial injustice can lead disadvantaged speakers to "lose confidence in his beliefs" (ibid.: 47–8) and "preventing him from developing certain intellectual virtues ... intellectual courage, 'impartiality', 'intellectual sobriety', and 'intellectual courage'" (ibid.: 49). Because systematic epistemic injustice is produced "specifically by those prejudices that track the subject through different dimensions of social activity," Fricker says it "renders one susceptible not only to testimonial injustice but to a gamut of different injustices" (ibid.: 27).
30. Bonilla-Silva 2018 [2003].
31. Kelderman 2023a; survey conducted by Next Generation Assessment (https://nextgenerationassessment.com/).
32. Rodrigues-Sherley 2022; Zalaznick 2022.
33. Pérez 2022.
34. Rodrigues-Sherley 2022.
35. Purdue Northwest University 2022: https://www.pnw.edu/purdue-north west-distinguished-as-diverse-metropolitan-university/.
36. Personal communication 2020, quoted anonymously with permission.
37. Personal communication 2020, quoted anonymously with permission.
38. My colleague also appears to think that including one reading *written by* a racial minority and woman means forcing all faculty to teach about race and gender. In my reply email, I had to do the racial labor of explaining to my White colleagues the very basic fact that minorities write articles and books on non-gender and non-race topics. I used the example of a Latina scholar whose methodological article on interviewing I assign in my Qualitative Research Methods course. Of course, I could have used myself as an example given that my first book was *The Sociology of Harry Potter* (Sims 2012).
39. Bonilla-Silva 2018 [2003]: 62.
40. Ibid.: 63.
41. Baldwin 1966.
42. Fricker 2007: 43.
43. Rodrigues-Sherley 2022.

Chapter 5: The Mens Rea Fallacy

1. Fricker 2007.
2. Hernández 2018.

3. Desmond and Emirbayer 2020 [2010]: 7.
4. Mills 1997: 36.
5. Prescod-Weinstein 2021: 159.
6. Rawls and Duck 2020.
7. As one of only a handful of minority students at my majority White private school, I had been advised by family members who worked in higher education not to waive my right to read the first letter of recommendation from a teacher precisely for this reason.
8. I say "used to" because I have not had students voice these objections in recent years. Gen Z have entered the classroom, and they have come of age with Band-Aids of many colors being available. In addition, makeup lines like Fenty have brought attention to the color issue in makeup. Now, most of my students can easily understand how limited options, especially combined with labeling light skinned ones "flesh," stem from Eurocentrism and racism.
9. Mueller 2017.
10. Ibid.: 225.
11. Ibid.: 230.
12. Personal communication 2023.
13. Rowling, "The Naga are snake-like mythical creatures." Twitter.
14. Sims 2022.
15. Ibid.
16. Rafalow 2020: 158.
17. Ibid.
18. Ibid.
19. Ibid.
20. Ibid.: 160.
21. Ibid.
22. Ibid.
23. Ibid.: 158.
24. Sims 2017.
25. Hernández 2018: 11.
26. Ibid.: 82.
27. Ibid.: 44, emphasis added.
28. Heilman 2022; Kolysh 2021.
29. FBI: https://www.fbi.gov/investigate/terrorism.
31. Benjamin 2019; Noble 2018.
32. Prescod-Weinstein 2021: 105.
33. Benjamin 2019: 62.
34. Allyn 2020.
35. Buolamwini 2018.
36. Benjamin 2019: 76.
37. Prescod-Weinstein 2021: 160.
38. Ibid.
39. Chapman and Brunsma (2020: 121–2).
40. Kolysh 2021: 50.

Chapter 6: The Innuendo Fallacy

1. Mills 1997: 73, emphasis in original.
2. Ibid., emphasis in original.
3. National Constitution Center. "South Carolina Declaration of Secession (1860)."
4. *The Italian Americans* (documentary) 2015.
5. "Executive Order 9066."
6. Kernahan 2019: 60.
7. https://www.urbandictionary.com.
8. Picca and Feagin 2007: xii.
9. Goffman 1959.
10. Picca and Feagin 2007.
11. Ibid.: 91.
12. Ibid.
13. Pérez 2022: 39.
14. Ibid.: 45.
15. Picca and Feagin 2007: 25, 21.
16. DiAngelo 2021: 50.
17. Ibid.: 53.
18. Desmond and Emirbayer 2020 [2010]; Kroskrity 2021; Haney López 2014.
19. Haney López 2014: ix.
20. Ibid.: 4.
21. Kroskrity 2021: 181.
22. Middleton and Franklin 2009.
23. After the campaign and his move to New York, it would come out that Ford did in fact have a serious girlfriend at the time who was White.
24. Middleton and Franklin 2009: 68.
25. Ibid.
26. Ibid.: 69
27. Desmond and Emirbayer 2020 [2010]: 111.
28. Ibid.
29. Kroskrity 2021: 183.
30. *Ghosts of Ole Miss* (documentary), 2012.
31. Biden, though White, nonetheless often receives racialized anger from conservatives for his "liberal" stances. In addition, Raúl Pérez (2022: 131–3) in his book *The Souls of White Jokes* explains that US Presidents back to Abraham Lincoln who are seen as "betraying" White interests become targets of racist jokes. See also chapter 2's section "The Non-Token Status of Race Traitors."
32. Mills 1997: 75.
33. Wingfield 2019: 91.
34. Rafalow 2020: 104.
35. Ibid.: 105.
36. Ibid.
37. Trump 2020 (Twitter). The end of Trump's tweet tagged the TV show *Fox and Friends* as well as one of their news anchors.

38. Bonilla-Silva 2018 [2003].
39. *Race – The power of an illusion*, 2003.
40. https://www.imdb.com.
41. Bowden 2020.
42. *Race – The power of an illusion*, 2003.
43. Weiner 2020.
44. Korver-Glenn 2021.
45. Rafalow 2020.
46. Desmond and Emirbayer 2020 [2010].

Chapter 7: The Recognition Fallacy

1. Tuan 1998.
2. Rhoden-Paul 2022.
3. Ibid.
4. Ibid.
5. Ibid.
6. Ibid.
7. Mendick and Leather 2022.
8. Ibid.
9. Davies 2023.
10. Ideas such as it takes hard work to "make it to the top" are perfect examples of this. The validity of their logic quickly weakens as soon as one observes how much hard work is done by poor people who need multiple jobs to survive compared to how infrequently hard work is required for survival of those born into generational wealth. Citing hard work rather than facts such as that up to a third of Ivy League admissions are legacies serves the interests of elites by obscuring the structural advantages they have over others due to accidents of birth not merit. Relatedly, accepting ruling ideas sets the mental stage to attribute lack of achievement to supposed lack of individual effort or talent.
11. Mills 1997: 95, emphasis in original.
12. Gregory 2023.
13. Berheide et al. 2022.
14. Collins 2000 [1990].
15. This woman blocked me after our exchange, so I cannot provide links as citations. I wrote this part of the chapter based on the screen shots I took on my phone at the time in anticipation of her either deleting her tweets or blocking me. As I've mentioned in talks on navigating academia as a Black woman, White fragility is predictable.
16. Collins 2000 [1990].
17. Buggs 2017: 386.
18. Ibid.
19. Ibid.; Rodriquez 2009.
20. Buggs 2017.

21. Mills 1997: 88, quoting Douglass' autobiography.
22. Ibid.: 89.
23. Buggs 2017; Marcano 2009.
24. Kernahan 2019: 43.
25. Thornhill 2019.
26. Mills 1997: 133.
27. Bonilla-Silva 2018 [2003]: 87; Allport 1954.
28. Prescod-Weinstein 2021: 121–2.
29. Kernahan 2019: 75; Crittle and Maddox 2017.
30. Ahmed 2021: 1.
31. Mehta 2023: 39, 114.
32. Ahmed 2021: 1; Collins 2000 [1990]: 279.
33. Song 2014: 107.
34. Ibid.
35. Andrews, quoted in Fuller 2022.
36. Fuller 2022.
37. Ibid.
38. Kernahan 2019: 16.
39. Ibid.
40. Ibid.; Hetter 2015.
41. Lentin 2016: 37.
42. Brooks 2020.
43. Ibid.: 410.
44. DiAngelo 2018; Kernahan 2019.
45. Zamudio-Suarez 2022.
46. Ibid.
47. Turner 2019.
48. Dow 2019; Sims and Njaka 2020.
49. Hagerman 2018.
50. Joseph-Salisbury and Connelly 2018.
51. Mills 1997: 93.
52. Yancy 2018: 1–2.
53. Ibid.: 1, 5.
54. Loewen 2018 [1995].
55. Mills (1997) explains that the "Racial Contract" that prescribes local (US) and global White privilege and non-White subordination came into being not through any one single act of writing and signing an actual contract but via "a series of acts" (p. 20). He offers as examples papal bulls, European discussions of their "discoveries," (broken) treaties with Native Americans, establishing unequal laws, failure to punish White vigilante exploitation of non-Whites, etc. beginning during sixteenth-century colonization and enslavement (pp. 20–1). In this way, the concepts of "White" and "US American" not only developed concomitantly and conflated together but were also foundationally constructed as beholden to White supremacy. Thus, when (White) people like Loewen "fail to live up to the civic and political responsibilities of Whiteness," such as his identifying textbooks' misinformation as problematic, thereby refusing to abide by

the epistemological terms of ignorance proscribed by White supremacy, "they are in dereliction of their duties" not just as White people but "as *citizens*" (Mills 1997: 14, emphasis added).

56. *Lies My Teacher Told Me* contains very little on the topic of religion, yet Loewen was called Anti-Christian by detractors. This shows how tightly White supremacy and Christianity are ideologically linked in the (White) US collective conscious.
57. Loewen 2018 [1995]: xxiii.
58. Yancy 2018: 53.
59. Ibid.
60. Loewen 2018 [1995]: 146.
61. Freedom in the World 2021: https://freedomhouse.org/country/united-states/freedom-world/2021.
62. Mills 1997: 87.
63. Ibid.: 40.
64. Chapman and Brunsma 2020: 9.
65. Mills 1997: 1, original emphasis removed.

Chapter 8: The Self-Defense Fallacy

1. Mills 1997: 89.
2. I originally called this the Defense Fallacy, but students told me that *self-defense* more clearly communicated that it represented a perspective on backlash to resisting domination.
3. Mitchell, personal communication, 2023.
4. White 2002.
5. Loewen 2018 [1995].
6. Metzl 2009.
7. Andrews 2023: 12.
8. Kolysh 2021: 144.
9. Medina 2011: 31–2.
10. Fricker 2007; Medina 2013.
11. Medina 2013: 31, emphasis in original.
12. Ibid.: 36, emphasis added.
13. Loewen 2018 [1995]: 175.
14. Ibid.
15. Ibid.: 251.
16. Ibid.: 268.
17. Medina 2013: 80.
18. Metzl 2019: 117.
19. She lost.
20. Pérez 2022: 8.
21. Ibid.: 32.
22. Ibid.: 8; educator Robin DiAngelo has noted that anti-Blackness in particular is enjoyable to the White majority (DiAngelo 2018).

23. Buggs 2017.
24. Pérez 2022: 159; Beltrán 2021.
25. Pérez 2022: 21.
26. Prescod-Weinstein 2021: 159.
27. In Chapman and Brunsma 2020: xv.
28. Anderson 2014.
29. Dawkins 2022.
30. American Sociological Association 2019.
31. Brown and Lemi 2021.
32. Ibid.: 23.
33. Ibid.: 31.
34. Joseph-Salisbury and Connelly 2018.
35. Kolysh 2021: 50.
36. Ibid.: 50, emphasis added.

Section III: Macro-Level Fallacies

1. Carr et al. 2021 [2018]: 38; Giddens et al. 2020 [1991]: 25.
2. Giddens et al. 2020 [1991]: 25.
3. Golash-Boza 2018 [2015]: 106.
4. Ibid.: 106.
5. Ibid.: 105; Feagin 2001: 16.
6. Bonilla-Silva 2021: 514.
7. Ibid.

Chapter 9: The Legalistic Fallacy

1. Desmond and Emirbayer 2020 [2010]: 7.
2. Childress 2013.
3. Mills 1997: 87.
4. At present, there are still laws that position abuses of minorities as legal, meaning that still today it is a part of the White supremacist serving epistemology of ignorance to use legality as a standard regarding racism. The strategically placed loophole in the 13th Amendment, that slavery is still legal "as a punishment for a crime," means that the labor of black and brown people is still being stolen for the profit of the White majority, e.g., firefighters in California to hand sanitizer in New York. With regard to legalized killing, so long as the person who kills is a police officer, it can be considered "lawful use of force" and thus legal. The epistemology of ignorance requires we ignore how this happens disproportionally by White cops against men of color.
5. Desmond and Emirbayer 2020 [2010]: 7.
6. Ibid.

7. Hirsch and Khan 2020.
8. Berrey 2021.
9. For more than a nutshell definition, see Victor Ray's *On Critical Race Theory: Why It Matters & Why You Should Care* (2022).
10. Whitmire 2022.
11. Ibid.
12. Ibid.
13. Goodfellow 2019.
14. Andrews 2023: 22–3, emphasis in original.
15. Kolysh 2021: 145.
16. Kelderman 2023b.
17. Ibid.
18. Ibid.
19. McMorris-Santoro and Edwards 2021.
20. Meckler and Natanson 2022.
21. Loewen 2018 [1995]: 237.
22. For example, Pager 2003; Bertrand and Mullainathan 2004; Pedulla 2016.
23. Hernández 2018.
24. Ibid.: 17; see also Clermont and Schwab 2009: 127.
25. American Psychological Association 2023.
26. Banks 2017; Hernández 2018.
27. Pérez 2022: 89.
28. Wells 2014.
29. Mills 1997: 75.
30. Ibid.: 84, emphasis in original.
31. Ibid.
32. Kolysh 2021: 140.
33. Mueller 2017.
34. Ibid.: 231.
35. Mills 1997: 15.
36. Fricker 2007: 73.

Chapter 10: The Fixed Fallacy

1. Desmond and Emirbayer 2020 [2010]: 8.
2. Lentin 2016: 35.
3. Mills 1997: 67; Deloria 1988 [1969].
4. Prescod-Weinstein 2021: 121.
5. Ibid.: 122.
6. Andrews 2021: 136.
7. Ibid.: 203–4.
8. Mills 1997: 72.
9. Other ideal types include Nazi Germany, Apartheid South Africa, and the Ancient Indian Caste System.

10. Andrews 2023: 165.
11. Sims 2016; Sims and Njaka 2020.
12. Lentin 2016: 35.

Chapter 11: The Ahistorical Fallacy

1. DuBois 1964 [1935]: 722.
2. Desmond and Emirbayer 2020 [2010]: 8.
3. Ibid.; elementary and high school textbooks in the US rarely broach events in the "recent" past let alone discuss how they contributed to present conditions of inequality (Loewen 2018 [1995]).
4. Cunningham et al. 2021: 9.
5. Darity 2021.
6. Andrews 2021: xiii.
7. I only learned about the events that occurred during my youth because I had parents who not only allowed me to watch the news with them but who would also answer my questions about it. My parents believed that "if a child is old enough to ask, she's old enough to have the answer."
8. Loewen 2018 [1995].
9. Ibid.
10. Mills 1997: 69.
11. Loewen 2018 [1995].
12. Desmond and Emirbayer 2020 [2010].
13. Sullivan 2007.
14. Yazdiha 2023.
15. Loewen 2018 [1995]: 171.
16. Fleming 2018; Bonilla-Silva 2018 [2003].
17. Andrews 2023: 20.
18. Benjamin 2022: 106.
19. Yazdiha 2023: 5.
20. Ibid.: 19.
21. Ibid.: 24.

Chapter 12: The Silence Fallacy

1. Kernahan 2019: 26.
2. Apfelbaum et al. 2008; Hagerman 2018.
3. Apfelbaum et al. 2008: 1515.
4. Ibid.: 1513.
5. Bonilla-Silva 2018 [2003].
6. Golash-Boza 2018 [2015]: 479; Giddens et al. 2020 [1991]: A13.
7. Kernahan 2019.
8. Ibid.: 25.

9. DiAngelo 2018: 1–2.
10. DiAngelo 2018: 2.
11. "Kevin's Parking Victory – The Office" 2020.
12. Lentin 2020: 5.
13. Adedoyin 2021.
14. Ibid. Prior to the resolution of the lawsuit, the school added dorm-level information to their dashboard.
15. *The Daily Show* 2021.
16. Rieger 2021.
17. Pew Research Center 2020.
18. Daniels 2021: 211.

Conclusion

1. Kernahan 2019: 54.
2. Andrews 2023: 19.
3. Yazdiha 2023: xiv.
4. McCormack 2011: 348.
5. de Boise 2015: 332.
6. Ibid.
7. Schalk 2022: 38.
8. Kolysh 2021: 48.
9. Cazenave 2016: 17.
10. Medina 2013; Fricker 2007: 91, emphasis in original.
11. Fricker 2007: 38.
12. Yancy 2018: 1–3.
13. Fricker 2007: 124.
14. DiAngelo 2021.
15. Fricker 2007: 92.
16. Mueller 2018: 5; Bonilla-Silva 2018 [2003].
17. Mills 1997: 107.
18. Andrews 2023: xii.
19. Tatum 2021.
20. Benjamin 2022.
21. Ibid.: 11.
22. Ibid.: 13. Benjamin's work here builds on sociologist Erik Olin Wright's book *How to Be an Anti-capitalist in the Twenty-First Century* (2019). Whereas Wright was focused on capitalism as the dominant species and various anti-capitalist efforts as the "alien species" he hoped would eventually "spill into the mainstream and displace the dominant species," Benjamin explains that she is adding "racism, ableism, sexism, and imperialism" to the ecosystem metaphor.
23. Daniels 2021; Pérez 2022; Picca and Feagin 2007.
24. Desmond and Emirbayer 2020 [2010]: 381.
25. Benjamin 2022: 18. In choosing to consciously and consistently reject the Racial Contract, though, one must take care not to lose epistemic humility

and fall into the self-serving hubris of "saviorism" or of calling out or even publicly shaming others just to show that "I am more enlightened, more 'woke,' less racist" (DiAngelo 2021: 66).

26. Lentin 2020: 5.
27. Yazdiha 2023.

References

"1921 Tulsa Race Massacre." Tulsa Historical Society and Museum. https://www.tulsahistory.org/exhibit/1921-tulsa-race-massacre/. Accessed June 4, 2023.

Acosta, Katie. 2021. *Queer Stepfamilies: The Path to Social and Legal Recognition*. New York: New York University Press.

Adedoyin, Oyin. 2021. "These student journalists uncovered their university's lack of covid data." *The Chronicle of Higher Education*, August 31. https://www.chronicle.com/blogs/live-coronavirus-updates/these-student-journalists-uncovered-their-universitys-lack-of-covid-data. Accessed June 2, 2023.

Ahmed, Sara. 2021. *Complaint!* Durham, NC: Duke University Press.

Alexander, Michelle. 2012 [2010]. *The New Jim Crow: Mass Incarceration in the Age of Colorblindness*. New York: The New Press.

Ali, Suki. 2003. *Mixed-Race, Post-Race: Gender, New Ethnicities and Cultural Practices*. Oxford: Berg.

Allport, Gordon. 1954. *The Nature of Prejudice*. Reading, MA: Addison-Wesley.

Allyn, Bobby. 2020. "'The computer got it wrong': How facial recognition led to false arrest of black man." National Public Radio, June 24. https://www.npr.org/2020/06/24/882683463/the-computer-got-it-wrong-how-facial-recognition-led-to-a-false-arrest-in-michig. Accessed May 24, 2023.

Ambrose, Susan A., Michael W. Bridges, Michele DiPietro, Marsha C. Lovett, and Marie K. Norman. 2010. *How Learning Works: Seven Research-Based Principles for Smart Teaching*. San Francisco, CA: Jossey-Bass.

American Psychological Association. 2023. "Health advisory on social media use in adolescence." https://www.apa.org/topics/social-media-internet/health-advisory-adolescent-social-media-use.pdf. Accessed May 30, 2023.

American Sociological Association. 2019. "Statement on Student Evaluations of Teaching." https://www.asanet.org/wp-content/uploads/asa_statement_on_student_evaluations_of_teaching_feb132020.pdf. Accessed October 31, 2023.

Anderson, Margaret. 2020. *Getting Smart About Race: An American Conversation*. Lanham, MD: Rowman & Littlefield.

Anderson, Steve. 2014. "A Christmas message from Chief Steve Anderson." Email. Transcript available at https://www.tennessean.com/story/news/

local/davidson/2014/12/26/nashville-police-chief-shares-message-responds-to-questions/20914171/. Accessed January 19, 2024.

Andrews, Kehinde. 2021. *The New Age of Empire: How Racism and Colonialism Still Rule the World*. New York: Bold Type Books.

Andrews, Kehinde. 2023. *The Psychosis of Whiteness: Surviving the Insanity of a Racist World*. London: Allen Lane.

Apfelbaum, Evan P., Kristin Pauker, Nalini Ambady, Samuel R. Sommers, and Michael I. Norton. 2008. "Learning (not) to talk about race: When older children underperform in social categorization." *Developmental Psychology* 44(5): 1513–28.

Associated Press. 2022. "Illinois Congresswoman calls Roe v. Wade Decision 'victory for white life' during Quincy Trump rally." NBC 5 Chicago. https://www.nbcchicago.com/news/local/illinois-rep-mary-miller-calls-roe-v-wade-decision-victory-for-white-life-during-quincy-trump-rally/2866885/. Accessed June 4, 2023.

Baldwin, James. 1966. "A report from occupied territory." *The Nation*, July 11.

Banks, Taunya Lovell. 2017. "Civil trials: A film illusion?" *Fordham Law Review* 85: 1969–85.

Beltrán, Cristina. 2021. "To understand Trump's support, we must think in terms of multiracial Whiteness." *Washington Post*, January 15. https://www.washingtonpost.com/opinions/2021/01/15/understand-trumps-support-we-must-think-terms-multiracial-whiteness/. Accessed December 4, 2023.

Benjamin, Ruha. 2019. *Race After Technology: Abolitionist Tools for the New Jim Code*. Cambridge: Polity.

Benjamin, Ruha. 2022. *Viral Justice: How We Grow the World We Want*. Princeton, NJ: Princeton University Press.

Berheide, Catherine White, Megan A. Carpenter, and David A. Cotter. 2022. "Teaching college in the time of COVID-19: Gender and race differences in faculty emotional labor." *Sex Roles* 86: 441–5.

Berrey, Stephen. 2021. "A discussion about the life and work of Dr. James Loewen and how we as educators, and as an organization, can continue his work." Panelist presentation to the Mid-South Sociological Association, October 22.

Bertrand, Marianne and Sendhil Mullainathan. 2004. "Are Emily and Greg more employable than Lakisha and Jamal? A field experiment on labor market discrimination." *The American Economic Review* 94(4): 991–1013.

Blumer, H. 1958. "Race prejudice as a sense of group position." *Pacific Sociological Review* 1(1): 3–7.

Bonilla-Silva, Eduardo. 2004. "From bi-racial to tri-racial: Towards a new system of racial stratification in the USA." *Ethnic and Racial Studies* 27(6): 931–50.

Bonilla-Silva, Eduardo. 2018 [2003]. *Racism Without Racists: Color-Blind Racism and the Persistence of Racial Inequality in America*, 5th edn. Lanham, MD: Rowman & Littlefield.

Bonilla-Silva, Eduardo. 2021. "What makes systemic racism *systemic*?" *Sociological Inquiry* 91(3): 513–33.

Bonvillian, Crystal. 2019. "Tennessee official's rant about 'queer' presidential candidate ignites call to #BoycottSevierCounty." WFTV9 News, October 23. https://www.wftv.com/news/deep-viral/tennessee-official-s-rant-about-queer-presidential-candidate-ignites-call-to-boycottseviercounty/1000737173/. Accessed May 10, 2023.

Bourdieu, Pierre. 1983. *Language and Symbolic Power*. Boston, MA: Harvard University Press.

Bowden, Ebony. 2020. "Trump: 'Suburban housewives' will vote for me over Joe Biden." *The New York Post*, August 12. https://nypost.com/2020/08/12/trump-suburban-housewives-will-vote-for-me-over-joe-biden/. Accessed May 16, 2023.

Brooks, Marcus. 2020. "It's okay to be White: Laundering White supremacy through a colorblind victimized White race-consciousness raising campaign." *Sociological Spectrum* 40(6): 400–16.

Brown, Nadia E. and Danielle Casarez Lemi. 2021. *Sister Style: The Politics of Appearance for Black Women Political Elites*. New York: Oxford University Press.

Budryk, Zach. 2019. "Trump renews attacks on Cummings: 'He should investigate himself'." The Hill, July 29. https://thehill.com/homenews/house/455254-trump-goes-after-cummings-again-he-should-investigate-himself/. Accessed May 16, 2023.

Buggs, Shantel Gabrieal. 2017. "'Your momma is day-glow white': Questioning the politics of racial identity, loyalty and obligation." *Identities: Global Studies in Culture and Power* 24(4): 379–97.

Buggs, Shantel Gabrieal. 2019. "Color, culture, or cousin?: Multiracial Americans and framing boundaries in interracial relationships." *Journal of Marriage & Family* 81(5); 1221–36.

Buolamwini, Joy. 2018. "When the robot doesn't see dark skin." *The New York Times*, June 21. https://www.nytimes.com/2018/06/21/opinion/facial-analysis-technology-bias.html. Accessed December 2, 2023.

Burke, Minyvonne and Marianna Sotomayor. 2018. "James Alex Fields found guilty of killing Heather Heyer during violent Charlottesville white nationalist rally." *NBC News*, December 7. https://www.nbcnews.com/news/crime-courts/james-alex-fields-found-guilty-killing-heather-heyer-during-violent-n945186. Accessed May 8, 2023.

Carr, Deborah, Elizabeth Heger Boyle, Benjamin Cornwell, Shlley Correll, Robert Crosnoe, Jeremy Freese, and Mary C. Waters. 2021 [2018]. *The Art and Science of Social Research*, 2nd edn. New York: W.W. Norton.

Cazenave, Noel. 2016. *Conceptualizing Racism: Breaking the Chains of Racially Accommodative Language*. Lanham, MD: Rowman and Littlefield.

Chapman, Nathanael and David Brunsma. 2020. *Beer and Racism*. Bristol: Bristol University Press.

Childress, Sarah. 2013. "Will the Violence Against Women Act close a tribal justice 'loophole'?" PBS Frontline, February 4. https://www.pbs.org/wgbh/frontline/article/will-the-violence-against-women-act-close-a-tribal-justice-loophole/. Accessed May 30, 2023.

Clermont, Kevin M. and Stewart J. Schwab. 2009. "Employment discrimination plaintiffs in federal court: From bad to worse?" *Harvard Law and Policy Review* 3: 103–32.

Coles, Tony. 2009. "Negotiating the field of masculinity: The production and reproduction of multiple dominant masculinities." *Men and Masculinities* 12: 30–44.

Collins, Patricia Hill. 2000 [1990]. *Black Feminist Thought Knowledge, Consciousness, and the Politics of Empowerment*. New York: Routledge.

Crenshaw, Kimberlé. 1989. "Demarginalizing the intersection of race and sex: A Black feminist critique of antidiscrimination doctrine, feminist theory and antiracist politics." *University of Chicago Legal Forum* 1989(1): article 8.

Crenshaw, Kimberlé. 1991. "Mapping the margins: Intersectionality, identity politics, and violence against women of color." *Stanford Law Review* 43(6): 1241–99.

Crittle, Chelsea and Keith B. Maddox. 2017. "Confronting bias through teaching: Insights from social psychology." *Teaching of Psychology* 44(2): 174–80.

Cunningham, David, Hedwig Lee, and Geoff Ward. 2021. "Legacies of racial violence: Clarifying and addressing the presence of the past." *The ANNALS of the American Academy of Political and Social Science* 694: 8–20.

Curington, Celeste Vaughan, Ken-Hou Lin, and Jennifer Hickes Lundquist. 2015. "Positioning multiraciality in cyberspace: Treatment of multiracial daters in an online dating website." *American Sociological Review* 80(4): 764–88.

Daniels, Jessie. 2021. *Nice White Ladies: The Truth About White Supremacy, Our Role in It, and How We Can Help Dismantle It*. New York: Seal Press.

Darity, Sandy. 2021. "'My family got here after slavery ended or after Jim Crow began' isn't absolution. If your ancestors . . ." Twitter, September 17. https://twitter.com/SandyDarity/status/1439061171156439041. Accessed September 17, 2021.

Davies, Caroline. 2023. "Charity boss at centre of royal race row steps down over abuse." *The Guardian*, March 8. https://www.theguardian.com/uk-news/2023/mar/08/ngozi-fulani-sistah-space-charity-boss-at-centre-of-royal-race-row-steps-down-over-abuse. Accessed March 14, 2023.

Davis, Emmalon. 2016. "Typecasts, tokens, and spokespersons: A case for credibility excess as testimonial injustice." *Hypatia* 31(3): 485–501.

Dawkins, Paul. 2022. "Neveruary 32nd." February 27. https://twitter.com/Paul__Dawkins/status/1497846158185668609?s=20&t=8rVI_CYk4lWEVXt41wU0wQ. Accessed February 27, 2022.

de Boise, Sam. 2015. "I'm not homophobic, 'I've got gay friends'": Evaluating the validity of inclusive masculinity." *Men and Masculinities* 18(3): 318–39.

Deloria, Vine Jr. 1988 [1969]. *Custer Died for Your Sins: An Indian Manifesto*. Norman, OK: University of Oklahoma Press.

Desmond, Matthew and Mustafa Emirbayer. 2020 [2010]. *Race in America*, 2nd edn. New York: W.W. Norton.

DiAngelo, Robin. 2018. *White Fragility: Why It Is So Hard for White People to Talk About Racism*. Boston, MA: Beacon Press.

DiAngelo, Robin. 2021. *Nice Racism: How Progressive White People Perpetuate Racial Harm*. Boston, MA: Beacon Press.

Dow, Dawn. 2019. *Mothering While Black: Boundaries and Burdens of Middle-Class Parenthood*. Oakland, CA: University of California Press.

Driscoll, Margarette. 2021. "'My friend Prince William is no racist.'" *The Telegraph*, March 20. https://www.telegraph.co.uk/royal-family/2021/03/20/friend-prince-william-no-racist/. Accessed May 17, 2023.

DuBois, W. E. B. 1964 [1935]. *Black Reconstruction*. Cleveland, OH: World Meridian.

Edelman, Lauren B., Sally Riggs Fuller and Iona Mara-Drita. 2001. "Diversity rhetoric and the managerialization of law." *American Journal of Sociology* 106(6): 1589–641.

"Executive Order 9066: Resulting in Japanese-American Incarceration (1942)." National Archives. https://www.archives.gov/milestone-documents/execu tive-order-9066. Accessed May 16, 2023.

Fanon, Frantz. 1961. *The Wretched of the Earth*. New York: Grove Press.

Federal Bureau of Investigation (FBI) "Terrorism." https://www.fbi.gov/investi gate/terrorism. Accessed March 17, 2023.

Feagin, Joe R. 2001. *Racist America: Roots, Current Realities, and Future Reparations*. New York: Routledge.

Fleming, Crystal. 2018. *How to Be Less Stupid About Race*. Boston, MA: Beacon Press.

Forsey, Zoe. 2020. "What it's like to work with Prince William – From man who has known him 10 years." *The Mirror*, June 21. https://www.mirror.co.uk/news /uk-news/what-its-like-work-prince-22182538.amp. Accessed May 17, 2023.

Freedom in the World 2021. 2021 The United States. https://freedomhouse.org /country/united-states/freedom-world/2021. Accessed March 14, 2023.

Fricker, Miranda. 2007. *Epistemic Injustice: Power and the Ethics of Knowing*. New York: Oxford University Press.

Friel, Mikhaila. 2019. "Meghan Markle is being criticized for doing the same things that Kate Middleton is praised for, and a royal expert says it wouldn't be happening if she were white." *Business Insider*, November 7. https:// www.insider.com/meghan-markle-criticized-kate-middleton-praised-double-standards-racism-2019-11. Accessed December 2, 2023.

Fuller, Pheobe. 2022. "GMB fans rush to defend Royal Family and slam guest as 'hate spreader'." December 1. https://www.examinerlive.co.uk/news/tv/gmb -fans-rush-defend-royal-25646306. Accessed December 20, 2022.

Ghosts of Ole Miss (documentary). 2012. ESPN. Partial transcript available at http:// www.espn.com/espn/eticket/story?page=mississippi62&num=2. Accessed June 4, 2023.

Giddens, Anthony, Mitchell Duneier, Richard P. Appelbaum, and Deborah Carr. 2020 [1991]. *Introduction to Sociology*, 12th edn. New York: W.W. Norton.

Goffman, Erving. 1959. *The Presentation of Self in Everyday Life*. New York: Anchor Books.

Golash-Boza, Tanya. 2018 [2015]. *Race and Racisms: A Critical Approach*. New York: Oxford University Press.

Goodfellow, Maya. 2019. "Put our colonial history on the curriculum – Then we'll understand who we really are." *The Guardian*, December 5. https://www.theguardian.com/commentisfree/2019/dec/05/britain-colonial-history-curriculum-racism-migration. Accessed May 30, 2023.

Gostanian, Ali and Suzanne Ciechalski. 2021. "Georgia sheriff's official under fire for remarks on spa shootings, anti-Asian Facebook post." *NBC News*, March 17. https://www.nbcnews.com/news/us-news/georgia-sheriff-s-official-under-fire-remarks-spa-shootings-anti-n1261359. Accessed June 4, 2023.

Govere, Linda and Ephraim M. Govere. 2016. "How effective is cultural competence training of healthcare providers on improving patient satisfaction of minority groups? A systematic review of literature." *Worldviews on Evidence-based Nursing* 13(6): 402–10.

Gregory, James. 2023. "Gary Lineker row goes to heart of BBC reputation – Ofcom boss." *BBC News*, March 14. https://www.bbc.com/news/uk-64953421. Accessed March 14, 2023.

Hagerman, Margaret. 2018. *White Kids: Growing Up with Privilege in a Racially Divided America*. New York: New York University Press.

Haney López, Ian. 2014. *Dog Whistle Politics: How Coded Racial Appeals Have Reinvented Racism and Wrecked the Middle Class*. New York: Oxford University Press.

Harry, The Duke of Sussex. 2023. *SPARE*. New York: Random House.

Hawkins, Billy. 2010. *The New Plantation: Black Athletes, College Sports, and Predominantly White NCAA Institutions*. New York: Palgrave Macmillan.

Heilman, Monica. 2022. "The racial elevator speech: How multiracial individuals respond to racial identity inquiries." *Sociology of Race and Ethnicity* 8(3): 370–85.

Hernández, Tanya Katerí. 2018. *Multiracials and Civil Rights: Mixed-Race Stories of Discrimination*. New York: New York University Press.

Hetter, Katia. 2015. "Online fury over Boston University professor's tweets on race." *CNN*, May 13.

Hill, Bailee. 2022. "Highland Park shooting witness demands answers on alleged shooter's mental health: 'Don't care about politics'." *Fox News*, July 5. https://www.foxnews.com/media/highland-park-shooting-witness-demands-answers-alleged-shooters-mental-health-care-politics. Accessed October 28, 2023.

Hirsch, Jennifer S. and Shamus Khan. 2020. *Sexual Citizens: Sex, Power, and Assault on Campus*. New York: W.W. Norton.

Ishizawa, Hiromi, Catherine T. Kenney, Kazuyo Kubo, and Gillian Stevens. 2006. "Constructing interracial families through intercountry adoption." *Social Science Quarterly* 87(5): 1207–24.

Joseph-Salisbury, Remi and Laura Connelly. 2018. "'If your hair is relaxed, white people are relaxed. If your hair is nappy, they're not happy': Black hair as a site of 'post-racial' social control in English schools." *Social Sciences* 7(11): 219.

Jost, John T. (2011). "System justification theory as compliment, complement, and corrective to theories of social identification and social dominance."

Pp. 223–63 in David Dunning (ed.), *Social Motivation*. New York: Psychology Press.

Kalev, Alexandra, Frank Dobbin and Erin Kelly. 2006. "Best practices or best guesses? Assessing the efficacy of corporate affirmative action and diversity policies." *American Sociological Review* 71(4): 589–617.

Kelderman, Eric. 2023a. "Many say they support DEI. Far fewer are meeting their goals." *Race on Campus. The Chronicle of Higher Education*, March 14. E-Newsletter.

Kelderman, Eric. 2023b. "Why are Trump and DeSantis talking about accreditation." *The Chronicle of Higher Education*, May 31. https://www.chronicle.com/article/why-are-trump-and-desantis-talking-about-accreditation. Accessed June 3, 2023.

Kernahan, Cyndi. 2019. *Teaching About Race and Racism in the College Classroom: Notes from a White Professor*. Morgantown, WV: West Virginia University Press.

"Kevin's Parking Victory – The Office." 2020. The Office YouTube Channel, June 20. https://www.youtube.com/watch?v=6EN3gJoc4-U. Accessed June 3, 2023.

Khanna, Nikki and Caitlin Killian. 2015. "'We didn't even think about adopting domestically': The role of race and other factors in shaping parents' decisions to adopt abroad." *Sociological Perspectives* 58(4): 570–94.

Kimmel, Michael and Matthew Mahler. 2003. "Adolescent masculinity, homophobia, and violence: Random school shootings, 1982–2001." *American Behavioral Scientist* 46(10): 1439–58.

Kolysh, Simone. 2021. *Everyday Violence: The Public Harassment of Women and LGBTQ People*. New Brunswick, NJ: Rutgers University Press.

Korver-Glenn, Elizabeth. 2021. *Race Brokers: Housing Markets and Segregation in 21st Century Urban America*. New York: Oxford University Press.

Kroskrity, Paul V. 2021. "Covert linguist racisms and the (re-)production of white supremacy." *Linguistic Anthropology* 31(2): 180–93.

Lentin, Alana. 2016. "Racism in public or public racism: Doing anti-racism in 'post-racial' times." *Ethnic and Racial Studies* 39(1): 33–48.

Lentin, Alana. 2020. *Why Race Still Matters*. Cambridge: Polity.

Loewen, James W. 2018 [1995]. *Lies My Teacher Told Me: Everything Your American History Textbook Got Wrong*. New York: The New Press.

Marcano, Donna-Dale. 2009. "White racial obligation and the false neutrality of political and moral liberalism." *The Southern Journal of Philosophy* 47: 16–24.

Marger, Martin. 2015. *Race and Ethnic Relations: American and Global Perspectives*, 10th edn. Stamford, CT: Cengage Learning.

McCormack, Mark. 2011. "The declining significance of homohysteria for male students in three sixth forms in the south of England." *British Educational Research Journal* 37: 337–53.

McMorris-Santoro, Evan and Meridith Edwards. 2021. "Tennessee parents say some books make students 'feel discomfort' because they're White. They say a new law backs them up." *CNN*, September 29. https://

www.cnn.com/2021/09/29/us/tennessee-law-hb-580-book-debate/index.html. Accessed October 7, 2023.

Meckler, Laura and Hannah Natanson. 2022. "New critical race theory laws have teachers scared, confused and self-censoring." *The Washington Post*, February 14. https://www.washingtonpost.com/education/2022/02/14/critical -race-theory-teachers-fear-laws/. Accessed October 7, 2023.

Medina, José. 2011. "The relevance of credibility excess in a proportional view of epistemic injustice: Differential epistemic authority and the social imaginary." *Social Epistemology* 25(1): 15–35.

Medina, José. 2013. *The Epistemology of Resistance: Gender and Racial Oppression, Epistemic Injustice, and Resistant Imaginations*. New York: Oxford University Press.

Meghji, Ali. 2022. *The Racialized Social System: Critical Race Theory as Social Theory*. Cambridge: Polity.

Mehta, Samira K. 2023. *The Racism of People Who Love You*. Boston, MA: Beacon Press.

Mendick, Robert and Jack Leather. 2022. "Ngozi Fulani: Palace race row accuser's charity given 'conflict of interest' advice by watchdog." *The Telegraph*, December 16. https://www.msn.com/en-gb/news/uknews/ngozi-fulani-palace -race-row-accuser-s-charity-given-conflict-of-interest-advice-by-watchdog/ ar-AA15mILT. Accessed June 5, 2023.

Metzl, Jonathan M. 2009. *The Protest Psychosis: How Schizophrenia Became a Black Disease*. Boston, MA: Beacon Press.

Metzl, Jonathan M. 2019. *Dying of Whiteness: How the Politics of Racial Resentment Is Killing America's Heartland*. New York: Basic Books.

Middleton, Richard T, IV and Sekou M. Franklin. 2009. "Southern racial etiquette and the 2006 Tennessee Senate race: The racialization of Harold Ford's deracialized campaign." *National Political Science Review* 12: 63–81.

Mills, Charles W. 1997. *The Racial Contract*. Ithaca, NY: Cornell University Press.

Mills, C. Wright. 1959. *The Sociological Imagination*. New York: Oxford University Press.

Mills, Charles W. 2007. "White ignorance." Pp. 13–38 in Shannon Sullivan and Nancy Tuana (eds.) *Race and Epistemologies of Ignorance*. Albany, NY: SUNY Press.

Mirrors of Privilege – Making Whiteness Visible. A documentary by Shakti Butler. World Trust. VHS.

Mitchell, Koritha. 2018. "Identifying white mediocrity and know-your-place aggression: A form of self-care." *African American Review* 51(4): 253–62.

Mueller, Jennifer. 2017. "Producing colorblindness: Everyday mechanisms of white ignorance." *Social Problems* 64(2): 219–38.

Mueller, Jennifer. 2018. "Advancing a sociology of ignorance in the study of racism and racial non-knowing." *Sociology Compass* 12(8): e12600.

Mueller, Jennifer. 2020. "Racial ideology or racial ignorance? An alternative theory of racial cognition." *Sociological Theory* 38(2): 142–69.

Mueller, Jennifer and DyAnna Katherine Washington. 2022. "Anticipating white futures: The ends-based orientation of white thinking." *Symbolic Interactionism* 45(1): 3–26.

National Constitution Center. "South Carolina Declaration of Secession (1860)." https://constitutioncenter.org/the-constitution/historic-document-library/ detail/south-carolina-declaration-of-secession-1860. Accessed June 5, 2023.

Noble, Safiya Umoja. 2018. *Algorithms of Oppression: How Search Engines Reinforce Racism.* New York: New York University Press.

North, Lili and Mindaugas Balčiauskas. 2020. "15 headlines show how differently the British press treat Meghan Markle vs Kate Middleton." *Bored Panda,* January 14. https://www.boredpanda.com/uk-media-double-standarts-royal -meghan-markle-kate-middleton/. Accessed December 2, 2023.

Omi, Michael and Howard Winant. 1994. *Racial Formation in the United States,* 2nd edn. New York: Routledge.

Pager, Devah. 2003. "The mark of a criminal record." *American Journal of Sociology* 108(5): 937–75.

Pascoe, C. J. 2005. "'Dude, you're a fag': Adolescent masculinity and the fag discourse." *Sexualities* 8: 329–46.

Pedulla, David S. 2016. "Penalized or protected? Gender and the consequences of nonstandard and mismatched employment histories." *American Sociological Review* 81(2): 262–89.

Pérez, Raúl. 2022. *The Souls of White Jokes: How Racist Humor Fuels White Supremacy.* Stanford, CA: Stanford University Press.

Pew Research Center. 2020. "In changing U.S. electorate, race and education remain stark dividing lines." Pew Research Center, June 2. https://www. pewresearch.org/politics/wp-content/uploads/sites/4/2020/06/PP_2020.06.02_ Party-ID_FINAL.pdf. Accessed June 3, 2023.

Picca, Leslie Houts and Joe R. Feagin. 2007. *Two-Faced Racism: Whites in the Backstage and Frontstage.* New York: Routledge.

Pollock, Mica. 2004. *Colormute: Race Talk Dilemmas in an American School.* Princeton, NJ: Princeton University Press.

Prescod-Weinstein, Chanda. 2021. *The Disordered Cosmos: A Journey into Dark Matter, Spacetime, & Dreams Deferred.* New York: Bold Type Books.

Purdue Northwest University. 2022. "Purdue Northwest distinguished as diverse metropolitan university." November 4. https://www. pnw.edu/purdue-northwest-distinguished-as-diverse-metropolitan-univer sity/. Accessed January 19, 2024.

Race – The Power of an Illusion. 2003. California News Reel.

Rafalow, Matthew H. 2020. *Digital Divisions: How Schools Create Inequality in the Tech Era.* Chicago, IL: University of Chicago Press.

Raleigh, Elizabeth. 2012. "Are same-sex and single adoptive parents more likely to adopt transracially? A national analysis of race, family structure, and the adoption marketplace." *Sociological Perspectives* 55(3): 449–71.

Rawls, Anne Warfield and Waverly Duck. 2020. *Tacit Racism.* Chicago, IL: University of Chicago Press.

Ray, Victor. 2019. "A theory of racialized organizations." *America Sociological Review* 84(1): 26–53.

Ray, Victor. 2022. *On Critical Race Theory: Why It Matters & Why You Should Care.* New York: Random House.

Rhoden, William C. 2006. *Forty Million Dollar Slaves: The Rise, Fall, and Redemption of the Black Athlete.* New York: Crown Publishers.

Rhoden-Paul, Andre. 2022. "Ngozi Fulani's charity Sistah Space stops work over safety." *BBC News*, December 10. https://www.bbc.com/news/uk-63925477. Accessed December 20, 2022.

Rieger, J. M. 2021. "Republicans claim they are being *silenced as they speak to millions of viewers.*" *The Washington Post*, February 4. https://www.washington post.com/politics/2021/02/04/republicans-claim-they-are-being-silenced-they-speak-millions-viewers/. Accessed June 3, 2023.

Robinson, Brandon. 2015. "'Personal preference' as the new racism: Gay desire and racial cleansing in cyberspace." *Sociology of Race and Ethnicity* 1(2): 317–30.

Rockquemore, Kerry Ann and Tracey Laszloffy. 2005. *Raising Biracial Children.* Lanham, MD: AltaMira Press.

Rodrigues-Sherley, Marchela. 2022. "Purdue U. Northwest Chancellor apologizes for speaking made-up 'Asian' language during commencement." *The Chronicle of Higher Education*, December 14. https://www.chronicle.com/article /purdue-u-northwest-chancellor-apologizes-for-speaking-made-up-asian-language-during-commencement Accessed December 15, 2022.

Rodriquez, Dalia. 2009. "The usual suspect: Negotiating white student resistance and teacher authority in a predominantly white classroom." *Cultural Studies Critical Methodologies* 9(4): 483–508.

Rowling, J. K. (@jk_rowling). "The Naga are snake-like mythical creatures of Indonesian mythology." Twitter, September 26, 2018. https://twitter.com/ jk_rowling/status/1044907311058358273.

Rucks-Ahidiana, Zawadi. "Covering gentrification, erasing race: Color-blind racism at work in the news." Unpublished manuscript.

Sarkar, Alisha Rahaman. 2023. "Trump recommits to banning Muslims from entering US if he is re-elected." *The Independent*, April 28. https://www. independent.co.uk/news/world/americas/us-politics/trump-election-muslim-travel-ban-b2328574.html. Accessed June 4, 2023.

Schalk, Sami. 2022. *Black Disability Politics.* Durham, NC: Duke University Press.

Sims, Jennifer Patrice. 2012. *The Sociology of Harry Potter.* Hamden, CT: Zossima.

Sims, Jennifer Patrice. 2016. "Reevaluation of the influence of appearance and reflected appraisals for mixed-race identity: The role of consistent inconsistent racial perception." *Sociology of Race and Ethnicity* 2(4): 569–83.

Sims, Jennifer Patrice. 2017. "An open letter to the black woman in the front row." Pp. 49–51 in Michelle Harris, Sherrill L. Sellers, Orly Clerge, and Frederick W. Gooding Jr. (eds.) *Stories from the Front of the Room: How Higher Education Faculty of Color Overcome Challenges and Thrive in the Academy.* Lanham, MD: Rowman & Littlefield.

Sims, Jennifer Patrice. 2022. "When the subaltern speak Parseltongue: Orientalism, racial re-presentation, and Claudia Kim as Nagini." Pp 105–18 in Sarah Park Dahlen and Ebony Elizabeth Thomas (eds.) *Harry Potter and the Other: Race, Justice, and Difference in the Wizarding World*. University of Mississippi Press.

Sims, Jennifer Patrice and Chinelo L. Njaka. 2020. *Mixed-Race in the US and UK: Comparing the Past, Present, and Future*. Bingley: Emerald Publishing.

Song, Miri. 2014. "Challenging a culture of racial equivalence." *British Journal of Sociology* 65(1): 107–29.

Sue, Derald Wing, Christina M. Capodilupo, Gina C. Torino, Jennifer M. Bucceri, Aisha M. B. Holder, Kevin L. Nadal, and Marta Esquilin. 2007. "Racial microaggressions in everyday life: Implications for clinical practice." *American Psychologist* 62(4): 271–86.

Sullivan, Shannon. 2007. "White ignorance and colonial oppression: Or, why I know so little about Puerto Rico." Pp. 153–72 in Shannon Sullivan and Nancy Tuana (eds.) *Race and Epistemologies of Ignorance*. Albany, NY: SUNY Press.

Tatum, Beverly Daniel. 2021. "Why are all the Black kids sitting together in the cafeteria." A conversation with Kehinde Andrews sponsored by Black Studies at Birmingham City University, May 27.

The Daily Show. 2021. "Republicans On National TV Being SILENCED." February 2. https://youtu.be/OP-lfWJNWpQ. Accessed June 3, 2023.

The Italian Americans (documentary). 2015. Public Broadcasting Station.

Thornhill, Ted. 2019. "We want Black students, just not you: How white admissions counselors screen Black prospective students." *Sociology of Race and Ethnicity* 5(4), 456–70.

Trump, Donald. 2020. https://twitter.com/realDonaldTrump/status/12935175147 98960640.

Tuan, Mia. 1998. *Forever Foreigners or Honorary Whites? The Asian Ethnic Experience Today*. New Brunswick, NJ: Rutgers University Press.

Turner, Cory. 2019. "Why all parents should talk with their kids about social identity." National Public Radio, October 8. https://www.npr.org/2019/10/08 /767205198/the-things-parents-dont-talk-about-with-their-kids-but-should. Accessed October 19, 2022.

US Census. "Explore Census Data." Searched "Sevier County, Tennessee" at https://data.census.gov. Accessed December 2, 2023.

Walsh, Joe. 2021. "FBI Director says Atlanta shooting 'does not appear' racially motivated." *Forbes*, March 19. https://www.forbes.com/sites/joewalsh/2021 /03/18/fbi-director-says-atlanta-shooting-does-not-appear-racially-motivated/. Accessed June 4, 2023.

Walton, Douglas and Thomas F. Gordon 2009. "Jumping to a conclusion: Fallacies and standards of proof." *Informal Logic* 29(2): 215–43.

Weiner, Jennifer. 2020. "Trump is dog-whistling. Are 'suburban housewives' listening?" *New York Times Opinion*, July 28. https://www.nytimes.com/2020/07 /28/opinion/trump-white-women.html. Accessed May 16, 2023.

Wells, Ida B. 2014. *The Light of Truth: Writings of an Anti-Lynching Crusader* (ed. by Mia Bay; gen. ed. Henry Luis Gates). New York: Penguin Classics.

White, Kevin. 2002. *An Introduction to the Sociology of Health and Illness*. Thousand Oaks, CA: SAGE.

Whitmire, Kyle. 2022. "Alabama's education system was designed to preserve white supremacy. I should know." AL.com, December 21. https://www.al.com/news/2022/12/alabamas-education-system-was-designed-to-preserve-white-supremacy-i-should-know.html. Accessed May 30, 2023.

Wingfield, Adia Harvey. 2019. *Flatlining: Race, Work, and Health Care in the New Economy*. Berkeley, CA: University of California Press.

Woodson, Carter G. 1933. *The Mis-Education of the Negro*. Washington, DC: The Associated Publishers.

Wright, Erik Olin. 2019. *How to Be an Anti-capitalist in the Twenty-First Century*. London: Verso.

WVLT News. 2019. "Sevier C. commissioner says 'queer' running for president is 'ugly.'" *WVLT News*, October 21. https://www.wvlt.tv/content/news/Fireworks-fly-at-Seveier-County. . . . Accessed October 23, 2019.

Yancy, George. 2018. *Backlash: What Happens When We Talk Honestly about Racism in America*. Lanham, MD: Rowman & Littlefield.

Yap, Audrey. 2017. "Credibility excess and the social imaginary in cases of sexual assault." *Feminist Philosophy Quarterly* 3(4), https://doi.org/10.5206/fpq/2017.4.1.

Yazdiha, Hajar. 2023. *The Struggle for the People's King: How Politics Transforms the Memory of the Civil Rights Movement*. Princeton, NJ: Princeton University Press.

Yuen, Nancy. 2021. "Because racism doesn't exist unless racists admit that they're racist." Twitter, March 18. https://twitter.com/nancywyuen/status/1372654573853155328. Accessed March 18, 2021.

Zalaznick, Matt. 2022. "Mockery of Asian language sparks calls for Purdue chancellor to step down." *University Business*, December 20. https://universitybusiness.com/purdue-university-northwest-chancellor-thomas-keon-resign-mock-asian-language/. Accessed May 24, 2023.

Zamudio-Suarez, Fernanda. 2022. "What we learned about equity this year." *Race on Campus. The Chronicle of Higher Education*, December 13.

Index